Discovering the American Past

Dr. Meyer - Pres, Trinity Grad. School

I Tim. 3: Key verse - know how to conduct ourselves in the House of God
Physical / Spiritual Check-up   7 Questions

3:1 - Do I have a heart for the ministry? - True Christian leadership?

3-6 - Am I caring for my spiritual life?   Do Private & Public lives match?
        3:5
  - Norm is the word of God - not today's standards

  - How am I doing w/ my relationship w/ others?   - The aqua color
      illustration - Both blue & green.

3:8-12 - Do I realize there are demands on leadership?   Leadership is obedience to God.
2 Kings 18   - Being glued / laminated to God
             - Knowing the presence of God is in your life.   Students have
                                                              Short-term success heroes
                                                              such as athletes

6:6-10   - Do I have a correct view of success?
  - The Wow & Now principles
  - Ears pierced while you wait - Huxley?   but
  - Success is not measured by our standards - Not GPA, spir. stuff
        "   "   is just glorify God - Judgment seat - The record in heaven counts -
                                                                not the record here.

3:16   - Am I still awed by the greatness of God?   Are we ready to
              be awed again?

       HE still holds the keys.

Discovering the American Past

A LOOK AT THE EVIDENCE

Volume I: To 1877

William Bruce Wheeler
University of Tennessee

Susan D. Becker
University of Tennessee

HOUGHTON MIFFLIN COMPANY   Boston

Dallas   Geneva, Illinois   Lawrenceville, New Jersey   Palo Alto

ACKNOWLEDGMENTS

Pages 5–17: Extracts from Lawrence S. Mayo, ed., *The History of the Colony and Province of Massachusetts Bay* reprinted by permission of Harvard University Press. Copyright 1936 by The President and Fellows of Harvard College.

Pages 27–28: Data in statistical sets 1–8 from *The Evolution of American Society, 1700–1815* by James A. Henretta. Copyright © 1973 by D. C. Heath and Company. Reprinted by permission of the publisher.

Pages 28–29: Data in statistical sets 9–12 reprinted from *The Journal of Interdisciplinary History*, VI (1976), 549, 557, 564, with permission of the editors of *The Journal of Interdisciplinary History* and The MIT Press, Cambridge, Massachusetts. Copyright © 1976, by the Massachusetts Institute of Technology and the editors of *The Journal of Interdisciplinary History*.

Acknowledgments continue following page 212.

Cover photograph courtesy of Historical Society of Pennsylvania

Printed in the U.S.A.
Library of Congress Catalog Card Number: 85–80136
ISBN: 0–395–35916–3

CDEFGHIJ-H-8987

Contents

Preface

Those of us who are historians find ourselves surrounded by a wealth of primary evidence that can be used to reconstruct American history. This evidence ranges from the more traditional sources such as letters, newspapers, public documents, speeches, and oral reminiscences to the less traditional sources such as photographs, buildings, statistics, film scripts, and cartoons. Moreover, as historians we know how exciting it can be to sort and analyze this evidence, arrange it in various ways, formulate a hypothesis, and arrive at a probable explanation for at least a part of our collective past.

In addition, the study of American history can contribute to an understanding of the contemporary world. It does this in two important ways: (1) it can put the present in perspective by giving us an appreciation of the trends, forces, and people who served to shape contemporary American life, and (2) it can teach us the skills we need in order to examine and analyze our present environment and culture. To be sure, other disciplines (sociology, psy-chology, political science, anthropology, computer science, to name but a few) can be of enormous help in understanding our contemporary world. It is our belief, however, that because of its dual function of teaching both perspective and skills, the study of American history can make a significant contribution to becoming a truly educated person. Our goals, then, are to interest students in historical issues and to help them develop and sharpen the crucial skills that people need to live in today's society.

Too often, however, students in the United States history survey course perceive American history as the story of *someone else's* distant past, not their own history, or they see history as only dry facts, names and dates. Yet we believe that the majority of college students really are interested in the past, their own history as well as those of other peoples. The immense popularity of historical fiction, films, and television miniseries is but one indication of that underlying but often untapped interest. Another indication is the number of unsolicited questions we receive from students, alumni, and other teachers concerning the historical background of some present issue or crisis. In sum, then, we firmly believe that the interest in history is strong, but that students curiously leave that interest outside when they enter an American history survey classroom.

We began this book with an urgent desire to tap the already existing interest students have in the past. In addition, we wanted our students to be more than just passive observers of the historical process, allowing others to do their thinking for them. We wanted our students to go beyond just reading about the past, that is, beyond merely watching historians' minds at work. To a certain degree, we wanted our students actually to *do* history, to reach *their own* conclusions based upon a guided examination of historical evidence.

In *Discovering the American Past: A Look at the Evidence,* we have tried to present a series of historical issues and events in a lively way so as to engage students' interest. We have also tried to provide a good mixture of types of historical situations and a balance among political, social, diplomatic, intellectual, and cultural history. In addition, each type of historical evidence is combined with an introduction to the appropriate methodology in an effort to teach students a variety of historical skills. As much as possible, we have tried

"to let the evidence speak for itself" and have avoided leading students to one particular interpretation or another. In this book, then, we have created a kind of historical sampler that we believe will help students learn the methods and skills historians use, as well as help them learn historical content. This approach is effective in many different classroom situations: seminars, small classes, large lecture classes with discussion sections.

Each chapter is divided into five parts: The Problem, The Method, The Evidence, Questions to Consider, and Epilogue. The section entitled "The Problem" gives the historical background and context for the evidence to be presented later in the chapter. The section called "The Method" gives students suggestions for studying and analyzing the evidence. "The Evidence" section is the heart of the chapter, providing a variety of primary source material on a particular historical event or issue. The section called "Questions to Consider" focuses students' attention on specific evidence and on linkages among different evidence material. The "Epilogue" section gives the aftermath or the historical outcome of the evidence — what happened to the people involved, who won the election, the results of a debate, and so on.

Discovering the American Past is not intended to replace a textbook or other reading material used in class. "The Problem" section in each chapter provides only a minimal factual context, and students are encouraged to return to their texts, readings, or lectures for information that will help them analyze the evidence presented in the chapter. An Instructor's Manual suggests ways that might be useful in guiding students through the evidence, questions students often ask, and a variety of ways in which the students' learning may be evaluated. By the time students complete this book, we believe they will know how to work with a great variety of historical evidence and how to use that evidence to answer historical questions about what happened and why.

We would like to thank the following people who read and critiqued the manuscript throughout its development. Their advice has been invaluable in helping to shape the book in its final form.

Frank Abbott, University of Houston
William Barney, University of North Carolina, Chapel Hill
John Cary, Cleveland State University
Howard Chudacoff, Brown University

Nancy Dye, University of Kentucky
Jack Elenbaas, California State University, Fullerton
Marcia Haubold, Triton College
Donald Jacobs, Northeastern University
James Lorence, University of Wisconsin
Robert McCaughey, Barnard College, Columbia University
Thomas G. Paterson, University of Connecticut
John Trickel, Richland College
William Walker, III, Ohio Wesleyan University
Darold Wax, Oregon State University

Our colleagues in the History Department at the University of Tennessee have been generous with both their ideas and their time, particularly Professors John R. Finger, Charles Johnson, Cathy Matson, and Jonathan Utley. The willing cooperation of our graduate teaching assistants enabled us not only to try out our ideas but also to evaluate their effectiveness in a variety of classroom situations. Finally, the staff of Houghton Mifflin Company have supported, encouraged, and helped us at every stage of this project.

Chapter 1

The Threat of Anne Hutchinson

The Problem

The Englishmen and women who came to the New World in the seventeenth and early eighteenth centuries did so for a variety of reasons. Many of those who arrived at Jamestown colony were motivated by the promise of wealth; at one point Virginians grew tobacco in the streets and even threatened their own existence by favoring tobacco over food crops. In contrast, the majority of the early settlers of Pennsylvania were Friends (Quakers) in search of religious freedom. In short, the American colonies represented for thousands of Englishmen and women a chance to make significant life-style changes.

Such was the case with the Puritans who settled and dominated the colony of Massachusetts Bay, founded in 1630. Though technically still members of the Church of England, the Puritans were convinced that many of that Church's beliefs and practices were wrongheaded and that the Church of England needed to be thoroughly purified (hence their name). For one thing, Puritans were convinced that the Church of England had become encrusted with unnecessary ceremony, rituals, and hierarchy — things they called "popery" because they associated them with the Roman Catholic Church. Popery, the Puritans believed, actually obstructed the ties between God and human beings and therefore should be eradicated.

But Puritans had deeper quarrels with the Church of England. More Calvinist than most of their English contemporaries, they believed that human salvation could not be earned by individual effort (like going to church, leading a good life, or helping one's neighbors). The Puritans called this type of salvation a "covenant of works," a notion they believed was simply wrong. Instead, they insisted that salvation came only as a free gift

[1]

① Compare voting records w/ those of the Virginia colonies.

where in history had this been tried? Is it practicable?

See John Calvin 20 Century ... treat preaching. 2:133

✱

selection by Winthrop

from God (a "covenant of grace"), and those few who received it were the true "saints." Those saints, Puritans felt, should be the only full members of the Church.

Believing it impossible to effect their reforms in England, many Puritans sought "voluntary banishment," as one of them called it, to the New World. Fired by the sense that God was using them to revolutionize human history, over one thousand men, women, and children arrived in New England to form their model community, based on the laws of God and following His commandments. "We shall be as a city upon a hill," exulted Puritan leader and colonial governor John Winthrop, "the eyes of all people are upon us."

Probably the best protection the Puritans had against the harsh New England environment was their sense of community and mission. Seeing themselves as the modern version of the ancient Israelites, Puritans believed that God had made a covenant (contract) with the Puritans of New England. As Winthrop explained, "Thus stands the cause between God and us: we are entered into covenant with Him. . . . The God of Israel is among us." Puritans believed the covenant stipulated that the entire community must follow God's laws as interpreted by Puritan leaders. If they did, God would reward them; if not, the community would be punished. Therefore, community solidarity was essential, and individual desires and

thoughts had to be subjugated to those of the community itself.

Thus, while Puritans sought religious freedom for themselves, they were not really willing to grant it to others. Dissent and discord, they reasoned, would lead to the breakdown of community cohesion, the inevitable violation of the covenant, and the punishment of the community in the same way God had punished the ancient Israelites when *they* had broken their covenant. Non-Puritans who migrated to Massachusetts Bay colony were required to attend the Puritan church, although they could not become members and hence could not vote in either church or civil elections. Those who refused to abide by these rules were banished from the colony. Moreover, those Puritans who were not saints also had to obey these regulations and similarly could not be church members and could not vote. Thus a comparatively small number of people in Massachusetts Bay controlled both the colony's church and government. To become a saint, one had to be examined by a committee and had to demonstrate to that committee's satisfaction that he or she had experienced a personal revelation from God and that the Holy Spirit resided in him or her. Fear of banishment or of God's displeasure at the breaking of the covenant kept the others in line.

This is not to say, however, that there was no dissension in Massachusetts Bay colony. Religious squabbles

✱ K

①

were not uncommon, often arising between saints over biblical interpretation, the theological correctness of one minister or another, or the behavior of certain fellow colonists. Indeed, to a limited extent Puritans actually welcomed these disputes, for they seemed to demonstrate that religion was still a vital part of the colonists' lives. As John Winthrop said, "The business of religion is the business of the Puritans." Weeknight gatherings at various church members' homes often engaged in these religious debates, and they were not disapproved of by either the ministers or the colony's civil leaders as long as the squabbles did not get out of control.

By the mid-1630s, however, one of the disputes had grown to such an extent that it threatened both the religious and secular unity of the colony. Some Puritans both in England and in Massachusetts Bay had begun to espouse an extreme version of the covenant of grace: they believed that, having been assured of salvation, an individual was virtually freed from the man-made laws of both church and state, taking his or her commands only from God who communicated His wishes to the saints. Called Antinomians (from *Anti*, "against," and *nomos*, "law"), these Puritan extremists attacked what one of them called the "deadness" of religious services and charged that several ministers were preaching the covenant of works. Carried to its logical extension, of course, Antinomianism threatened

to overthrow the authority of the ministers and even the power of the colonial government itself. Growing in numbers and intensity, the Antinomians in 1636 were able to elect one of their followers to replace Winthrop as colonial governor, although Winthrop was able to return to the office the next year.

Into this highly charged atmosphere stepped Anne Hutchinson, age forty-three, who had arrived in Massachusetts Bay in 1634 and soon became embroiled in the Antinomian controversy, or, as other Puritans called it, the "Antinomian heresy." The daughter of a clergyman who had been imprisoned twice for his religious unorthodoxy, Anne had married prosperous businessman William Hutchinson in 1612, when she was twenty-one years old. Before arriving in Massachusetts Bay, she had given birth to fourteen children, eleven of whom were alive in 1634.

Anne Hutchinson's many duties at home, however, did not prevent her from remaining very active in the church. Extremely interested in religion and theological questions, she was particularly influenced by John Cotton, a Puritan minister who had been forced to flee from England to Massachusetts Bay in 1633 because of his religious ideas. Upon arrival in the colony, Cotton said he was shocked by the extent to which colonists had been "lulled into security" by their growing belief that they could earn salvation through good works. Attacking this in sermons and in letters to other clergymen, Cotton helped to fuel the Antinomian cause as well as Anne Hutchinson's religious ardor.

At first the Hutchinsons were seen as welcome additions to the community, largely because of William's prosperity and Anne's knowledge of midwifery. Soon, however, Anne Hutchinson began to drift into religious issues. She began to hold weeknight meetings in her home, at first to expand upon the previous Sunday's sermons and later to expound her own religious notions — ideas very close to those of the Antinomians. In November 1637 Anne's brother-in-law (John Wheelwright, another Puritan minister) was banished from the colony because of his radical sermons, and Anne was brought to trial before the General Court of Massachusetts Bay. With Governor Winthrop presiding, the Court met to decide the fate of Mrs. Hutchinson. Privately, Winthrop called Anne Hutchinson a person of "nimble wit and active spirit and a very voluble [fluent] tongue." Publicly, however, the governor was determined to be rid of her.

Why were Winthrop and other orthodox Puritans so opposed to her? What crime had she committed? Some of Wheelwright's followers had been punished for having signed a petition supporting him, but Anne Hutchinson had not signed the petition. Many other Puritans had held religious discussions in their homes, and more than a few had opposed the views of their ministers. Technically, Anne Hutchinson had broken no law. Why, then, was she considered such a threat that she was brought to trial and ultimately banished from the colony? Your task is to answer that question.

The Method

For two days Anne Hutchinson stood before the General Court, presided over by the unsympathetic Governor John Winthrop. Fortunately, a fairly complete transcript of the proceedings has been preserved. Contained in that transcript are the clues that you as the historian-detective will need to answer the question. While spelling and punctuation have been modernized in most cases, the portions of the transcript you are about to read have been reproduced verbatim. At first, some of the seventeenth-century phraseology might seem a bit strange. Like most spoken languages, English is constantly changing — think of how much English has changed since Chaucer's day. Yet if you read slowly and carefully, the transcript should give you no problem.

Before you begin studying the transcript, keep two additional instructions in mind:

1. Be careful not to lose sight of the central question you are seeking to an-

Central Question

swer: why was Anne Hutchinson such a threat to Massachusetts Bay colony? The transcript raises several other questions, some of them so interesting that they might pull you off the main track. As you read through the transcript, make a list of the various ways you think Anne might have threatened Massachusetts Bay.

2. Be willing to read between the lines. As you read each statement, ask yourself what is being said. Then try to deduce what is actually meant by what is being said. Sometimes people say exactly what they mean, but often they don't. They might intentionally or unintentionally disguise the real meaning of what they are saying, but the real meaning can usually be found. In conversation with a person face to face, voice inflection, body language, and other visual clues often provide the real meaning to what is being said. In this case, where personal observation is impossible, you must use both logic and imagination to read between the lines.

The Evidence

Excerpt of the examination from Thomas Hutchinson (Anne's great-grandson), The History of the Colony and Province of Massachusetts-Bay, *Vol. II, edited by Lawrence Shaw Mayo (Cambridge, Mass.: Harvard University Press, 1936), pp. 366–391.*

November 1637

The Examination of Mrs. Anne Hutchinson at the Court at Newton[1]

CHARACTERS

Mrs. Anne Hutchinson, *the accused*
General Court, *consisting of the governor, deputy governor, assistants, and deputies*
Governor, *John Winthrop, chair of the court*
Deputy Governor, *Thomas Dudley*
Assistants, *Mr. Bradstreet, Mr. Nowel, Mr. Endicott, Mr. Harlakenden, Mr. Stoughton*

1. Normally the trial would have been held in Boston, but Anne Hutchinson had numerous supporters in that city and therefore the proceedings were moved to the small town of Newton, where she had few allies.

[5]

Outline
1 - Arg. bet. Winthrop & Hutchinson
2 - Breaking the 5th Command
3 - Meetings in Anne's home
4 - Nature of Anne's preaching

Deputies, *Mr. Coggeshall, Mr. Bartholomew, Mr. Jennison, Mr. Coddington, Mr. Colborn*

Clergymen and Ruling Elders,
  Mr. Peters, minister in Salem;
  Mr. Leveret, a ruling elder in a Boston church;
  Mr. Cotton, minister in Boston;
  Mr. Wilson, minister in Boston, who supposedly made notes of a previous meeting between Anne Hutchinson, Cotton, and the other ministers;
  Mr. Sims, minister in Charlestown

MR. WINTHROP, GOVERNOR: Mrs. Hutchinson, you are called here as one of those that have troubled the peace of the commonwealth and the churches here; you are known to be a women that hath had a great share in the promoting and divulging of those opinions that are causes of this trouble, and to be nearly joined not only in affinity and affection with some of those the court had taken notice of and passed censure upon, but you have spoken divers things as we have been informed very prejudicial to the honour of the churches and ministers thereof, and you have maintained a meeting and an assembly in your house that hath been condemned by the general assembly as a thing not tolerable nor comely in the sight of God nor fitting for your sex, and notwithstanding that was cried down you have continued the same. Therefore we have thought good to send for you to understand how things are, that if you be in an erroneous way we may reduce you that so you may become a profitable member here among us. Otherwise if you be obstinate in your course that then the court may take such course that you may trouble us no further. Therefore I would intreat you to express whether you do assent and hold in practice to those opinions and factions that have been handled in court already, that is to say, whether you do not justify Mr. Wheelwright's sermon and the petition.

MRS. HUTCHINSON: I am called here to answer before you but I hear no things laid to my charge.

GOV.: I have told you some already and more I can tell you.

MRS. H.: Name one, Sir.

GOV.: Have I not named some already?

MRS. H.: What have I said or done?

[*Here, in a portion of the transcript not reproduced, Winthrop accused Hutchinson of harboring and giving comfort to a faction that was dangerous to the colony.*]

MRS. H.: Must not I then entertain the saints because I must keep my conscience?

GOV.: Say that one brother should commit felony or treason and come to his brother's house. If he knows him guilty and conceals him he is guilty of the same. It is his conscience to entertain him, but if his conscience comes into act in giving countenance and entertainment to him that hath broken the law he is guilty too. So if you do countenance those that are transgressors of the law you are in the same fact.

MRS. H.: What law do they transgress?

GOV.: The law of God and of the state.

MRS. H.: In what particular?

GOV.: Why in this among the rest, whereas the Lord doth say honour thy father and thy mother.[2]

MRS. H.: Ey, Sir, in the Lord.

GOV.: This honour you have broke in giving countenance to them.

MRS. H.: In entertaining those did I entertain them against any act (for there is the thing) or what God hath appointed?

GOV.: You knew that Mr. Wheelwright did preach this sermon and those that countenance him in this do break a law.

MRS. H.: What law have I broken?

GOV.: Why the fifth commandment.[3]

MRS. H.: I deny that for he [Wheelwright] saith in the Lord.

GOV.: You have joined with them in the faction.

MRS. H.: In what faction have I joined with them?

GOV.: In presenting the petition.

MRS. H.: Suppose I had set my hand to the petition. What then?

GOV.: You saw that case tried before.

MRS. H.: But I had not my hand to the petition.

GOV.: You have councelled them.

MRS. H.: Wherein?

GOV.: Why in entertaining them.

MRS. H.: What breach of law is that, Sir? Fathers of the Commonwealth

2. Exodus 20:12. Anne Hutchinson's natural father was in England and her natural mother was dead. To what, then, was Winthrop referring?

3. "Honour thy father and thy mother: that thy days may be long upon the land which the Lord thy God giveth thee." Exodus 20:12.

GOV.: Why dishonouring of parents.

MRS. H.: But put the case, Sir, that I do fear the Lord and my parents. May not I entertain them that fear the Lord because my parents will not give me leave?

GOV.: If they be the fathers of the commonwealth, and they of another religion, if you entertain them then you dishonour your parents and are justly punishable.

MRS. H.: If I entertain them, as they have dishonoured their parents I do.

GOV.: No but you by countenancing them above others put honor upon them.

MRS. H.: I may put honor upon them as the children of God and as they do honor the Lord.

GOV.: We do not mean to discourse with those of your sex but only this: you do adhere unto them and do endeavor to set forward this faction and so you do dishonour us.

MRS. H.: I do acknowledge no such thing. Neither do I think that I ever put any dishonour upon you.

GOV.: Why do you keep such a meeting at your house as you do every week upon a set day? . . .

MRS. H.: It is lawful for me so to do, as it is all your practices, and can you find a warrant for yourself and condemn me for the same thing? The ground of my taking it up was, when I first came to this land because I did not go to such meetings as those were, it was presently reported that I did not allow of such meetings but held them unlawful and therefore in that regard they said I was proud and did despise all ordinances. Upon that a friend came unto me and told me of it and I to prevent such aspersions took it up, but it was in practice before I came. Therefore I was not the first.

GOV.: For this, that you appeal to our practice you need no confutation. If your meeting had answered to the former it had not been offensive, but I will say that there was no meeting of women alone, but your meeting is of another sort for there are sometimes men among you.

MRS. H.: There was never any man with us.

GOV.: Well, admit there was no man at your meeting and that you was sorry for it, there is no warrant for your doings, and by what warrant do you continue such a course?

MRS. H.: I conceive there lies a clear rule in Titus that the elder women should instruct the younger and then I must have a time wherein I must do it.

GOV.: All this I grant you, I grant you a time for it, but what is this to the pur-

pose that you Mrs. Hutchinson must call a company together from their call-
ings to come to be taught of you?

MRS. H.: Will it please you to answer me this and to give me a rule for then I
will willingly submit to any truth. If any come to my house to be instructed in
the ways of God what rule have I to put them away?

GOV.: But suppose that a hundred men come unto you to be instructed. Will
you forbear to instruct them?

MRS. H.: As far as I conceive I cross a rule in it.

GOV.: Very well and do you not so here?

MRS. H.: No, Sir, for my ground is they are men.

GOV.: Men and women all is one for that, but suppose that a man should come
and say, "Mrs. Hutchinson, I hear that you are a woman that God hath given
his grace unto and you have knowledge in the word of God. I pray instruct me
a little." Ought you not to instruct this man?

MRS. H.: I think I may. Do you think it not lawful for me to teach women and
why do you call me to teach the court?

GOV.: We do not call you to teach the court but to lay open yourself.

[*In this portion of the transcript not reproduced, Anne Hutchinson and Governor
Winthrop continued to wrangle over specifically what law she had broken.*]

GOV.: Your course is not to be suffered for. Besides that we find such a course
as this to be greatly prejudicial to the state. Besides the occasion that it is to
seduce many honest persons that are called to those meetings and your opinions
being known to be different from the word of God may seduce many simple
souls that resort unto you. Besides that the occasion which hath come of late
hath come from none but such as have frequented your meetings, so that now
they are flown off from magistrates and ministers and since they have come to
you. And besides that it will not well stand with the commonwealth that families should be neglected for so many neighbours and dames and so much time
spent. We see no rule of God for this. We see not that any should have authority to set up any other exercises besides what authority hath already set up and
so what hurt comes of this you will be guilty of and we for suffering you.

MRS. H.: Sir, I do not believe that to be so.

GOV.: Well, we see how it is. We must therefore put it away from you or re-
strain you from maintaining this course.

MRS. H.: If you have a rule for it from God's word you may.

GOV.: We are your judges, and not you ours and we must compel you to it.

[Here followed a discussion of whether or not men as well as women attended Anne Hutchinson's meetings. In response to one question, Hutchinson denied that women ever taught at men's meetings.]

DEPUTY GOVERNOR: I would go a little higher with Mrs. Hutchinson. About three years ago we were all in peace. Mrs. Hutchinson from that time she came hath made a disturbance, and some that came over with her in the ship did inform me what she was as soon as she was landed. I being then in place dealt with the pastor and teacher of Boston and desired them to enquire of her, and then I was satisfied that she held nothing different from us. But within half a year after, she had vented divers of her strange opinions and had made parties in the country, and at length it comes that Mr. Cotton and Mr. Vane[4] were of her judgment, but Mr. Cotton hath cleared himself that he was not of that mind. But now it appears by this woman's meeting that Mrs. Hutchinson hath so forestalled the minds of many by their resort to her meeting that now she hath a potent party in the country. Now if all these things have endangered us as from that foundation and if she in particular hath disparaged all our ministers in the land that they have preached a covenant of works,[5] and only Mr. Cotton a covenant of grace,[6] why this is not to be suffered, and therefore being driven to the foundation and it being found that Mrs. Hutchinson is she that hath depraved all the ministers and hath been the cause of what is fallen out, why we must take away the foundation and the building will fall.

MRS. H.: I pray, Sir, prove it that I said they preached nothing but a covenant of works.

DEP. GOV.: Nothing but a covenant of works. Why a Jesuit[7] may preach truth sometimes.

MRS. H.: Did I ever say they preached a covenant of works then?

DEP. GOV.: If they do not preach a covenant of grace clearly, then they preach a covenant of works.

MRS. H.: No, Sir. One may preach a covenant of grace more clearly than another, so I said.

4. Henry Vane, an ally of the Antinomians, was elected governor of Massachusetts Bay colony in 1636 and lost that office to Winthrop in 1637.

5. For an explanation of the covenant of works, see the introduction to this chapter.

6. For an explanation of the covenant of grace, see the introduction to this chapter.

7. The Society of Jesus (Jesuits) was a Roman Catholic order that placed special emphasis on missionary work and on combatting Protestantism. The Jesuits were particularly detested by many Protestants, including the Puritans.

DEP. GOV.: We are not upon that now but upon position.

MRS. H.: Prove this then Sir that you say I said.

DEP. GOV.: When they do preach a covenant of works do they preach truth?

MRS. H.: Yes, Sir. But when they preach a covenant of works for salvation, that is not truth.

DEP. GOV.: I do but ask you this: when the ministers do preach a covenant of works do they preach a way of salvation?

MRS. H.: I did not come hither to answer to questions of that sort.

DEP. GOV.: Because you will deny the thing.

MRS. H.: Ey, but that is to be proved first.

DEP. GOV.: I will make it plain that you did say that the ministers did preach a covenant of works.

MRS. H.: I deny that.

DEP. GOV.: And that you said they were not able ministers of the New Testament, but Mr. Cotton only.

MRS. H.: If ever I spake that I proved it by God's word.

COURT: Very well, very well.

MRS. H.: If one shall come unto me in private, and desire me seriously to tell then what I thought of such an one, I must either speak false or true in my answer.

[*In this lengthy section Hutchinson was accused of having gone to a meeting of ministers and accusing them all — except John Cotton — of preaching a covenant of works rather than a covenant of grace. The accusation, if proven, would have been an extremely serious one. Several of the ministers testified that Hutchinson had made this accusation.*]

DEP. GOV.: I called these witnesses and you deny them. You see they have proved this and you deny this, but it is clear. You said they preached a covenant of works and that they were not able ministers of the New Testament; now there are two other things that you did affirm which were that the scriptures in the letter of them held forth nothing but a covenant of works and likewise that those that were under a covenant of works cannot be saved.

MRS. H.: Prove that I said so.

GOV.: Did you say so?

MRS. H.: No, Sir. It is your conclusion.

DEP. GOV.: What do I do charging of you if you deny what is so fully proved?

GOV.: Here are six undeniable ministers who say it is true and yet you deny that you did say that they did preach a covenant of works and that they were not able ministers of the gospel, and it appears plainly that you have spoken it, and whereas you say that it was drawn from you in a way of friendship, you did profess then that it was out of conscience that you spake and said, "The fear of man is a snare. Wherefore shall I be afraid, I will speak plainly and freely."

MRS. H.: That I absolutely deny, for the first question was thus answered by me to them: They thought that I did conceive there was a difference between them and Mr. Cotton. At the first I was somewhat reserved. Then said Mr. Peters, "I pray answer the question directly as fully and as plainly as you desire we should tell you our minds. Mrs. Hutchinson we come for plain dealing and telling you our hearts." Then I said I would deal as plainly as I could, and whereas they say I said they were under a covenant of works and in the state of the apostles why these two speeches cross one another. I might say they might preach a covenant of works as did the apostles, but to preach a covenant of works and to be under a covenant of works is another business.

DEP. GOV.: There have been six witnesses to prove this and yet you deny it.

MRS. H.: I deny that these were the first words that were spoken.

GOV.: You make the case worse, for you clearly shew that the ground of your opening your mind was not to satisfy them but to satisfy your own conscience.

[*There was a brief argument here about what Hutchinson actually said at the gathering of ministers, after which the Court adjourned for the day.*]

The next morning.

GOV.: We proceeded the last night as far as we could in hearing of this cause of Mrs. Hutchinson. There were divers things laid to her charge: her ordinary meetings about religious exercises, her speeches in derogation of the ministers among us, and the weakening of the hands and hearts of the people towards them. Here was sufficient proof made of that which she was accused of in that point concerning the ministers and their ministry, as that they did preach a covenant of works when others did preach a covenant of grace, and that they were not able ministers of the New Testament, and that they had not the seal of the spirit, and this was spoken not as was pretended out of private conference, but out of conscience and warrant from scripture alleged the fear of man is a snare and seeing God had given her a calling to it she would freely speak. Some other speeches she used, as that the letter of the scripture held forth a covenant of works, and this is offered to be proved by probable grounds. If there be any thing else that the court hath to say they may speak.

[*At this point a lengthy argument erupted when Hutchinson demanded that the ministers who testified against her be recalled as witnesses, put under oath, and repeat their accusations. One member of the Court said that "the ministers are so well known unto us, that we need not take an oath of them."*]

GOV.: I see no necessity of an oath in this thing seeing it is true and the substance of the matter confirmed by divers. Yet that all may be satisfied, if the elders will take an oath they shall have it given them. . . .

MRS. H.: I will prove by what Mr. Wilson hath written[8] that they [the ministers] never heard me say such a thing.

MR. SIMS: We desire to have the paper and have it read.

MR. HARLAKENDEN: I am persuaded that is the truth that the elders do say and therefore I do not see it necessary how to call them to oath.

GOV.: We cannot charge any thing of untruth upon them.

MR. HARLAKENDEN: Besides, Mrs. Hutchinson doth say that they are not able ministers of the New Testament.

MRS. H.: They need not swear to that.

DEP. GOV.: Will you confess it then?

MRS. H.: I will not deny it or say it.

DEP. GOV.: You must do one.

[*More on the oath followed.*]

DEP. GOV.: Let her witnesses be called.

GOV.: Who be they?

MRS. H.: Mr. Leveret and our teacher and Mr. Coggeshall.

GOV.: Mr. Coggeshall was not present.

MR. COGGESHALL: Yes, but I was. Only I desired to be silent till I should be called.

GOV.: Will you, Mr. Coggeshall, say that she did not say so?

MR. COGGESHALL: Yes, I dare say that she did not say all that which they lay against her.

---

8. Wilson had taken notes at the meeting between Mrs. Hutchinson and the ministers. Hutchinson claimed that these notes would exonerate her. They were never produced and are now lost.

MR. PETERS: How dare you look into the court to say such a word?

MR. COGGESHALL: Mr. Peters takes upon him to forbid me. I shall be silent.

MR. STOUGHTON: Ey, but she intended this that they say.

GOV.: Well, Mr. Leveret, what were the words? I pray, speak.

MR. LEVERET: To my best remembrance when the elders did send for her, Mr. Peters did with much vehemency and intreaty urge her to tell what difference there was between Mr. Cotton and them, and upon his urging of her she said, "The fear of man is a snare, but they that trust upon the Lord shall be safe." And being asked wherein the difference was, she answered that they did not preach a covenant of grace so clearly as Mr. Cotton did, and she gave this reason of it: because that as the apostles were for a time without the spirit so until they had received the witness of the spirit they could not preach a covenant of grace so clearly.

[Here Hutchinson admitted that she might have said privately that the ministers were not able ministers of the New Testament.]

GOV.: Mr. Cotton, the court desires that you declare what you do remember of the conference which was at the time and is now in question.

MR. COTTON: I did not think I should be called to bear witness in this cause and therefore did not labour to call to remembrance what was done; but the greatest passage that took impression upon me was to this purpose. The elders spake that they had heard that she had spoken some condemning words of their ministry, and among other things they did first pray her to answer wherein she thought their ministry did differ from mine. How the comparison sprang I am ignorant, but sorry I was that any comparison should be between me and my brethren and uncomfortable it was. She told them to this purpose that they did not hold forth a covenant of grace as I did. . . . I told her I was very sorry that she put comparisons between my ministry and theirs, for she had said more than I could myself, and rather I had that she had put us in fellowship with them and not have made the discrepancy. She said she found the difference. . . . And I must say that I did not find her saying they were under a covenant of works, nor that she said they did preach a covenant of works.

[Here John Cotton tried to defend Hutchinson, mostly by saying he did not remember most of the events in question.]

MRS. H.: If you please to give me leave I shall give you the ground of what I know to be true. Being much troubled to see the falseness of the constitution of the Church of England, I had like to have turned Separatist. Whereupon I kept a day of solemn humiliation and pondering of the thing, the scripture was brought unto me — he that denies Jesus Christ to be come in the flesh is antichrist. This I considered of and in considering found that the papists[9] did not deny him to come in the flesh, nor we did not deny him. Who then was antichrist? Was the Turk antichrist only? The Lord knows that I could not open scripture; he must by his prophetical office open it unto me. So after that being unsatisfied in the thing, the Lord was pleased to bring this scripture out of the Hebrews. He that denies the testament denies the testator, and in this did open unto me and give me to see that those which did not teach the new covenant had the spirit of antichrist, and upon this he did discover the ministry unto me, and ever since, I bless the Lord. He hath let me see which was the clear ministry and which the wrong. Since that time I confess I have been more choice and he hath left me to distinguish between the voice of my beloved and the voice of Moses, the voice of John Baptist and the voice of antichrist, for all those voices are spoken of in scripture. Now if you do condemn me for speaking what in my conscience I know to be truth I must commit myself unto the Lord.

MR. NOWEL: How do you know that that was the spirit?

MRS. H.: How did Abraham know that it was God that bid him offer his son, being a breach of the sixth commandment?

DEP. GOV.: By an immediate voice.

MRS. H.: So to me by an immediate revelation.

DEP. GOV.: How! an immediate revelation.

MRS. H.: By the voice of his spirit to my soul. . . .

[*In spite of the general shock that greeted her claim that she had experienced an immediate revelation from God, Hutchinson went on to state that God had compelled her to take the course she had taken and that God had said to her, as He had to Daniel of the Old Testament, that "though I should meet with affliction, yet I am the same God that delivered Daniel out of the lion's den, I will also deliver thee."*]

MRS. H.: You have power over my body but the Lord Jesus hath power over my body and soul, and assure yourselves thus much: you go on in this course you begin you will bring a curse upon you and your posterity, and the mouth of the Lord hath spoken it.

9. *Papists* is a Protestant term for Roman Catholics, referring to the papacy.

DEP. GOV.: What is the scripture she brings?

MR. STOUGHTON: Behold I turn away from you.

MRS. H.: But now having seen him which is invisible I fear not what man can do unto me.

GOV.: Daniel was delivered by miracle. Do you think to be deliver'd so too?

MRS. H.: I do here speak it before the court. I look that the Lord should deliver me by his providence.

MR. HARLAKENDEN: I may read scripture and the most glorious hypocrite may read them and yet go down to hell.

MRS. H.: It may be so.

[*Anne Hutchinson's "revelations" were discussed among the stunned Court.*]

MR. BARTHOLOMEW: I speak as a member of the court. I fear that her revelations will deceive.

[*More on revelations followed.*]

DEP. GOV.: I desire Mr. Cotton to tell us whether you do approve of Mrs. Hutchinson's revelations as she hath laid them down.

MR. COTTON: I know not whether I do understand her, but this I say: If she doth expect a deliverance in a way of providence, then I cannot deny it.

DEP. GOV.: No, Sir. We did not speak of that.

MR. COTTON: If it be by way of miracle then I would suspect it.

DEP. GOV.: Do you believe that her revelations are true?

MR. COTTON: That she may have some special providence of God to help her is a thing that I cannot bear witness against.

DEP. GOV.: Good Sir, I do ask whether this revelation be of God or no?

MR. COTTON: I should desire to know whether the sentence of the court will bring her to any calamity, and then I would know of her whether she expects to be delivered from that calamity by a miracle or a providence of God.

MRS. H.: By a providence of God I say I expect to be delivered from some calamity that shall come to me.

[*Revelations were further discussed.*]

DEP. GOV.: These disturbances that have come among the Germans have been all grounded upon revelations, and so they that have vented them have stirred up their hearers to take up arms against their prince and to cut the throats of one another, and these have been the fruits of them, and whether the devil may inspire the same into their hearts here I know not, for I am fully persuaded that Mrs. Hutchinson is deluded by the devil, because the spirit of God speaks truth in all his servants.

GOV.: I am persuaded that the revelation she brings forth is delusion.

[*All the court but some two or three ministers cried out, "We all believe it — we all believe it." Hutchinson was found guilty. Coddington made a lame attempt to defend Hutchinson but was silenced by Governor Winthrop.*]

GOV.: The court hath already declared themselves satisfied concerning the things you hear, and concerning the troublesomeness of her spirit and the danger of her course amongst us, which is not to be suffered. Therefore if it be the mind of the court that Mrs. Hutchinson for these things that appear before us is unfit for our society, and if it be the mind of the court that she shall be banished out of our liberties and imprisoned till she be sent away, let them hold up their hands.

[*All but three did so.*]

GOV.: Those that are contrary minded hold up yours.

[*Only Mr. Coddington and Mr. Colborn did so.*]

MR. JENNISON: I cannot hold up my hand one way or the other, and I shall give my reason if the court require it.

GOV.: Mrs. Hutchinson, the sentence of the court you hear is that you are banished from out of our jurisdiction as being a woman not fit for our society, and are to be imprisoned till the court shall send you away.

MRS. H.: I desire to know wherefore I am banished?

GOV.: Say no more. The court knows wherefore and is satisfied.

Questions to Consider

Now that you have examined the evidence, at least one point is very clear: the political and religious authorities of Massachusetts Bay were determined to get rid of Anne Hutchinson, whether she actually had broken any law or not. They tried to bait her, force admissions of guilt from her, confuse her, browbeat her. Essentially, they had already decided on the verdict before the trial began. So we

① Anne - threat - subverting colonial order
   but having broken a specific law
② Criticized the ministry implied they were in violation
   of the covenants
③ violated the 'place' assign. to women.

know that Anne Hutchinson was a threat — and a serious one — to the colony.

And yet the colony had dealt quite differently with Roger Williams, a Puritan minister banished in 1635 because of his extreme religious beliefs. Williams was given every chance to mend his ways, Governor Winthrop remained his friend throughout Williams' appearances before the General Court, and it was only with great reluctance that the Court finally decided to send him out into the "wilderness."

Why, then, was Anne Hutchinson such a threat and why was her trial such an ordeal? Obviously, she did pose a religious threat. As you look back through the evidence, try to clarify the exact points of difficulty between Hutchinson and the ministers. What was the basis of the argument over covenants of grace and works? What was Hutchinson supposed to have said? Under what circumstances had she allegedly said this? To whom? What was the role of her own minister, John Cotton, in the trial?

One must remember that Anne Hutchinson's trial took place in the midst of the divisive Antinomian controversy. What threat did the Antinomians pose to Massachusetts Bay and to Puritanism? Was Anne Hutchinson an Antinomian? How would you prove whether she was or was not?

Hutchinson's place or role in the community also seems to have come into question during the trial. What do the questions about the meetings she held in her home reveal? Look beyond what the governor and members of the Court are actually saying. Try to imagine what they might have been thinking. In what ways might Hutchinson's meetings have eventually posed a threat to the larger community?

Finally, look through the transcript one more time. It provides some clues, often subtle ones, about the relationships between men and women in colonial Massachusetts. Puritan law and customs gave women approximately equal status with men, and of course women could join the church just as men could. But in every society there are unspoken assumptions about how men and women should behave. Can you find any evidence that Anne Hutchinson violated these assumptions? If so, what did she do? Again, why would this be dangerous?

In conclusion, try to put together all you know from the evidence to answer the central question: why was Anne Hutchinson such a threat to Massachusetts Bay colony?

Epilogue

Even after their banishment, misfortune continued to plague the Hutchinson family. Anne, William, and their children moved to an island in Narragansett Bay, where Anne once

Epilogue

again became pregnant. However, by then she was over forty-five years old and had begun her menopause. Therefore the fetus did not develop naturally and was aborted into a hydatidiform mole (resembling a cluster of grapes), which was expelled with considerable pain and difficulty. Many believed that the "birth" of this "monster baby" was proof of Anne Hutchinson's religious heresy.

In 1642 Anne's husband died, and she moved with her six youngest children to the Dutch colony of New Netherland in what is now the Bronx borough of New York City. The next year she and all but one of her children were massacred by Indians.

Massachusetts Bay continued to try to maintain community cohesion for years after the expulsion of Anne Hutchinson and her family. But as the colony grew and prospered, change ultimately did come. New generations were born that seemed unable to embrace the original zeal of the colony's founders. New towns were formed, which increased the colony's size and made uniformity more difficult. Growth and prosperity also seemed to bring an increased interest in individual wealth and a corresponding decline in religious fervor. Reports of sleeping during sermons, fewer conversions of young people, blasphemous language, and growing attention to physical pleasures were numerous, as were reports of election disputes, intrachurch squabbling, and community bickering.

To those who remembered the old ways of Massachusetts Bay, such straying from the true path was more than unfortunate. The Puritans felt that as the ancient Israelites had been punished by God when they broke their covenant, so they would have to pay for their indiscretions. As one Puritan minister put it, "In the time of their prosperity, see how the Jews turn their backs and shake off the authority of the Lord." The comparision was lost on almost no one.

Hence it is not surprising that by the late 1680s (more than forty years after Anne Hutchinson's death) a wave of religious hysteria swept across Massachusetts Bay colony. Convinced that they had broken their covenant with God, many Puritans grimly awaited their punishment, spending long hours in churches listening to sermons with such ominous titles as "Day of Doom" or "God's Quarrel with New England." When in 1692 a few young girls in Salem Village began accusing some of their neighbors of being possessed by Satan, many were convinced that the day of punishment finally had arrived. Before that incident had run its course, twenty people had been killed, nineteen of them by hanging, and many more temporarily imprisoned. Although the Puritans' congregational church remained the official established church of Massachusetts until 1822, the original community cohesion was destroyed long before that.

[19]

Chapter 2

Rhythms of Colonial Life: The Statistics of Colonial New England

The Problem

The years between the settlement of the colonies and the American Revolution are critical ones in American history. In those years, which in some colonies stretched to over a century,[1] stability was gradually achieved, economic bases were laid, political institutions were established, social structures and institutions evolved, and intellectual and cultural life eventually thrived. As population increased and as older settlements matured, new towns and settlements were founded on the edge of the receding wilderness, thus repeating the process of settlement, stability, growth, and maturation. And, while the vast majority of colonists were still tied to England by bonds of language, economics, government, and affection, over the years those bonds gradually loosened until the colonists, many without fully realizing it, had become something distinctly different than simply Englishmen and women who happened to reside in another land. In some ways, then, the American Revolution was the political realization of earlier economic, social, cultural, and political trends and events in colonial life.

The three best words to describe the period between settlement and Revolution are growth, change, and maturation. Unquestionably, the once tiny and fragile colonies did grow, at

1. The following colonies had been in existence for a century or more when the American Revolution broke out in 1775: Virginia, Massachusetts Bay, Rhode Island, Connecticut, Maryland, New York, and New Jersey. Settlements of Europeans also existed in New Hampshire and Delaware areas over a century before the Revolution, although they did not formally become colonies until later.

[20]

first through a continual influx of new colonists from Europe and later largely through natural increase. In New England alone, the growth rate was phenomenal; the region that had contained approximately 18,000 people in 1640 contained 80,000 people by 1690 and over 500,000 people by 1760. In the South, growth rates initially had been more modest, due to high mortality. By the mid-eighteenth century, however, movement away from the unhealthy coastal areas, the digging of deeper wells to get uncontaminated water, and a more nutritional diet had lowered death rates significantly, and population grew correspondingly. In the Middle Colonies (especially Pennsylvania and New York), the ethnic and religious diversity of the population necessitated a kind of religious and cultural toleration that in turn attracted even more settlers from Europe, thus supplementing the region's natural increase.

Indeed, each time a colony became successful or experienced extensive growth, it was all that much easier for other colonies to be founded in nearby geographical locations. Throughout the colonies, population increased so rapidly that Benjamin Franklin boasted in the 1760s that the number of Americans had doubled every twenty-two years.

As the colonies grew in population, they tended to change and mature. Economically, the southern colonies slowly developed a system of commercial agriculture in which cash crops such as tobacco, rice, and indigo were grown, harvested, and exported to England. At first labor was provided by white indentured servants, but this labor was gradually supplanted by African slaves.[2] In the Middle Colonies, wheat and forest products were exported to England. Hence both the Southern and Middle Colonies fit well into the English mercantile system, in which raw materials were raised in the colonies and shipped to England where they were processed into goods and returned to the colonies for purchase. In New England, however, comparatively rocky soil and a short growing season kept crop yields low and agricultural surpluses meager. Many New England colonists, therefore, had to find other ways to make a living. They turned either to the sea as fishermen, traders, shippers, and seamen or to some native manufacturing such as iron products, rum, shipbuilding, and ropemaking. With the exception of fishing, none of these activities fit into England's mercantile plans for her Empire.

At the same time that the colonists were developing their economic bases, they were creating social structures and institutions as well. In the South a

2. According to historian Edmund Morgan, slavery was adopted in Virginia when white indentured servants began living longer and upon gaining freedom began to pose a threat to the established planter elite. Africans too were living longer, but posed no threat to the planter elite and hence became a better investment.

relatively small number of planters dominated the region's social and political institutions, and although they were sometimes challenged by newer planters (as the Virginia planter elite was in 1676 in Bacon's Rebellion), their control of these institutions was almost complete. Below this group were the yeomanry, small farmers who raised some surpluses for sale but who spent the majority of their efforts raising their own food. The institution of slavery discouraged the existence of a free lower class, and the planters' preference for European-made goods prevented the rise of a sizable group of skilled artisans. In the Middle Colonies and in New England, most people lived on small family farms. As in the South, however, large landowners (especially in New York) and increasingly wealthy merchants dominated social and political life. Both regions possessed numerous skilled artisans who resided mostly in the larger towns and port cities. Altogether, the colonists had developed a system of social stratification in which different socioeconomic classes possessed different rights and privileges. But social status was based more on wealth than on a person's hereditary position, and thus mobility was possible if not generally prevalent.

As the colonies grew, changed, and matured, they became more and more politically aware. From the beginning the colonists showed an intense and active interest in politics. But that interest sharpened as they gradually came to see the societies they were creating as permanent ones and not just temporary outposts of Europe. Not only did they realize that their colonies were directly affected by the difficulties the English monarchy was encountering, but also, like their counterparts in the mother country, they became convinced that they had to guard their rights as English citizens against the encroachments of any government — including their own (the English monarchy). Although the colonial governments differed somewhat on the surface (for example, Virginia called its assembly the House of Burgesses, while Massachusetts named its lower house the General Court), these governments were actually quite similar in substance. Representation of the people, limited though it might have been, was very important to the colonists, as were the power to tax and the traditional protections for the individual, such as the rights of free speech, jury trial, and assembly. In fact, the American colonists would react very strongly, sometimes even violently, to the British efforts after 1763 to make the colonies share the increasing costs of empire. From the colonists' viewpoint, laws such as the Stamp Act and the Quartering Act seemed to endanger and possibly even violate their traditional rights.

Not only had the colonists' political ideas been sharpened and refined during the period before the American Revolution, but their other ways of thinking were also greatly affected. In the period immediately preceding the Revolution, the Enlightenment encouraged an optimistic, scientific, more rational outlook on life, and the Great Awakening forced both people and churches to raise serious, often divisive, questions about their religious beliefs and practices. The Enlightenment and the Great Awakening generally affected different groups of colonists, with the former being espoused by the literate and educated and the latter embraced by the middling and poorer sorts.[3] Both movements, however, contained a strong streak of individualism: the Enlightenment in its emphasis on the potential of the individual mind, and the Great Awakening in its concentration on the individual soul. Each, in its own way, increased the colonists' sense of themselves as individuals who possessed individual rights as well as individual futures. Once huddled together for protection and mutual assistance in tiny settlements, by the mid-eighteenth century colonists had grown, changed, and matured, as had the settlements they had built. They harbored new attitudes about themselves, their society, their individual futures, and, almost inevitably, their government.

It should be evident by now that the period between colonial settlement and the American Revolution was a crucial one. Growth, change, maturation, increased political awareness, the Enlightenment, and the Great Awakening all had played important roles in shaping American society. And yet there were other significant contributions to the trends of growth, change, and maturation — contributions somewhat less visible than the economic, social, and political occurrences described earlier. What were these other contributions? How important were they? Did they interact with the already-discussed economic, social, and political trends and with the rise in political consciousness, the Enlightenment, and the Great Awakening? And finally, what role did each of these trends and events play in the growing separation from the mother country?

When most people think of the colonial period in America, they invariably think of the colonial leaders, men and women who held the economic, social, and political reins of the society. But these leaders — the John Winthrops and Anne Hutchinsons, the Jonathan Edwardses and Benjamin Franklins, the William Penns and Nathaniel Bacons — represent only a tiny fraction of the men and women who lived in the colonies between 1607 and 1775. And yet, in order to understand the processes of growth, change, and maturation more fully, it is necessary for us to study the lives of the "ordinary" men, women, and children as well as those of their eco-

3. Most people in the eighteenth century did not use the term *class* but instead referred to people as belonging to the "better," "middling," or "poorer" sort.

nomic, social, and political "betters." How did the processes of growth, change, and maturation affect small farmers and artisans, their spouses, sons, and daughters? How did the situations of these people change over time? How did they react to those changes? Indeed, if we can learn more about the lives of all Americans and not just those of the prominent colonists, we will be able to better understand the extent to which growth, change, and maturation helped affect the coming of the American Revolution.

As you can imagine, it is considerably easier to collect information about the leading colonial figures than it is for the "average" men and women. Few of the farmers, artisans, or laborers left diaries or letters to provide clues to their thoughts and behavior; fewer made speeches or participated in decision making; fewer still talked with leaders like Washington and Jefferson, so their thoughts and actions were much less likely to be recorded for us by others. In some ways, then, a curtain has been drawn across a large part of American colonial history, obscuring the lives, thoughts, and feelings of the vast majority of the colonists. Sometimes even their names have been lost.

The Method

How can we hope to reconstruct the lives, thoughts, and feelings of people who left no letters, diaries, sermons, speeches, or votes for us to analyze? Recently historians have become more imaginative in using the relatively limited records at their disposal to examine the lives of "ordinary" men, women, and children who lived during the colonial period. Almost every person, even the poorest, left some record that he or she existed. That person's name may appear in any of a number of records, including church records stating when he or she was baptized, marriage records, property-holding records, civil- or criminal-court records, military records, tax records, and death or cemetery records. It is in these records that the lives of the "ordinary" men, women, and children of colonial America can be examined. An increasing number of historians have been carefully scrutinizing those records to re-create the lives and attitudes of those who left no other evidence.

How is this done? Most historians interested in the lives of the "ordinary" colonists have come to rely heavily on statistics. Instead of trying to uncover all of the records having to do with one person or family (which might not be representative of the whole population), these historians use statistics to create *collective biographies,* that is, biographies of population *groups* (farmers in Andover, Massachusetts, for example) rather than biographies of certain individuals. The historians collect all (or a sample of all) of the birth, death, and marriage records of a community and

TABLE 1

Type of Record	Questions
Marriage	At what age are women marrying? Is that age changing over time?
Wills, probate	How are estates divided? Is that method changing over time?
Land, tax	What percentage of the adult male population owns land? Is that percentage changing over time? Is the land evenly distributed among the adult male population? Does the population change over time?

look at all (or a sample of all) of the wills, probate records,[4] tax and land-holding records, and census returns. What these historians are doing is forming an aggregate or collective picture of a community and how that community has changed over time. Are women marrying later? Are women having fewer children now than they were in another time? Are inheritance patterns (the methods of dividing estates among heirs) changing over time? Are farms increasing or decreasing in size? To the historian, each statistical summary of records (each set of statistics or *aggregate* picture) contains information that will increase understanding of the community being studied.

But after the statistics are compiled, what does the historian do next? As shown above, each set of statistics is examined separately to see what changes are occurring over time. Table 1 shows the types of questions historians would ask of several different types of records.

Having examined each set of statis-

tics, the historian places the sets in some logical order, which may vary depending on the available evidence, the central questions the historian is attempting to answer, and the historian's own preferences. Some historians prefer a "birth-to-death" ordering, actually beginning with age-at-marriage statistics for females and moving chronologically through the collective life of the community's population. Others prefer to isolate the demographic statistical sets (birth, marriage, migration, and death) from the economic sets (such as landholding and division of estates). With a few exceptions, we have arranged the statistical sets in a rough chronological format.

Up to this point the historian has (1) collected the statistics and arranged them into sets, (2) examined each set and measured tendencies or changes over time, and (3) arranged the sets in some logical order. Now the historian must begin to ask "why" for each set. For example:

1. Why does the method of dividing estates change over time?

2. Why are women marrying later?

---

4. Probate records are public records of processed wills.

3. Why are premarital pregnancies increasing?

In many cases, the answer to each of these questions (and other "why" questions) can be found in one of the other statistical sets. That may cause the historian to alter his or her ordering of the sets to make the story more clear.

The historian is actually linking the sets to one another to form a chain. When two sets have been linked (because one set answers the "why" question of another set), then the historian repeats the process until all the sets have been linked to form one chain of evidence. At that point the historian can summarize the tendencies that have been discovered and, if desired, can connect those trends or tendencies with other events occurring in the period, such as the American Revolution.

Your task in this chapter is to use the statistics provided to identify important trends affecting the men, women, and children of colonial New England in the century preceding the American Revolution. Use the process described above:

1. Examine each statistical set, especially for a change over time.

2. Ask why that change took place.

3. Find the answer in another set, thereby establishing a linkage.

4. Repeat the process until all the sets have been linked together.

5. Then ask the central questions: What important trends affected the men, women, and children of colonial New England in the century preceding the American Revolution? How were people likely to think and feel about those trends?

At first the statistics will appear cold and impersonal and would seem to tell us little that is worth knowing. Can't we just skip this problem and get on to the political events leading up to the American Revolution (like the Boston Massacre) and the important battles of the Revolution? And yet, it is crucial to remember that some of the men and boys who were on the streets of Boston on the evening of March 5, 1770, are counted in these statistics. And some of the men who participated in the Battles of Lexington and Concord also appear in these statistics. Are there any links between what the statistics represent and the subsequent behaviors of these people?

Handwritten top:
1 What do the statistics measure?
2 How does it change over time?
3 Why does change take place?

The Evidence

Statistical set 1 reprinted from James A. Henretta, The Evolution of American Society, 1700–1815: An Interdisciplinary Approach *(Lexington, Mass.: D. C. Heath, 1973), p. 27. Data for statistical sets 2–8 from Henretta, pp. 13, 15, 19, 25, 29–30, 12, and 133, respectively. Data for statistical sets 9–12 from Gary B. Nash, "Urban Wealth and Poverty in Pre-Revolutionary America,"* Journal of Interdisciplinary History, *6 (Spring 1976), 545–584.*

1. Population Increase in New England, by Decade

Handwritten: 1 – Rapid Pop. Growth   3 – Link to #

1700–1710	24%	1740–1750	24%
1710–1720	48%	1750–1760	25%
1720–1730	27%	1760–1770	29%
1730–1740	33%		

2. Child Mortality[5]

Handwritten: 1 – Low child mortality   3 – No statistical answer

Sweden: 50% of those born did not reach 15 years, 1751–1799
France: 50% of those born did not reach 21 years, 1750–1800
Andover, Mass.: 10% of those born did not reach 21 years, 1650–1700

Handwritten left: Go to #6, then 3, 4, 5

3. New England Farm Size

Handwritten: 1 – Farms smaller & more intensely cultivated   3 – Link to 1 & 2 – More children to divide the land – thus more intensely cultivated

1650s: 200–300 acres (one-third cultivated)
1750s: under 100 acres (mostly cultivated)

4. Period of Fallow,[6] New England Farms

Handwritten: 1 – Fallow period down & yields surely down   3 – See 1, 2, 3

1650: field left fallow between 7 and 15 years
1770: field left fallow between 1 and 2 years

5. Abbot Family, Andover, Mass.

Handwritten: 1 – Abbot Family growing   3 – Proof of what would have happened if land continued to be divided.

1650: George Abbot was only adult male
1750: 25 adult male Abbots in Andover

5. Normally historical demographers use the term *child mortality* to refer to the deaths of children under five years old. Note that this is not the way the term is used here.

6. Fallow land is plowed and tilled but left unseeded during a growing season. Land is left fallow to replenish the soil's nutrients. Colonial farmers as a rule did not use fertilizer.

Handwritten bottom: used to emphasize what Abbots farm might have looked like if equally divided among all male heirs. – if that were possible

[handwritten top margin: 1- Fewer estates divided among all male heirs]
[handwritten: 3- Link to 1-4 (inability to div. land among all male heirs)]

6. Division of Estates, Andover, Mass.

[handwritten left margin: Consequences of #6.]
[handwritten: 1- Changing inheritance patterns obliged young people to defer marriage]

1st generation: 95% of all estates divided among all male heirs
2nd generation: 75% of all estates divided among all male heirs
3rd generation: 58% of all estates divided among all male heirs
4th generation (which came to maturity after 1750): under 50% of all estates divided among all male heirs

[handwritten left margin: 2- At same time premarital conceptions increased.]

7. Average Age at Marriage for Females

[handwritten: 1- Age increasing]
[handwritten: 3- See 6]

Andover, Mass., 1650s: 19 years
Andover, Mass., 1750s: 23–24 years

[handwritten left margin: 3- Migration - to Boston - not westward (towns had to be est. & land approved from town govt.)]

8. Premarital Conceptions

[handwritten: 1- Increase]
[handwritten: 3 - See 6 & 7]
[handwritten: Is this the only reason? Rel. ideas waning?]

Hingham, Mass.
  1660: under 10%
  1700: 10%
  1750: 30%
Bristol, R.I.
  1740–1760: 50%

[handwritten left margin: 4- migrants coming into the economic bottom of Boston &]

9. Migration[7] into Boston, 1747–1771, by Group

[handwritten: 1- Migration increasing]
[handwritten: 3- See 6]

Group	1747	1759	1771
Single men	3.0%	8.5%	23.4%
Single women	4.0%	16.8%	20.0%
Widows and widowers	7.9%	8.9%	4.4%
Married couples	33.6%	27.4%	27.5%
Children	51.5%	38.4%	24.7%

[handwritten left margin: 5- Wealth concentrated in fewer + fewer hands.]

10. Wealth Distribution[8] in Boston, 1687 and 1771

Wealth Distribution	1687	1771
Wealth possessed by the richest 5% of the people	30.2%	48.7%
Wealth possessed by the next wealthiest 5% of the people	16.1%	14.7%

7. Migration refers to internal migration, and not to immigration from Europe.
8. See Questions to Consider for assistance in reading this set.

[Handwritten: Wealthiest Bostonians controlled an increasing share of towns property. Poorer 60% controlling less & less]

[Handwritten: 3 - Poverty of migrants]

Wealth possessed by the next wealthiest 30% of the people	39.8%	27.4%
Wealth possessed by the next wealthiest 30% of the people	11.3%	9.1%
Wealth possessed by the poorest 30% of the people	2.6%	0.1%

11. Taxables[9] in Boston, 1728–1771

[Handwritten: 1 - Pop. increasing. Taxables decreasing]

[Handwritten: 3 - see #9 Greater proportion of Bostonians are without property]

Year	Population	Taxables
1728	12,650	c. 3,000
1733	15,100	c. 3,500
1735	16,000	3,637
1738	16,700	3,395
1740	16,800	3,043
1741	16,750	2,972
1745	16,250	2,660
1750	15,800	c. 2,400
1752	15,700	2,789
1756	15,650	c. 2,500
1771	15,500	2,588

12. Poor Relief in Boston, 1700–1775

[Handwritten: 1 - Poor relief increasing faster than pop.]

[Handwritten: 3 - See 9–11]

Year	Population	Average Annual Expenditure	Expenditure per 1,000 Pop.
1700–10	7,500	£ 173	£ 23
1711–20	9,830	181	18
1721–30	11,840	273	23
1731–40	15,850	498	31
1741–50	16,240	806	50
1751–60	15,660	1204	77
1761–70	15,520	1909	123
1771–75	15,500	2478	156

[Handwritten: 2x, ?x]

9. *Taxables* refers to the number of people who owned a sufficient amount of property (real estate and buildings) to be taxed.

answer the
3 Question)
for each
statistical
set)

Questions to Consider

When using statistics, one must first look at each set individually. For each set, ask the following questions:

1. What does this set of statistics measure?

2. How does what is being measured change over time?

3. Why does that change take place?

For example, the first set of statistics deals with population increase in New England. With the exception of the 1710–1720 decade, population growth was steady and rapid. Why was this so? Look at the second set, on child mortality. Could this set help to answer the "why" question for the first set? It is important for you to know that immigration to New England from Europe declined drastically in the 1640s. Therefore, the population growth can be attributed to both natural increase and low child mortality.

Why was child mortality so low? No other statistical sets can answer this question definitely. Based on other things you know about colonial New England, such as climate and population density, can you make some educated guesses? Since we have no other set that can answer the "why" question, we must begin our chain of evidence again, starting with a different set of statistics.

Look at the set dealing with New England farm size. Ask the three questions. Look for a set that answers the third question. Can the earlier sets plus the sets on the Abbot family and the division of estates help? How? As you can see, you have linked the earliest two sets (population increase and child mortality) to some of the subsequent sets in a different way.

But we have overlooked an important set, that on the period of fallow. Ask the three questions. Does the third question link that set into your emerging chain?

Now complete the links of your chain:

1. Why were women marrying later? (Find the set or sets that answer this.)

2. Why were premarital conceptions increasing? (Look at the other sets and make some educated guesses.)

3. How did the types of people moving to Boston change? Why? Where did they come from?

At this point we have come to the set on wealth distribution in Boston. Note that Boston is not a farming village like Andover and Hingham. Read the set in this way: The richest 5% of those living in Boston in 1687 owned 30.2% of the town's taxable wealth (essentially real estate and buildings), but by 1771 the richest 5% owned 48.7% of the town's taxable wealth; the poorest 30% of those living in Boston in 1687 owned 2.6% of the town's taxable wealth, but by 1771 the poorest 30% owned 0.1%

of the town's taxable wealth. Read the chart the same way for the groups in-between. As you examine the chart, note which groups were gaining in wealth and which groups were losing in wealth.

The last three sets of statistics are different ways of looking at the same problem. How are these sets related to one another? How can you link them back to the chain you have made?

At this point, you should be able to answer the central questions,

1. What were the important trends having to do with growth, change, and maturation that affected the people of colonial New England?

2. How were people likely to think and feel about those trends?

Epilogue

Many of the men who fought on the Patriot side either in the Continental Line (the troops under the central government, the United States Army) or the Massachusetts Bay militia came from the towns, farms, and seaports of the troubled New England colonies. If asked why they had endured such hardships to fight against the mother country, most probably they would have said that they were fighting for liberty and independence — and undoubtedly they were. But we now re-alize that a number of other factors were present that may very well have provided strong reasons for these men to contest the British. Whether they fully understood these forces can never be known with certainty, since very few left any written record that might help us to comprehend their behavior.

The American Revolution was a momentous event not just for Americans but ultimately for many other people as well. As Ralph Waldo Emerson wrote years later, it was a "shot heard 'round the world." The American Revolution was the first anticolonial rebellion that was successful on the first try, and as such it provided a model for others in Latin America and elsewhere. As a revolt against authority, the American Revolution made many European rulers tremble, for if the ideas contained in the Declaration of Independence (especially that of the right of revolution against unjust rulers) ever became widespread, their own tenures might well be doomed. And, beginning with the French Revolution, this is precisely what happened; gradually, crowns began to topple all across the Continent. Indeed, many would have agreed with the Frenchman Turgot who, writing of America in the 1780s, noted

This people is the hope of the human race. It may become the model. It ought to show the world, by facts, that men can be free and yet peace-

[31]

ful, and may dispense with the chains in which tyrants and knaves . . . have presumed to bind them. . . . The Americans should be an example of political, religious, commercial and industrial liberty. The asylum they offer to the oppressed of every nation, the avenue of escape they open, will compel governments to be just and enlightened.[10]

The Revolution obviously brought independence and in the long run became one of the significant events in world history. But did it alter or re-

10. Richard Price, *Observations on the Importance of the American Revolution, and the Means of Making It a Benefit to the World* (London: printed for T. Cadell, 1785), pp. 102, 123.

verse the economic and social trends that, as we have seen, were affecting the men, women, and children of colonial New England? In 1818 the United States Congress passed an act providing pensions for impoverished veterans of the War of Independence and their widows. Congressmen believed that there were approximately 1,400 poor veterans and widows who were still alive. Yet an astounding 30,000 applied for pensions, 20,000 of whom were ultimately approved to receive these benefits. Clearly the American Revolution, while it was an event that had worldwide significance, did not necessarily change the lives of all the men and women who participated in it. Or did it?

Chapter 3

What Really Happened in the Boston Massacre? The Trial of Captain Thomas Preston

---

The Problem

The town of Boston[1] had been uneasy throughout the first weeks of 1770. Tension had been building since the early 1760s, as the town was increasingly affected by the forces of migration, change, and maturation. The protests against the Stamp Act had been particularly bitter there, and men like Samuel Adams were encouraging their fellow Bostonians to be even bolder in their remonstrances. In response, in 1768 the British government ordered two regiments of soldiers to Boston to restore order and enforce the laws of Parliament. "They

will not *find* a rebellion," quipped Benjamin Franklin of the soldiers, "they may indeed *make* one" (italics added).

The troops in Boston made a difficult situation even more difficult. Incidents between Bostonians and redcoats were common on the streets, in taverns, and at the places of employment of British soldiers who sought part-time jobs to supplement their meager salaries. Known British sympathizers and informers were harassed, and crown officials were openly insulted. Indeed, the town of Boston seemed to be a powder keg just waiting for a spark to set off an explosion.

On February 22, 1770, British sympathizer and informer Ebenezer

1. Although Boston was one of the largest urban centers in the colonies, the town was not incorporated as a city. Several attempts were made, but residents opposed them, fearing they would lose the institution of the town meeting.

Chapter 3
What Really
Happened in the
Boston Massacre?
The Trial of
Captain Thomas
Preston

Richardson tried to tear down an anti-British sign. He was followed to his house by an angry crowd that proceeded to taunt him and break his windows with stones. One of the stones struck Richardson's wife. Enraged, he grabbed a musket and fired almost blindly into the crowd. Eleven-year-old Christopher Seider[2] fell to the ground with eleven pellets of shot in his chest. The boy died eight hours later. The crowd, by now numbering around one thousand, dragged Richardson from his house and through the streets, finally delivering him to the Boston jail. Four days later the town conducted a huge funeral for Christopher Seider, probably arranged and organized by Samuel Adams. Seider's casket was carried through the streets by children, and approximately two thousand mourners (one-seventh of Boston's total population) took part.

All through the next week Boston was an angry town. Gangs of men and boys roamed the streets at night looking for British soldiers foolish enough to venture out alone. Similarly, off-duty soldiers prowled the same streets looking for someone to challenge them. A fight broke out at a ropewalk between some soldiers who worked there part-time and some unemployed colonists.

Then, on the chilly evening of March 5, 1770, the spark that many feared and a few longed for was pro-

vided. A small group of men and boys began taunting a British sentry (called a "Centinel" or "Sentinel") stationed in front of the Custom House. Pushed to the breaking point by this goading, the soldier struck one of his tormenters with his musket. Soon a crowd of fifty or sixty gathered around the frightened soldier, prompting him to call for help. The officer of the day, Captain Thomas Preston, and seven British soldiers hurried to the Custom House to protect the sentry.

Upon arriving at the Custom House, Captain Preston must have sensed how precarious his position was. The crowd had swelled to several hundred, some anxious for a fight, others simply curiosity seekers, and still others called from their homes by the town's church bells, a traditional signal that a fire had broken out. Efforts by Preston and others to calm the crowd proved useless. And because the crowd had enveloped Preston and his men as it had the lone sentry, escape was nearly impossible.

What happened next is a subject of considerable controversy. One of the soldiers fired his musket into the crowd, and the others followed suit one by one. The colonists scattered, leaving five dead[3] and six wounded,

---

2. Christopher Seider is sometimes referred to as Christopher Snider.

3. Those killed were Crispus Attucks (a black seaman in his forties, who also went by the name of Michael Johnson), James Caldwell (a sailor), Patrick Carr (an immigrant from Ireland who worked as a leather-breeches maker), Samuel Gray (a ropemaker), and Samuel Maverick (a seventeen-year-old apprentice).

some of whom were probably innocent bystanders. Preston and his men quickly returned to their barracks where they were placed under house arrest. They were later taken to jail and charged with murder.

Both sides sought to use the event to support their respective causes. But Samuel Adams, Patriot leader and master of propaganda, clearly had the upper hand. The burial of the five "martyrs" was attended by almost every resident of Boston, and Adams used the event to push his demands for British troop withdrawal and to heap abuse on the mother country. Therefore, when the murder trial of Captain Thomas Preston finally opened in late October, emotions had hardly diminished.

Crowd disturbances had been an almost regular feature of life, both in England and America. Historian John Bohstedt has estimated that England was the scene of at least one thousand crowd disturbances and riots between 1790 and 1810. Colonial America was no more placid; demonstrations and riots were almost regular features of the colonists' lives. Yet in almost no cases were there any deaths, and the authorities seldom fired on the crowds. Destruction of property was widespread in these disturbances, and officials seem to have been content to allow the crowd to vent its anger almost unchecked. Indeed, it was almost as if the entire community was willing to countenance demonstrations and riots, as long as they were confined to parades, loud gatherings, and limited destruction of property. Yet on March 5, 1770, both the crowd and the soldiers acted uncharacteristically. The result was the tragedy that colonists dubbed the "Boston Massacre." Why did the crowd and the soldiers behave as they did?

Preston's trial began on October 24, 1770, delayed by the authorities in an attempt to cool the emotions of the townspeople. John Adams, Josiah Quincy, and Robert Auchmuty had agreed to defend Preston, even though the former two were staunch Patriots. They believed that the captain was entitled to a fair trial and did their best to defend him. After a difficult jury selection, the trial began. It lasted for four days, an unusually long trial for the times. The case went to the jury at 5:00 P.M. on October 29. Although it took the jury only about three hours to reach a verdict, the decision was not announced until the following day.

Your task is to use portions of the transcript of the murder trial of Captain Thomas Preston to reconstruct what actually happened on that March 5, 1770, evening in Boston, Massachusetts. Was Preston guilty as charged? Or was he innocent? Only by reconstructing the events that we have come to refer to as the Boston Massacre will you be able to answer those questions. Spelling and punctuation in the transcript have been modernized only where it is otherwise difficult to understand the meaning.

Chapter 3
What Really
Happened in the
Boston Massacre?
The Trial of
Captain Thomas
Preston

The Method

Many students (and some historians) like to think that facts speak for themselves. This is especially tempting when analyzing a single incident, like the Boston Massacre, where there were many eyewitnesses who testified at the trial. However, discovering what really happened, even when there are eyewitnesses, is never quite that easy. Witnesses may be confused at the time, they may see only part of the incident, or they may unconsciously "see" only what they expect to see. Obviously, witnesses may also have some reasons to lie. Thus the testimony of witnesses must be carefully scrutinized, both for what the witnesses *mean* to tell us and for other relevant information as well.

All of the witnesses (except the reporter from the *Boston Gazette*) were at the scene in Boston, yet not all of their testimony is equally valuable. First try to reconstruct the scene itself — the actual order in which the events occurred and where the various participants were standing. Whenever possible, look for corroborating testimony — two or more reliable witnesses who heard or saw the same things.

Be careful to use all of the evidence. You should be able to develop some reasonable explanation for the conflicting testimony and those things that do not fit into your reconstruction very well.

Almost immediately you will discover that some important pieces of evidence are missing. For example, it would be useful to know the individual backgrounds and political views of the witnesses. Unfortunately, we know very little about the witnesses themselves, and we can reconstruct the political ideas of only about one-third of them. Therefore, you will have to rely on the testimonies given, deducing which witnesses were telling the truth, which were lying, and which were simply mistaken.

Likewise, it would be helpful to read the transcripts of the defense attorneys' summary so we could know what their principal arguments were. Unfortunately, that evidence too has been lost.

However, the fact that significant portions of the evidence are missing is not the disaster it may seem to be. Historians seldom have all the evidence they need when they attempt to tackle a historical problem. Instead, they must be able to do as much as they can with the evidence that is available, using it as completely and imaginatively as they can. They do this by asking questions of the available evidence. Where were the witnesses standing? Which one(s) seem more likely to be telling the truth? Which witnesses were probably lying? A rough sketch of the scene has been provided. How can it help you?

Keep the central question in mind: what really happened in the Boston Massacre? Throughout this exercise, one thing you will be trying to determine is whether or not an order to fire was actually given. If so, by whom? If not, how can you explain why shots were fired? As commanding officer, Thomas Preston was held responsible and charged with murder. You might want to consider the evidence available to you as either a prosecution or defense attorney. Which side had the stronger case?

The Evidence

FIGURE 1   Site of the Boston Massacre. Town House Area, 1770.

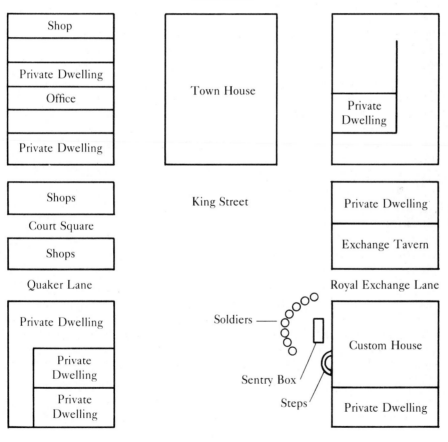

*Chapter 3
What Really
Happened in the
Boston Massacre?
The Trial of
Captain Thomas
Preston*

TESTIMONY

Excerpt of testimony from Hiller B. Zobel, ed., The Legal Papers of John Adams, *Vol. II (Cambridge, Mass.: Belknap Press of Harvard University Press, 1965), pp. 46–98.*

ALEXANDER CRUIKSHANKS

As the Clock struck 9 I saw two Boys abusing the Centinel. They said you Centinel, damned rascally Scoundrel Lobster[4] Son of a Bitch and desired him to turn out. He told them it was his ground and he would maintain it and would run any through who molested or attempted to drive him off. There was about a dozen standing at a little distance. They took no part. He called out Guard several times and 7 or 8 Soldiers with Swords Bayonets and one with a large Tongs in his hand came. I saw the two Boys going to the Men who stood near the Centinel. They returned with a new Edition of fresh Oaths, threw Snow Balls at him and he then called Guard several times as before.

PETER CUNNINGHAM

Upon the cry of fire and Bells ringing went into King Street, heard the Capt. say Turn out the Guard. Saw the Centinel standing on the steps of the Custom house, pushing his Bayonet at the People who were about 30 or 40. Captain came and ordered the Men to prime and load.[5] He came before 'em about 4 or 5 minutes after and put up their Guns with his Arm. They then fired and were priming and loading again. I am pretty positive the Capt. bid 'em Prime and load. I stood about 4 feet off him. Heard no Order given to fire. The Person who gave Orders to Prime and load stood with his back to me, I did not see his face only when he put up their Guns. I stood about 10 or 11 feet from the Soldiers, the Captain about the midway between.

WILLIAM WYATT

I heard the Bell, coming up Cornhill, saw People running several ways. The largest part went down to the North of the Town house. I went the South side,

---

4. The British soldiers' coats from the rear bore a slight resemblance to the back of a lobster.

5. Muskets were loaded with powder, wadding, a ball, and more wadding from the muzzle. Then the hammer (see Figure 3) was drawn back halfway, and powder was poured into the small pan under the hammer. A small piece of flint was attached to the cock (see Figure 3) so that, when the trigger was pulled, the cock would come down and the flint would make a spark that would ignite the gunpowder in the pan. The fire would then travel into the breech to ignite the powder there and fire the gun. If the powder in the pan exploded but did not ignite the powder in the breech, the result was a "flash in the pan" and a musket that did not fire.

saw an Officer leading out 8 or 10 Men. Somebody met the officer and said, Capt. Preston for Gods sake mind what you are about and take care of your Men. He went down to the Centinel, drew up his Men, bid them face about, Prime and load. I saw about 100 People in the Street huzzaing, crying fire, damn you fire. In about 10 Minutes I heard the Officer say fire. The Soldiers took no notice. His back was to me. I heard the same voice say fire. The Soldiers did not fire. The Officer then stamped and said Damn your bloods fire be the consequences what it will. Immediately the first Gun was fired. I have no doubt the Officer was the same person the Man spoke to when coming down with the Guard. His back was to me when the last order was given. I was then about 5 or 6 yards off and within 2 yards at the first. He stood in the rear when the Guns were fired. Just before I heard a Stick, which I took to be upon a Gun. I did not see it. The officer had to the best of my knowledge a cloth coloured Surtout[6] on. After the firing the Captain stepd forward before the Men and struck up their Guns. One was loading again and he damn'd 'em for firing and severely reprimanded 'em. I did not mean the Capt. had the Surtout but the Man who spoke to him when coming with the Guard.

JOHN COLE

I saw the officer after the firing and spoke to the Soldiers and told 'em it was a Cowardly action to kill men at the end of their Bayonets. They were pushing at the People who seemed to be trying to come into the Street. The Captain came up and stamped and said Damn their bloods fire again and let 'em take the consequence. I was within four feet of him. He had no Surtout but a red Coat with a Rose on his shoulder. The people were quarrelling at the head of Royal Exchange lane.[7] The Soldiers were pushing and striking with the Guns. I saw the People's Arms moving but no Sticks.

THEODORE BLISS

At home. I heard the Bells for fire.[8] Went out. Came to the Town House. The People told me there was going to be a Rumpus with the Soldiers. Went to the Custom house. Saw Capt. Preston there with the Soldiers. Asked him if they were loaded. He said yes. If with Ball. He said nothing. I saw the People

6. *Surtout* is the name of a certain type of overcoat.

7. See Figure 1 for location of Royal Exchange Lane.

8. No town in colonial America had a municipal fire department. Whenever a fire broke out, the church bells would be rung and citizens would gather with buckets to put out the fire. In Boston, citizens were required to keep two buckets in their homes and to turn out when the bells were rung.

Chapter 3
What Really
Happened in the
Boston Massacre?
The Trial of
Captain Thomas
Preston

throw Snow Balls at the Soldiers and saw a Stick about 3 feet long strike a Soldier upon the right. He sallied and then fired. A little time a second. Then the other[s] fast after one another. One or two Snow balls hit the Soldier, the stick struck, before firing. I know not whether he sallied on account of the Stick or step'd back to make ready. I did not hear any Order given by the Capt. to fire. I stood so near him I think I must have heard him if he had given an order to fire before the first firing. I never knew Capt. Preston before. I can't say whether he had a Surtout on, he was dressed in red. I know him to be the Man I took to be the Officer. The Man that fired first stood next to the Exchange lane. I saw none of the People press upon the Soldiers before the first Gun fired. I did after. I aimed a blow at him myself but did not strike him. I am sure the Captain stood before the Men when the first Gun was fired. I had no apprehension the Capt. did give order to fire when the first Gun was fired. I thought, after the first Gun, the Capt. did order the Men to fire but do not certainly know. I heard the word fire several times but know not whether it came from the Captain, the Soldiers or People. Two of the People struck at the Soldiers after the first Gun. I don't know if they hit 'em. There were about 100 People in the Street. The muzzles of the Guns were behind him. After the first Gun the Captain went quite to the left and I to the right.

HENRY KNOX

I saw the Captain coming down with his party. I took Preston by the Coat, told him for Gods sake take care of your Men for if they fire your life must be answerable. In some agitation he replied I am sensible of it. A Corporal was leading them. The Captain stopd with me and the Party proceeded to the Centinel the People crying stand by. The Soldiers with their Bayonets charged[9] pushing through the People in order to make way — make way damn your Bloods. The Captain then left me and went to the Party. I heard the Centinel say damn their bloods if they touch me I will fire. In about 3 minutes after this the party came up. I did not see any thing thrown at the Centinel. I stood at the foot of the Town house when the Guns were fired. I heard the People cry damn your bloods fire on. To the best of my recollection the Corporal had a Surtout on. I had none.

9. *Bayonets charged* was a position in the manual of arms (see Figure 2) in which the musket, with bayonet fixed, was held outward and slightly upward. It would be exceedingly difficult to fire a musket accurately from this position because of the recoil upon firing.

BENJAMIN BURDICK

When I came into King Street about 9 o'Clock I saw the Soldiers round the Centinel. I asked one if he was loaded and he said yes. I asked him if he would fire, he said yes by the Eternal God and pushd his Bayonet at me. After the firing the Captain came before the Soldiers and put up their Guns with his arm and said stop firing, dont fire no more or dont fire again. I heard the word fire and took it and am certain that it came from behind the Soldiers. I saw a man passing busily behind who I took to be an Officer. The firing was a little time after. I saw some persons fall. Before the firing I saw a stick thrown at the Soldiers. The word fire I took to be a word of Command. I had in my hand a highland broad Sword which I brought from home. Upon my coming out I was told it was a wrangle between the Soldiers and people, upon that I went back and got my Sword. I never used to go out with a weapon. I had not my Sword drawn till after the Soldier pushed his Bayonet at me. I should have cut his head off if he had stepd out of his Rank to attack me again. At the first firing the People were chiefly in Royal Exchange lane, there being about 50 in the Street. After the firing I went up to the Soldiers and told them I wanted to see some faces that I might swear to them another day. The Centinel in a melancholy tone said perhaps Sir you may.

DANIEL CALEF

I was present at the firing. I heard one of the Guns rattle. I turned about and lookd and heard the officer who stood on the right in a line with the Soldiers give the word fire twice. I lookd the Officer in the face when he gave the word and saw his mouth. He had on a red Coat, yellow Jacket and Silver laced hat, no trimming on his Coat. The Prisoner is the Officer I mean. I saw his face plain, the moon shone on it. I am sure of the man though I have not seen him since before yesterday when he came into Court with others. I knew him instantly. I ran upon the word fire being given about 30 feet off. The officer had no Surtout on.

DIMAN MORTON

Between 9 and 10 I heard in my house the cry of fire but soon understood there was no fire but the Soldiers were fighting with the Inhabitants. I went to King Street. Saw the Centinel over the Gutter, his Bayonet breast high. He retired to the steps — loaded. The Boys dared him to fire. Soon after a Party came down, drew up. The Captain ordered them to load. I went across the Street. Heard

Chapter 3
What Really
Happened in the
Boston Massacre?
The Trial of
Captain Thomas
Preston

one Gun and soon after the other Guns. The Captain when he ordered them to load stood in the front before the Soldiers so that the Guns reached beyond him. The Captain had a Surtout on. I knew him well. The Surtout was not red. I think cloth colour. I stood on the opposite corner of Exchange lane when I heard the Captain order the Men to load. I came by my knowledge of the Captain partly by seeing him lead the Fortification Guard.

JOSEPH PETTY

Between nine and ten of the clock last evening I harked thither, and saw a number of soldiers by the Custom House with their guns leveled; and in an instant of time I heard the word fire: and a number of guns were immediately discharged one after another by the said soldiers. . . . The whole time I was there I saw no insult or abuse offered the soldiers, excepting one stick that was sent among them after the firing.

ROBERT GODDARD

[Preston] ordered his men to stand with their bayonets charged. He then said, "Boys stand off or we shall wound some of you; you had better stand off." A sailor then struck the officer, upon which he said, "Damn you I will not be used in such a manner." Immediately he said Fire upon which the Soldiers stood for a short space. The officer then said "Damn your Blood fire." I immediately heard and saw one musket discharged, which was directly followed by several others.

BOSTON GAZETTE REPORTER

They took place by the custom house and, continued to push to drive the people off, pricked some in several places, on which they were Clamorous and, it is said, threw snow balls. On this, the Captain commanded them to fire; and more snow balls coming, he again said, damn you, fire, be the consequence what it will! One soldier then fired.

CAPTAIN THOMAS PRESTON

The mob still increased and were outrageous, striking their clubs or bludgeons one against another, and calling out, come on you rascals, you bloody backs, you lobster scoundrels, fire if you dare, G-d damn you, fire and be damned, we know you dare not, and much more such language was used. At this time I was between the soldiers and the mob, parleying with, and endeavoring all in my power to persuade them to retire peaceably, but to no purpose. They advanced to the points of the bayonets, struck some of them and even the muzzles of the pieces, and seemed to be endeavoring to close with the soldiers. On which some well behaved persons asked me if the guns were charged. I replied yes. They then asked me if I intended to order the men to fire. I answered no, by no means, observing to them that I was advanced before the muzzles of the men's pieces, and must fall a sacrifice if they fired; that the soldiers were upon the half cock[10] and charged bayonets, and my giving the word fire under those circumstances would prove me to be no officer. While I was thus speaking, one of the soldiers having received a severe blow with a stick, stepped a little to one side and instantly fired. . . . On this a general attack was made on the men by a great number of heavy clubs and snowballs being thrown at them, by which all our lives were in imminent danger, some persons at the same time from behind calling out, damn your bloods — why don't you fire. Instantly three or four of the soldiers fired. . . . On my asking the soldiers why they fired without orders, they said they heard the word fire and supposed it came from me. This might be the case as many of the mob called out fire, fire, but I assured the men that I gave no such order; that my words were, don't fire, stop your firing.

HUGH WHITE, JAMES HARTIGAN, MATHEW KILLROY *(soldiers)*

May it please your Honours, we poor distressed prisoners beg that ye would be so good as to let us have our trials at the same time with our Captain, for we did our Captain's orders & if we don't obey his commands should have been confined & shot for not doing of it.

ISAAC PIERCE

The Lieut. Governor asked Capt. Preston didn't you know you had no power to fire upon the Inhabitants or any number of People collected together unless you had a Civil Officer to give order. The Captain replied I was obliged to, to save my Sentry.

EDWARD HILL

After all the firing Captain Preston put up the Gun of a Soldier who was going to fire and said fire no more you have done mischief enough.

---

10. The cock of a musket had to be fully drawn back (cocked) in order to fire. In half cock, the cock was drawn only halfway back so that priming powder could be placed in the pan. The musket, however, would not fire at half cock. This is the origin of "Don't go off half cocked."

Chapter 3
What Really
Happened in the
Boston Massacre?
The Trial of
Captain Thomas
Preston

RICHARD PALMES

I said to Preston are your Soldiers' Guns loaded. He answered with powder and ball. Sir I hope you don't intend the Soldiers shall fire on the Inhabitants. He said by no means. The instant he spoke I saw something resembling Snow or Ice strike the Grenadier on the Captain's right hand being the only one then at his right. He instantly stepped one foot back and fired the first Gun. I had then my hand on the Captain's shoulder. After the Gun went off I heard the word fire. The Captain and I stood in front about half between the breech and muzzle of the Guns.

MATTHEW MURRAY

I heard no order given. I stood within two yards of the Captain. He was in front talking with a Person, I don't know who. I was looking at the Captain when the Gun was fired.

DANIEL CORNWALL

Capt. Preston was within 2 yards of me — before the Men — nearest to the right — facing the Street. I was looking at him. Did not hear any order. He faced me. I think I should have heard him. I directly heard a voice say Damn you why do you fire. Don't fire. I thought it was the Captain's then. I now believe it. . . .

WILLIAM SAWYER

The people kept huzzaing. Damn 'em. Daring 'em to fire. Threw Snow balls. I think they hit 'em. As soon as the Snow balls were thrown and a club a Soldier fired. I heard the Club strike upon the Gun and the corner man next the lane said fire and immediately fired. This was the first Gun. As soon as he had fired he said Damn you fire. I am so sure that I thought it was he that spoke. The next Gun fired and so they fired through pretty quick.

JANE WHITEHOUSE

A Man came behind the Soldiers walked backwards and forward, encouraging them to fire. The Captain stood on the left about three yards. The man touched one of the Soldiers upon the back and said fire, by God I'll stand by you. He was dressed in dark colored clothes. . . . He did not look like an Officer. The man fired directly on the word and clap on the Shoulder. I am positive the man was not the Captain. . . . I am sure he gave no orders. . . . I saw one man take a chunk of wood from under his Coat throw it at a Soldier and knocked him. He fell on his face. His firelock[11] was out of his hand. . . . This was before any firing.

JAMES WOODALL

I saw one Soldier knocked down. His Gun fell from him. I saw a great many sticks and pieces of sticks and Ice thrown at the Soldiers. The Soldier who was knocked down took up his Gun and fired directly. Soon after the first Gun I saw a Gentleman behind the Soldiers in velvet of blue or black plush trimmed with gold. He put his hand toward their backs. Whether he touched them I know not and said by God I'll stand by you whilst I have a drop of blood and then said fire and two went off and the rest to 7 or 8. . . . The Captain, after, seemed shocked and looked upon the Soldiers. I am very certain he did not give the word fire.

CROSS-EXAMINATION OF CAPTAIN JAMES GIFFORD

Q: Did you ever know an officer order men to fire with their bayonets charged [Figure 2]?

A: No, Officers never give order to fire from charged bayonet. They would all have fired together, or most of them.

NEWTON PRINCE, *a Negro, a member of the South Church*

Heard the Bell ring. Ran out. Came to the Chapel. Was told there was no fire but something better, there was going to be a fight. Some had buckets and bags and some Clubs. I went to the west end of the Town House where [there] were a number of people. I saw some Soldiers coming out of the Guard house with their Guns and running down one after another to the Custom house. Some of the people said let's attack the Main Guard, or the Centinel who is gone to King street. Some said for Gods sake don't lets touch the main Guard. I went down. Saw the Soldiers planted by the Custom house two deep. The People were calling them Lobsters, daring 'em to fire saying damn you why don't you fire. I saw Capt. Preston out from behind the Soldiers. In the front at the right. He spoke to some people. The Capt. stood between the Soldiers and the Gutter about two yards from the Gutter. I saw two or three strike with sticks on the Guns. I was going off to the west of the Soldiers and heard the Guns fire and

---

11. *Firelock* is a synonym for a musket.

[45]

Chapter 3
What Really
Happened in the
Boston Massacre?
The Trial of
Captain Thomas
Preston

saw the dead carried off. Soon after the Guard Drums beat to arms. The People whilst striking on the Guns cried fire, damn you fire. I have heard no Orders given to fire, only the people in general cried fire.

CONCLUSION OF PROSECUTION'S SUMMARY TO THE JURY

Now Gentlemen the fact being once proved, it is the prisoner's part to justify or excuse it, for all killing is, *prima facie*, Murder. They have attempted to prove, that the People were not only the aggressors, but attacked the Soldiers with so much Violence, that an immediate Danger of their own Lives, obliged them to fire upon the *Assailants*, as they are pleased to call them. Now this *violent Attack* turns out to be nothing more, than a few Snow-balls, thrown by a parcel of *Boys*; the most of them at a considerable distance, and as likely to hit the Inhabitants as the Soldiers (*all this is but* which is a common Case in the Streets of Boston at that Season of the Year, when a Number of People are collected in a Body), and one Stick, that struck a Grenadier, but was not thrown with sufficient force to wound, or even sally him; whence then this Outrage, fury and abuse so much talk'd of? The Inhabitants collected, Many of them from the best of Motives, to make peace; and some out of mere Curiosity, and what was the Situation of Affairs when the Soldiers begun the fire? In addition to the Testimony of many others, you may collect it from the Conduct of Mr. Palmes, a Witness on whom they principally build their Defence. Wou'd he place himself before a party of Soldiers, and risque his Life at the Muzzels of their Guns, when he thought them under a Necessity of firing to defend their Life? 'Tis absurd to suppose it; and it is impossible you should ever seriously believe, that their Situation could either justify or excuse their . . . Conduct. I would contend, as much as any Man, for the tenderness and Benignity of the Law; but, if upon such trifling and imaginary provocation, Men may o'erleap the Barriers of Society, and carry havock and Desolation among their defenceless Fellow Subjects; we had better resign an unmeaning title to protection in Society and range the Mountains uncontrol'd. Upon the whole Gentlemen the facts are with you, and I doubt not, you will find such a Verdict as the Laws of God, of Nature and your own Conscience will ever approve.

Figures 2, 3, and 4 from Anthony D. Darling, Red Coat and Brown Bess, *Historical Arms Series, No. 12 (Bloomfield, Ontario). Courtesy of Museum Restoration Service, © 1970, 1981.*

FIGURE 2   The Position of "Charged Bayonets."

FIGURE 3   Detail of a Musket.

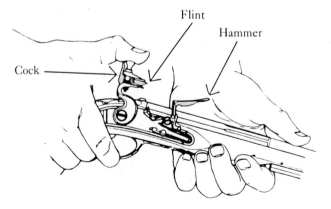

Chapter 3
What Really
Happened in the
Boston Massacre?
The Trial of
Captain Thomas
Preston

FIGURE 4   Diagram of a Musket.

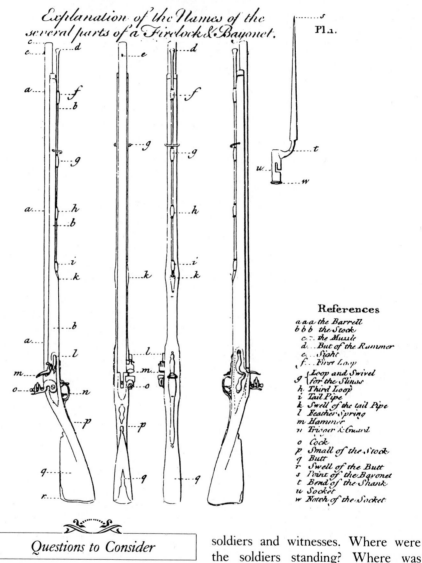

Explanation of the Names of the several parts of a Firelock & Bayonet.

Pl.1.

References

a a a the Barrell
b b b the Stock
c . . . the Muzzle
d . . . But of the Rammer
e . . . Sight
f . . . First Loop
g { Loop and Swivel
     for the Slings
h Third Loop
i Tail Pipe
k Swell of the tail Pipe
l Feather Spring
m Hammer
n Trigger & Guard
o Cock
p Small of the Stock
q Butt
r Swell of the Butt
s Point of the Bayonet
t Bend of the Shank
u Socket
w Notch of the Socket

Questions to Consider

In reconstructing the event, try to picture the positions of the various soldiers and witnesses. Where were the soldiers standing? Where was Captain Preston? Which witnesses were closest to Preston? Where were the other witnesses?

Now look at the testimony. What were the major points Preston made in his own defense? Do the witnesses who were closest to Preston agree or disagree with one another and with Preston? On what points? Be specific — you are trying to clarify what these witnesses heard and saw, and compare it with Preston's account.

Next consider the other witnesses, those who were not so near. What did they hear? What did they see? To what degree do their testimonies agree or disagree, both with each other and with Preston and those closest to him?

Look once again at all the testimony. Is there any other relevant or helpful information given by any of the witnesses? What? Why might it be important?

After you have answered these questions and carefully weighed the evidence provided by the eyewitnesses, you should be ready to answer the central question: what really happened in the Boston Massacre?

Epilogue

In the trial of Thomas Preston, the jury took only three hours to reach its verdict: not guilty. The British officer was quickly packed off to England where he received a pension of £200 per year from the King "to compensate him for his suffering." Of the eight soldiers (the sentry plus the seven men Preston brought to the Custom House), six were acquitted, while two were convicted of manslaughter and punished by being branded on the thumb. From there they disappeared into the mists of history.

On the road to the American Revolution, many events stand out as important or significant. The Boston Massacre is one such event. However, we must be careful in assessing its importance. After all, the colonists and the mother country did not finally resort to arms until five years after this dramatic event. By that time, most of those killed on King Street on March 5 had been forgotten.

Yet the Boston Massacre and other events helped to shape an attitude held by Americans as to what their own revolution had been all about. To most Americans, the British were greedy, heartless tyrants who terrorized a peaceful citizenry. Over one hundred years after the event, the Massachusetts legislature authorized a memorial honoring the "martyrs" to be placed on the site of the "massacre" (over the objections of the Massachusetts Historical Society). The Bostonians' convictions were bolstered by Irish immigrants whose ancestors had known British "tyranny" at first hand, and the Bostonians remained convinced that the American Revolution had been caused by the selfishness and oppression of Britain. As we can see in the Boston Mas-

Chapter 3
What Really
Happened in the
Boston Massacre?
The Trial of
Captain Thomas
Preston

sacre, the road to revolution was considerably more complicated than that.

Today the site of the Boston Massacre is on a traffic island beside the Old State House (formerly called the Town House and seen in the background of Paul Revere's famous engraving[12]) in the midst of Boston's financial district. With the exception of the State House (now a tasteful museum), the site is ringed by skyscrapers that house, among others, the Bank of Boston and the Bank of New England. Thousands of Bostonians and tourists stand on the Boston Massacre site every day, waiting for the traffic to abate.

Many years ago John Adams said that "the foundation of American independence was laid" on the evening of March 5, 1770. While he may have overstated the case, clearly many Americans have come to see the event as a crucial one in the coming of their revolution against Great Britain.

But few have stopped to ponder what actually happened on that fateful evening. Like the American Revolution itself, the answer to that question may well be more complex than we think.

12. The actual title of Revere's engraving is "The BLOODY MASSACRE perpetrated in King Street, BOSTON, on March 5th, 1770 by a party of the 29th Regt."

Chapter 4

The Philadelphia Congressional Election of 1794: Who Won and Why?

The Problem

The years between 1789 and 1801 were crucial ones for the young nation. To paraphrase a comment of Benjamin Franklin, Americans by 1789 (the first year of the Washington administration) had proved themselves remarkably adept at *destroying* governments: in the American Revolution they had ended British rule of the thirteen colonies, and in the Constitutional Convention of 1787 they had ultimately destroyed the United States' first attempt at self-government, the Articles of Confederation. But they had yet to prove that they could *build* a central government that could protect their rights and preserve order and independence. For that reason the period from 1789 to 1801 was important in terms of the survival of the new Republic.

Many important questions confronted the nation's citizens during those difficult years. Could the new government create a financial system that would pay off the public debt, encourage commerce, manufacturing, and investments, and establish a workable federal tax program? Was the central government strong enough to maintain order and protect citizens on the expanding frontier? Could the nation's leaders conceive a foreign policy that would maintain peace, protect international trade, and honor previous treaty commitments? To what extent should national interests overrule the interests and views of the several states?

A much larger question had to do with republicanism itself. No republican experiment of this magnitude had ever been tried before, and there were considerable fears expressed by a

Chapter 4
The Philadelphia
Congressional
Election of 1794:
Who Won and
Why?

number of Americans that the experiment might not survive. Some, like Rufus King of New York,[1] wondered whether the people possessed sufficient intelligence and virtue to be trusted to make wise decisions and choose proper leaders. Others, like John Adams of Massachusetts, doubted that a government without titles, pomp, or ceremony would command the respect and allegiance of common men and women. Still others, like William L. Smith of South Carolina,[2] feared that the new government was not strong enough to maintain order and enforce its will throughout the huge expanse of its domain. And finally, men like Patrick Henry of Virginia and Samuel Adams of Massachusetts were afraid that the national government would abandon republican principles in favor of an aristocratic despotism. Hence, although most Americans were republican in sentiment, they strongly disagreed over the best ways to preserve republicanism and over the dangers it faced. Some Americans openly distrusted "the people" — Alexander Hamilton of New York once called them a "headless beast." Others were wary of the government itself, even though George Washington had been chosen as its first president.

1. Rufus King (1755–1827) was a native of Massachusetts but moved to New York after the Revolution.
2. William L. Smith (1758–1812) was a Federalist congressman from South Carolina and later United States minister to Portugal. He was a staunch supporter of Alexander Hamilton.

Much of the driving force of the new government was provided by Alexander Hamilton, the first secretary of the Treasury. Hamilton used his closeness to Washington as well as his boldness and imagination to fashion a set of policies that set the new nation on its initial course. His scheme for paying the national and state debts, creating a semipublic national bank, and instituting a policy of taxation tended to bind the people and the states closer to the central government. His forcefulness concerning the Whiskey Rebellion of 1794 made it clear that the government could protect its citizens and enforce its laws on the vast and faraway frontier. His favoritism toward Great Britain caused him to meddle in the business of Secretary of State Thomas Jefferson and served to redirect American foreign policy from a pro-French to a pro-British orientation. Indeed, using the popular Washington as a shield (as he later admitted), Hamilton became the most powerful figure in the new government and the one most responsible for making that new government workable.

It is not surprising, however, that these issues and policies provoked sharp disagreements that eventually created two rival political factions, the Federalists (led by Hamilton) and the Democratic-Republicans (led by James Madison and Thomas Jefferson). Federalists generally advocated a strong central government, a broad interpretation of the Constitution, full payment of national and state debts, the establishment of the Bank of the United States, encouragement of commerce, and a pro-British foreign policy. Democratic-Republicans generally favored a central government with limited powers, a strict interpretation of the Constitution, and a pro-French foreign policy, and opposed the Bank.[3]

First appearing in Congress in the early 1790s, these two relatively stable factions gradually began to take their ideas to the voters, thus creating the seeds of what would become by the 1830s America's first political party system. Although unanticipated by the men who drafted the Constitution, this party system became a central feature of American political life, so much so that today it would probably be impossible to conduct the affairs of government or hold elections without it.

Yet that evolution was not foreseen by Americans of the 1790s. Many feared the rise of these political factions, believing that the new government was not strong enough to withstand their increasingly vicious battles. Most people did not consider themselves members of either political faction, and no highly organized campaigns or platforms existed to bind voters to one faction or another. It was considered bad form for candidates to openly seek office (one *stood* for office but never *ran* for office), and

appeals to voters were usually made by friends or political allies of the candidates. Different property qualifications for voting in each state limited the size of the electorate, and most states in the 1790s did not allow the voters to select presidential electors.[4] All of these factors impeded the rapid growth of the modern political party system.

In spite of this, however, political battles during the 1790s grew in intensity and ferocity. As Hamilton's economic plans and Federalism's pro-British foreign policy (the climax of which was the Jay Treaty of 1795) became more clear, Democratic-Republican opposition grew more bitter. Initially the Federalists had the upper hand, largely perhaps because of that group's identification with President Washington. But gradually the Democratic-Republicans gained strength, so much so that by 1800 their titular leader Thomas Jefferson was able to win the presidential election and put an end to Federalist control of the national government.

How can we explain the success of the Democratic-Republicans over their Federalist opponents? To answer this question it would be necessary to study in depth some key elections of

3. These are general tendencies. Some Federalists and Democratic-Republicans did not stand with their respective factions on all of these issues.

4. Pennsylvania, the state under consideration in this chapter, had the most liberal voting requirements. All freemen and freeholders (that is, all taxpayers and property owners) could vote. In Philadelphia, this meant that roughly 50 to 75 percent of the adult males would have been eligible to vote in 1794. Voter turnout, however, was often low.

Chapter 4
The Philadelphia
Congressional
Election of 1794:
Who Won and
Why?

the 1790s. While many such contests could be seen as important ones for understanding the eventual Democratic-Republican victory in 1800, we have selected for further examination the 1794 race for the federal congressional seat from the city of Philadelphia. Because that seat had been held by a Federalist since the formation of the new government, this election was both an important test of strength of the rival Democratic-Republicans and representative of similar important contests being held in that same year in New York, Massachusetts, Maryland, and elsewhere. In the Philadelphia race, Federalist incumbent Thomas Fitzsimons was pitted against Democratic-Republican challenger John Swanwick. Your task is to find out who won this election and why.

The Method

Observers of modern elections employ a variety of methods to analyze political contests and to determine why particular candidates won or lost. Some of the most important of these methods are the following:

1. *Study the candidates* — How a candidate projects him- or herself may be crucial to the election's outcome. Candidates have backgrounds, voting records, personalities, and idiosyncracies that can be assessed by voters. Candidates travel extensively, are seen either in person or on television

by voters, and have several opportunities to appeal to the electorate. Post-election polls have shown that many voters respond as much to the candidates as people (a strong leader, a warm person, a confident leader, and so forth) as they do to the candidates' ideas. For example, in 1952 voters responded positively to Dwight Eisenhower even though many were not sure of his positions on a number of important issues.

2. *Study the issues* — Elections often give citizens a chance to clarify their thinking on some of the leading questions of the day. To make matters more complicated, certain groups (economic, ethnic, and interest groups, for example) respond to issues in different ways. The extent to which candidates can identify the issues that concern voters and can speak to these issues in an acceptable way could well mean the difference between victory and defeat. For example, in 1976 candidate Jimmy Carter was able to tap voters' post-Watergate disgust with corruption in the federal government and defeat incumbent Gerald Ford by speaking to that issue.

3. *Study the campaigns* — Success in devising and implementing a campaign strategy in modern times has been a crucial factor in the outcomes of elections. How does the candidate propose to deal with the issues? How are various interest groups to be lured under the party banner? How will money be raised, and how will it be

spent? Will the candidate debate his or her opponent? Will the candidate make a lot of personal appearances or will he or she conduct a "front-porch" campaign? How will the candidate's family, friends, and political allies be used? Which areas (neighborhoods, regions, states, sections) will be targeted for special attention? To many political analysts it is obvious that a number of superior candidates have been unsuccessful because of poorly run campaigns. By the same token, many less-than-superior candidates have won elections because of effectively conducted campaigns.

4. *Study the voters* — Recently the study of elections has become more scientific. Sophisticated polling techniques have revealed that people similar in demographic variables such as age, sex, race, income, marital status, ethnic group, and religion tend to vote in similar fashions. For example, urban blacks voted overwhelmingly for Jimmy Carter in 1976.

These sophisticated polling techniques, also used for Gallup polls, Nielsen television ratings, and predicting responses to new consumer products, rest upon some important assumptions about human behavior. One assumption is that human responses tend to be strongly influenced (some would go so far as to say *determined*) by demographic variables. Put another way, similar people tend to respond similarly to certain stimuli (such as candidates and campaigns). Another assumption is that these

demographic patterns are constant and do not change rapidly. Lastly, it is assumed that if we know how some of the people responded to certain stimuli, we can calculate how others possessing the same demographic variables will respond to those same stimuli.

Though there are many such patterns of voting behavior, they are easily observable. After identifying the demographic variables that influence these patterns, a demographic sample of the population is created. Thus fifty white, male, middle-aged, married, Protestant, middle-income voters included in a sample might represent perhaps 100,000 people who possess these same variables. The fifty in the sample would then be polled to determine how they voted, and from this information we could infer how the 100,000 voted. Each population group in the sample would be polled in similar fashion. By doing this we can know with a fair amount of precision who voted for whom, thereby understanding which groups within the voting population were attracted to which candidate. Of course the answer to why they were attracted still must be sought with one of the other methods: studying the candidates, studying the issues, and studying the campaigns.

The above four approaches are methods for analyzing modern electoral contests. In fact, most political analysts employ a combination of these approaches. But can these

Chapter 4
The Philadelphia
Congressional
Election of 1794:
Who Won and
Why?

methods be used to analyze the 1794 congressional election in Philadelphia? Neither of the candidates openly sought the office and neither made appearances in his own behalf. Although there certainly were important issues, neither political faction drew up a platform to explain to voters where its candidate stood on those issues. No organized campaign was conducted by either political faction. No polls were taken to see what the concerns of the voters were. At first glance, then, it would appear that most if not all of these approaches to analyzing modern elections would be useless in any attempt to analyze the 1794 Fitzsimons-Swanwick congressional contest.

These approaches, however, may not be as useless as they initially appear. For one thing, Philadelphia in 1794 was not a large city — it contained only about 45,000 people — and many voters knew the candidates personally, since both were prominent figures in the community. Their respective backgrounds were generally well known. Moreover, Fitzsimons, as the incumbent, had a voting record in Congress, and how Swanwick stood on the issues would have been known by most voters, revealed either through Swanwick's friends or through the positions he took as a member of the Democratic Society. Furthermore, the Federalists and Democratic-Republicans had taken general positions on some of the important issues. In addition, we are able to establish with a fair amount of cer-

tainty which voters cast ballots for Fitzsimons and which supported Swanwick. Finally, it is possible to identify some important trends and events occurring in Philadelphia. In sum, although we might not have all the evidence we would like to have (historians almost never do), imaginative uses of the evidence at our disposal may allow us to analyze the 1794 election with all or most of the approaches used in analyzing modern political contests.

In this chapter you will be working with several types of evidence:

1. Biographical material on the two candidates, to help you in comparing their respective backgrounds

2. Statements by Alexander Hamilton and Thomas Jefferson on the Whiskey Rebellion, one important issue in the congressional race

3. Some miscellaneous information that will prove helpful in analyzing some other important issues

4. Two graphs, one on household budgets and the other on real wages

5. A map of Philadelphia showing ward divisions in 1794

6. A table showing the occupations of Philadelphians by wards, to assist you in characterizing the wards by socioeconomic class

7. A first-person account of the yellow fever epidemic in Philadelphia in 1793

[56]

8. A map of Philadelphia showing a sampling of yellow fever deaths in 1793

9. A map of Philadelphia showing congressional voting by wards, 1794

When analyzing the 1794 congressional election in Philadelphia, it will be extremely helpful to divide the task into manageable parts and then put those parts into a logical order. This allows you to reorder the evidence, arranging it so that you can accomplish your task without excess time or confusion. For example, it might be convenient for you to work backward chronologically, answering the questions in this order:

1. Who won the election?

2. Who voted for each candidate?

3. Why did people vote for the candidates they did?

Once you have divided the task, you can arrange the evidence in the order that will answer the questions.

As you examine each piece of evidence, think of the four general approaches used in analyzing elections explained above. Try to group the evidence by approach. For example, statements by Hamilton and Jefferson are presented and information on the yellow fever epidemic of 1793 is provided. Under what general approach would you put each of these pieces of evidence? Such an arrangement of the evidence will give you four ways to analyze why the 1794 congressional election in Philadelphia turned out the way it did.

The Evidence

THE CANDIDATES

THOMAS FITZSIMONS (1741–1811) was born in Ireland and migrated to the colonies sometime before the Revolution. He entered commerce as a clerk in a Philadelphia countinghouse and worked his way up to merchant status. He was a member of the Continental Congress in 1782 and 1783 and a member of Pennsylvania state House of Representatives in 1786 and 1787. He was a delegate to the Constitutional Convention in 1787 and was elected to the federal Congress in 1789. He was a Federalist and a firm supporter of Alexander Hamilton's policies, including the excise tax. He was a Roman Catholic.

JOHN SWANWICK (1740–1798) was born in England and came with his family to the colonies where his father secured work as a minor government official. During the Revolution his father became a Tory, though John Swanwick em-

Chapter 4
The Philadelphia
Congressional
Election of 1794:
Who Won and
Why?

braced the Patriot cause. During the war (1777) he became a clerk in a merchant firm in Philadelphia, rising rapidly to become a full partner by 1783. He held a number of minor offices before being elected to the state legislature in 1792. He opposed the excise tax but thought the rebellion in western Pennsylvania was the wrong method of protest. He was an officer in the Democratic Society and an officer in a society that aided immigrants. He wrote poetry and was considered politically ambitious by those who knew him. He belonged to the Protestant Episcopal Church. He was a Democratic-Republican.

THE WHISKEY REBELLION — TWO OPINIONS

From Harold C. Syrett, ed., The Papers of Alexander Hamilton, *Vol. XVII (New York: Columbia University Press, 1972), pp. 15–19.*

ALEXANDER HAMILTON *to President Washington, August 2, 1794*

If the Judge shall pronounce that the case described in the second section of that Act [authorizing the calling out of the militia] exists, it will follow that a competent force of Militia should be called forth and employed to suppress the insurrection and support the Civil Authority in effectuating Obedience to the laws and punishment of Offenders.

It appears to me that the very existence of Government demands this course and that a duty of the highest nature urges the Chief Magistrate to pursue it.

From Paul L. Ford, ed., Writings of Thomas Jefferson, *Vol. VI (New York: G. P. Putnam's Sons, 1895), pp. 516–519.*

THOMAS JEFFERSON *to James Madison, December 28, 1794*

And with respect to the transactions against the excise law [the Whiskey Rebellion], it appears to me that you are all swept away in the torrent of governmental opinion, or that we do not know what these transactions have been. We knew of none which, according to the definitions of the law, have been anything more than riotous. . . . The excise law is an infernal one. . . . The information of our militia, returned from the Westward, is uniform, that the people there let them pass quietly; they were objects of their laughter, not of their fear.

MISCELLANEOUS INFORMATION

There were a number of sugar and tobacco factories in Philadelphia, which employed many workers. These factories manufactured items that came under the excise tax.

Swanwick was a member of the Democratic Society, a political pressure group organized by Democratic-Republican leaders to get artisans and laborers involved in protest against the policies of the Washington administration. The society passed a resolution opposing the excise tax. The president condemned the society in 1794, saying that he believed that it and other similar societies were responsible for the Whiskey Rebellion. The society endorsed Swanwick in 1794 and worked actively in his behalf.

FIGURE 1 Household Budgets. Both household budgets and real wages (shown in Figure 2) were calculated by Billy G. Smith in his "Struggles of the 'Lower Sort' in Late Eighteenth Century Philadelphia," *Working Papers from the Regional Economic History Research Center* (Wilmington, Del.: Eleutherian Mills-Hagley Foundation, 1979), pp. 1–30. For household budgets, Smith calculated the costs of food, rent, fuel, and clothing and then established how much of these items were consumed. See *ibid.*, pp. 4–5. The base year of the index (100) was 1762. The estimated expenditure for food, rent, fuel, and clothing for the family of a workingman in 1762 was £55.

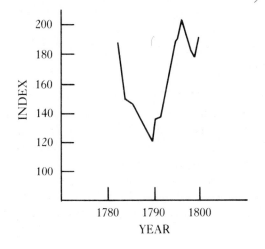

Chapter 4
The Philadelphia
Congressional
Election of 1794:
Who Won and
Why?

FIGURE 2   Real Wages. The base year for the index (100) is 1762. If fully employed, a workingman in Philadelphia in 1762 would have earned approximately £59. By the 1790s a skilled workingman in Philadelphia earned approximately $1.00 per day. Unskilled workers earned approximately 60 cents per day.

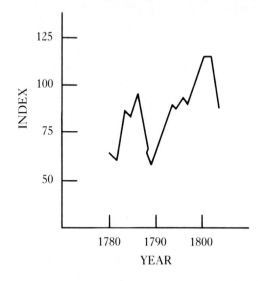

FIGURE 3 **Philadelphia Wards, 1794.**

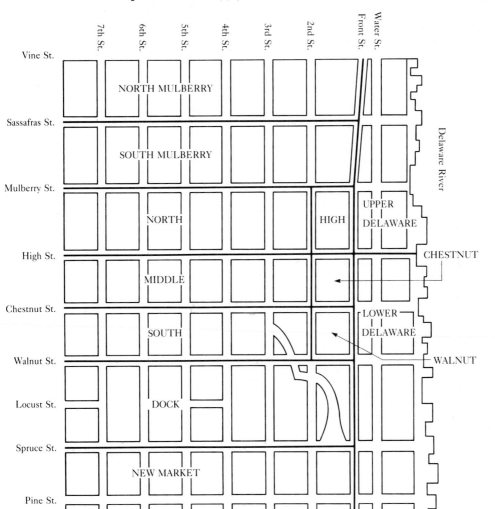

Chapter 4
The Philadelphia
Congressional
Election of 1794:
Who Won and
Why?

TABLE 1   A Sample of Occupations by Ward (Males Only), Philadelphia, 1794*

	Upper Delaware	North Mulberry	South Mulberry	High	North	Chestnut	Middle	Walnut	South	Dock	New Market	Lower Delaware
Gentleman	3	22	31	7	21	1	15	2	8	17	25	5
Merchant	76	47	65	47	90	38	63	20	26	101	83	43
Artisan	95	353	338	33	183	46	164	48	73	131	222	71
Laborer	18	93	103	10	70	7	27	8	12	38	56	1
Shopkeeper	13	24	39	24	44	9	23	4	6	7	35	8
Inn and Tavern Keeper	8	17	12	3	13	5	22	3	4	12	11	6
Captain	6	17	14	0	3	0	1	4	1	7	37	0
Government Employee	2	12	13	0	16	2	13	1	7	14	18	0
Seaman	7	15	5	1	3	1	2	2	2	9	21	2
Teacher	1	5	12	0	6	0	2	0	3	5	6	0
Doctor	1	3	10	3	5	3	2	3	6	10	9	0
Grocer	10	22	20	3	37	2	20	0	5	25	34	6
Clergy	0	5	8	0	0	0	3	0	3	4	4	0
Lawyer	0	3	11	2	1	0	4	1	13	12	5	1
Clerk	5	16	18	3	7	1	12	1	4	10	12	1
Broker	0	1	2	0	3	2	4	4	3	2	1	0
Other	1	5	0	1	3	1	0	0	1	1	2	0
Unknown	1	7	14	1	1	0	2	0	1	2	8	0

* Sample taken from the Philadelphia city directory for 1794. Poor people were notoriously undercounted in city directories. So also were nonpermanent residents, like seamen.

FIRST-PERSON
ACCOUNT

From James Hardie, The Philadelphia Directory and Register *(Philadelphia, 1794).*

Of the Yellow Fever

Having mentioned this disorder to have occasioned great devastation in the year 1793, a short account of it may be acceptable to several of our readers. . . .

This disorder made its first appearance toward the latter end of July, in a lodging house in North Water Street; and for a few weeks seemed entirely confined to that vicinity. Hence it was generally supposed to have been imported and not generated in the city. This was the opinion of Doctors Currie, Cathrall and many others. It was however combated by Dr. Benjamin Rush, who asserts that the contagion was generated from the stench of a cargo of damaged coffee. . . .

But from whatever fountain we trace this poisoned stream, it has destroyed the lives of many thousands — and many of those of the most distinguished worth. . . . During the month of August the funerals amounted to upwards of three hundred. The disease had then reached the central streets of the city and began to spread on all sides with the greatest rapidity. In September its malignance increased amazingly. Fear pervaded the stoutest heart, flight became general, and terror was depicted on every countenance. In this month 1,400 more were added to the list of mortality. The contagion was still progressive and towards the end of the month 90 & 100 died daily. Until the middle of October the mighty destroyer went on with increasing havoc. From the 1st to the 17th upwards of 1,400 fell victims to the tremendous malady. From the 17th to the 30th the mortality gradually decreased. In the whole month, however, the dead amounted to upwards of 2,000 — a dreadful number, if we consider that at this time near one half of the inhabitants had fled. Before the disorder became so terrible, the appearance of Philadelphia must to a stranger have seemed very extraordinary. The garlic, which chewed as a preventative[,] could be smelled at several yards distance, whilst other[s] hoped to avoid infection by a recourse to smelling bottles, handkerchiefs dipped in vinegar, camphor bags, &c. . . .

During this melancholy period they city lost ten of her most valuable physicians, and most of the others were sick at different times. The number of deaths in all amounted to 4041.

Chapter 4
The Philadelphia
Congressional
Election of 1794:
Who Won and
Why?

FIGURE 4 Sampling of Deaths from Yellow Fever, Philadelphia, 1793 Epidemic. Sample taken from Philadelphia newspapers. After a time, officials simply stopped recording the names of those who died, except for prominent citizens. Therefore, although James Hardie reported that 4,041 people had died, one scholar has estimated the death toll to have been as high as 6,000, roughly one out of every seven Philadelphians.

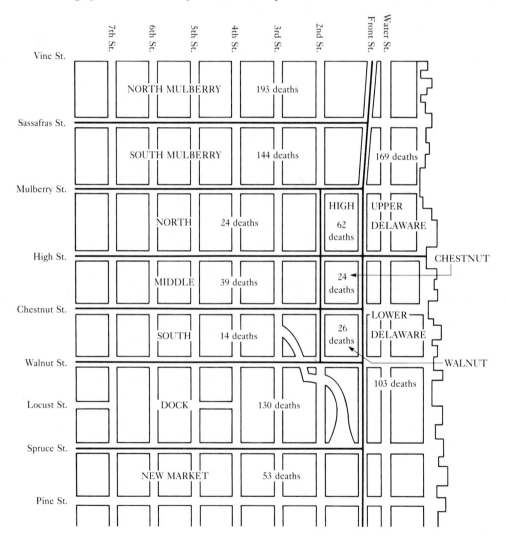

FIGURE 5 Congressional Election, Philadelphia, 1794.

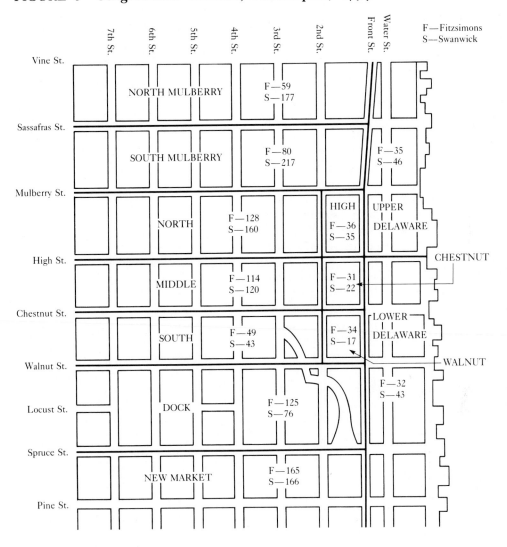

Chapter 4
The Philadelphia
Congressional
Election of 1794:
Who Won and
Why?

Questions to Consider

No single method of analyzing elections will provide you with the answer to the central question of who won and why. Instead, you must examine each piece of evidence separately. See what each piece of evidence is trying to tell you and how that piece relates to the rest of the pieces.

Once you have determined which of the candidates won the election, you should try to discover who tended to vote for each candidate. One piece of evidence available to you is a chart showing occupations by wards. Although there are exceptions, occupations can often be used to establish a person's wealth and status. Today many people introduce themselves by telling their name, occupation, and address. What are these people really saying? Examine carefully the occupational makeup of each ward. Then look at one of the maps. Where do the bulk of laborers live? Artisans (skilled laborers)? Merchants? How could you use this evidence to determine who tended to support Fitzsimons and Swanwick?

Having established who tended to vote for Fitzsimons and who tended to vote for Swanwick, you are ready to answer the question of why one of the candidates was more appealing to the majority of Philadelphia voters. It is here that the four major approaches explained earlier can be brought into play.

1. *Candidates* — Biographical information on the two candidates is included. Don't neglect to study the additional material on Swanwick under "Miscellaneous Information." This is material that voters not personally acquainted with the candidates would have known. What are the significant points of comparison and contrast between the candidates?

One of the significant points of difference is religion. Fitzsimons was a Roman Catholic, and Swanwick belonged to the Protestant Episcopal Church. Most of Philadelphia's voters were Protestant, the two largest denominations being Lutheran and Quaker. Was religion a factor in this election? How can you prove that it was or that it was not?

2. *Issues* — There were a number of issues in this election, and it was fairly clear how each faction stood on those issues. Two of the most important issues were the excise tax and the Whiskey Rebellion.

In its efforts to raise money the national government had settled on, among other things, an excise tax on selected products manufactured in the United States. The taxes on tobacco products, sugar products, and distilled spirits raised storms of protest, especially in western Pennsylvania where whiskey was an important commodity. In that area, farmers tried to prevent the collection of the tax, a protest that eventually grew into the Whiskey Rebellion of 1794. In a sense, this was the first real test of the ability of the central government to enforce its laws.

a. Which groups in Philadelphia did the excise tax affect most? How?

b. How did each candidate stand on the excise tax?

c. Which groups of Philadelphians would have been likely to favor their respective positions?

d. How did each faction stand on the Whiskey Rebellion?

e. How did the candidates stand on this issue?

f. Which groups of Philadelphians would have been likely to favor their respective positions?

3. *Campaign* — Although there were a few mass meetings and some distribution of literature, there was no real campaign in the modern sense. In the absence of an organized campaign, how did voters make up their minds?

4. *Voters* — At the time of the election, other important trends were occurring in Philadelphia that might have influenced voters. For example, review the evidence on household budgets and real wages, compiled by the historian Billy Smith. What general trends can you observe? Which groups would be most affected by these trends? How would they feel?

Also review the material on the 1793 yellow fever epidemic, in which there were over four thousand re-

corded deaths (not quite one-tenth of the city's total population). Why has this material been included in the evidence? How does the evidence on the fever relate to other pieces of evidence? Think about where the epidemic broke out. Who lived in that area? James Hardie said that many people fled the city. Who would tend to leave? Who could not leave? What impact might this event have had on the election a year later?

Now you are ready to answer the question of why the 1794 congressional election in Philadelphia turned out the way it did. Make sure, however, that your opinion is solidly supported by evidence.

Epilogue

As the temporary national capital in 1794, Philadelphia was probably somewhat more advanced than the rest of the nation in the growth of political factions. However, by the presidential election of 1800 most of the country had become involved in the gradual process of party building. Yet it took a number of important elections before the Democratic-Republicans could truly claim to be the dominant faction. Each one of these elections can be analyzed, much as you have analyzed the 1794 congressional election in Philadelphia.

For his part, John Swanwick never

Chapter 4
The Philadelphia
Congressional
Election of 1794:
Who Won and
Why?

saw the ultimate triumph of Democratic-Republicanism, for he died in the 1798 yellow fever epidemic in Philadelphia. Fitzsimons never again sought national political office, preferring to concentrate his energies on his already successful mercantile and banking career. Hamilton died in a duel with Aaron Burr in 1804. After he left the presidency in 1809, Jefferson retired to his estate Monticello to bask in the glories of being an aging founding father. He died in 1826 at the age of eighty-three.

By 1826 many of the concerns of the Federalist era had been resolved. The War of 1812 had further secured American independence, and the death of the Federalist faction had put an end to the notion of government by an entrenched (established) and favored elite. At the same time, however, new issues had arisen to test the durability of the Republic and the collective wisdom of its people. After a brief political calm, party battles once again were growing more fierce, as the rise of Andrew Jackson threatened to split the brittle Jeffersonian coalition. Westward expansion was carrying Americans into territories owned by other nations, and few doubted that an almost inevitable conflict lay ahead. American cities, like Philadelphia, were growing both in population and in socioeconomic problems. The twin specters of slavery and sectional conflict were claiming increasing national attention. Whether the political system fashioned in the 1790s could address these crucial issues and trends and at the same time maintain its republican principles was a question that soon would have to be addressed.

Chapter 5

The Clash of Political and Economic Philosophies: Jackson's Veto of the Bank Recharter (1832)

The Problem

The election of General Andrew Jackson to the presidency in 1828 was seen by many Americans as a victory of the people over the forces of political privilege and vested interests. Although a man of considerable wealth by 1828, Jackson had begun his life in humbler circumstances and had achieved his prosperity through hard work and a measure of good luck. Hence, to many Americans, Jackson was the model of what they too could achieve. Moreover, in the War of 1812 the Tennessean had given Americans a genuine war hero and a thrilling victory at New Orleans. Indeed, even Jackson's faults (his legendary stubbornness and hot temper, his tyrannical behavior at New Or-

leans and later in Florida,[1] his lack of cultural refinements) were turned by many Americans into political assets, evidence that General Jackson was one of them. The first president to whom people felt close enough to give a nickname, "Old Hickory," Andrew Jackson was thought of by his contemporaries as the first "people's president."

In many ways, however, Jackson was the heir of important political trends and forces that he did not create. To begin with, the two-party sys-

1. In an expedition against the Seminole Indians in 1818 Jackson had apprehended and hanged two British agents, causing a brief international incident.

[69]

Chapter 5
The Clash of
Political and
Economic
Philosophies:
Jackson's Veto
of the Bank
Recharter

tem had deteriorated steadily ever since Thomas Jefferson became president in 1801, until by the early 1820s only Jefferson's party, the Democratic-Republican party, remained. Yet that single party was hardly united, as personal and sectional conflicts kept the Democratic-Republicans divided against themselves. Such fissures made it increasingly difficult for the party to select a nominee for president. Up to 1824 Democratic-Republican congressmen had gathered in a caucus and simply named the nominee, always, incidentally, from 1800 to 1820, a Virginian. In 1824, however, personal and sectional animosities virtually destroyed the caucus system, and several other presidential candidates entered the contest, nominated by state legislatures.[2] The resulting campaign saw what was left of party unity dissolve completely. Jackson won a plurality of popular and electoral votes but was denied the presidency by the House of Representatives, where his opponents united against him to make John Quincy Adams the next president. Believing that he had been robbed of the nation's highest office, Jackson and his supporters began a four-year quest to unseat Adams, an effort that was ultimately successful.

Paralleling the disintegration of party unity was the movement toward universal white manhood suffrage. When Jefferson won the presidency in 1800, none of the states provided for universal white manhood suffrage, and only a few allowed voters to select presidential electors. Between 1812 and 1821, however, six western states entered the Union, all of which granted all adult white males the right to vote. In addition, four of the older states virtually eradicated property qualifications for votes. Finally, by 1828 all but one state[3] provided for the selection of presidential electors by popular vote.

The rapid extension of the suffrage and the movement toward selecting presidential electors by popular vote had a profound and lasting impact on American politics in general and presidential campaigns in particular. Newly enfranchised voters now felt they had more of a stake in the elections and wanted the candidates to speak to issues that concerned them. To give all voters the sense of being included, campaigns had to be more broadly based. Issues were important, but so were campaign symbols and tactics, and a candidate with great popular appeal or charisma would have a tremendous advantage. In such a new political atmosphere, created in part by the rapid extension of the suffrage, Andrew Jackson would be turned from a military hero into a national political symbol.

2. The presidential candidates in 1824 were Jackson, John Quincy Adams, Henry Clay, John C. Calhoun, and William Crawford (the caucus selection). Calhoun quickly withdrew to become candidate for vice-president.

3. South Carolina.

Along with the disintegration of the Democratic-Republican party and the extension of the suffrage to the common white man was another important trend that affected American politics. In 1800 so-called professional politicians had been few in number, probably no more than a handful in the entire country. With the extension of the suffrage, however, an opportunity arose for men who could manage campaigns, create "images" for candidates, use the press, and organize the new voters. In addition, the party divisions and the collapse of the caucus system gave these men the wedge they needed to break into politics. One such group of ambitious and farsighted men approached Andrew Jackson about running for president. After some brief hesitation ("I'm not fit to be President," he remarked), the Hero of New Orleans consented to allow these men to help build a national movement to sweep him into the presidency. By 1828 this group included several of Jackson's Tennessee friends as well as a number of knowledgeable figures in Virginia, Pennsylvania, South Carolina, and New York. This is not to say that these men manipulated Jackson (indeed, it actually may have been the other way around) or that the people were duped. Rather, these men took Jackson's already widespread popularity and channeled it toward the 1828 presidential election. As the beneficiary of these important changes in American politics, Jackson won easily.

Yet, even after he was elected overwhelmingly, it was not entirely clear what Jackson's presidential priorities were or what his program would be. The general's friends had avoided issues that might offend certain groups of voters and had instead concentrated on Jackson's mass popularity. Even political "insiders" and "experts" were not sure what to expect from Jackson as president. As Senator Daniel Webster, not a friend of Jackson, wrote, "Gen. J. will be here about 15 Feb. — Nobody knows what he will do when he comes. My opinion is that when he comes he will bring a breeze with him. Which way it will blow, I cannot tell. My fear is stronger than my hope."

Paralleling the changes in American political institutions were changes in American economic life. After the War of 1812 rapid westward expansion had created economic opportunities not only for farmers but also for those engaged in commerce, transportation, and manufacturing. The spread of cotton throughout the Gulf States was accompanied by the dramatic expansion of other commercial crops into the Old Northwest, bringing both sections of the country into the increasingly pervasive market economy in which farmers produced agricultural products more for the marketplace than for home consumption. Meanwhile in the Northeast the modern factory system, still in its infancy, was gradually replacing homemade goods and the "putting out"

Chapter 5
The Clash of
Political and
Economic
Philosophies:
Jackson's Veto
of the Bank
Recharter

system.[4] Privately financed toll roads, canals, and railroad enterprises were beginning to tie these economic components together into what would ultimately become a national economy.

It was almost inevitable that these two important trends, political and economic, would become intertwined. The central issue uniting them was what role the federal government should play in the nation's economic growth. Initially Jeffersonians had rejected Federalist notions that the government — through Hamilton's Bank of the United States,[5] tariffs to protect infant industries, federal protection and encouragement of American commerce, and publicly financed internal improvements — take an active part in the direction of the American economy. Indeed, Democratic-Republicans in 1811 had refused to renew the Bank's charter and in other areas had advocated a more laissez-faire approach to the private economic sector. However, the War of 1812 convinced many, principally younger Democratic-Republicans, that they had been mistaken and that strong ties between the federal government and private economic interests were necessary. Led by new political figures like

Henry Clay of Kentucky, this group succeeded in rechartering the Bank of the United States in 1816, raising tariffs, and making ambitious plans for government-financed transportation facilities.

However other Democratic-Republicans viewed such actions as neo-Federalist heresies. Claiming themselves to be true heirs of Thomas Jefferson, these Democratic-Republicans believed that the benefits of American economic growth were being enjoyed disproportionately by rich and powerful businessmen with close connections to key political figures who protected their interests. Therefore, they felt these men held an unfair advantage over the vast majority of farmers, businessmen, merchants, and bankers without such connections. Their alternative was to return to Jefferson's policies of laissez-faire, believing that unfettered economic competition was far preferable to an economic system in which those of the financial and political establishment received most of the benefits of the nation's economic growth. While they did not believe that all men were equal, they did insist that all men should begin their economic lives in an approximately equal position, unaided by government favoritism. Competition, free of "unnatural" advantages, would prove who was truly best.

To these men the most visible symbol of the neo-Federalist economic

4. In the "putting out" system, partially finished materials were taken to workers in their homes, hence "put out." The workers, usually women, then performed their part of the work.

5. The brainchild of Alexander Hamilton, the first Bank of the United States was chartered in 1791 for twenty years.

policies was the Bank of the United States. By the time that Jackson claimed the presidency, the Bank, aided significantly by being the sole repository of federal revenues, dwarfed all its competitors, holding approximately 20 percent of the nation's loans and one-third of all bank deposits and specie (hard money). The Bank, whose headquarters was in Philadelphia, had twenty-nine branches in the country's principal cities and was able by its sheer size to control local and state banks and strongly influence the direction the American economy would take. Furthermore, it was a poorly kept secret that in order to maintain its unique position, the Bank regularly paid several congressmen and senators (Henry Clay, Daniel Webster, and Tennessee's Davy Crockett being but three) to protect its interests and further its policies. As a result, traditional Democratic-Republicans were joined by a number of farmers, southern planters, businessmen who felt injured by the Bank's policies or who had been denied loans, and smaller bankers in their opposition to the Bank of the United States. Together they looked to Andrew Jackson, the product of changes in American political institutions, to correct the abuses of American economic institutions.

Temperamentally, President Jackson sympathized with this group. In his annual messages to Congress in 1829, 1830, and 1831 Jackson suggested revisions in the Bank's charter that would provide for a more competitive banking system. Congress, however, consistently exonerated the Bank and its president, Nicholas Biddle, of the president's charges and in July 1832 passed a bill rechartering the Bank for twenty more years. The intial charter was not due to expire until 1836, but Henry Clay, looking for an issue to use in opposing Jackson in the presidential election of 1832, convinced Biddle to push for recharter four years early.

Assisted by four of his most trusted advisers,[6] Jackson composed a message to accompany his veto of the recharter bill. Your task is to analyze that veto message, answering the following questions:

1. What reasons did Jackson give for opposing the recharter of the Bank of the United States?

2. What does the veto message show about the economic and social thought of the Jacksonian Democrats?

Following the veto message are some reactions to it both by members of Congress and by the press. What other (noneconomic) issues were raised by Jackson's veto of the Bank recharter bill? How do those points help to clarify the political and social situations in America in the 1830s?

6. These were Roger Brooke Taney, Amos Kendall, Andrew J. Donelson, and Levi Woodbury.

Chapter 5
The Clash of
Political and
Economic
Philosophies:
Jackson's Veto
of the Bank
Recharter

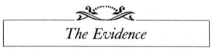

The Method

President Jackson's veto message has been reproduced for you almost in its entirety. (A few parts not central to Jackson's argument have been omitted.) The written message was delivered to Congress by one of Jackson's subordinates. Indeed, not since the days of President Washington had a president appeared in person before Congress.

Ever since the American Revolution, many people have criticized the legal profession in general and lawmakers in particular for using tortuous language and strange reasoning to make the law virtually unintelligible to all but lawyers. While there probably is some truth to the charges, careful reading at a slow pace will allow you to grasp the basic reasoning Jackson used to arrive at his decision as well as the principal points of those who reacted to his message. Since such opinions are usually constructed like building blocks, don't skip ahead or skim, but be sure you understand the meaning of each paragraph. It would be helpful if, as you read, you make an outline of the main points for future reference. Then consult a text as well as the introduction to this chapter to place the incident in its economic, social, and political context.

The Evidence

From James D. Richardson, A Compilation of the Messages and Papers of the Presidents, 1789–1897, *Vol. 2 (Washington, D.C.: Government Printing Office, 1896), pp. 576–577, 580–582, 589–591.*

Veto Message — Bank of the United States

TO THE SENATE: The bill "to modify and continue" the act entitled "An act to incorporate the subscribers to the Bank of the United States" was presented to me on the 4th July instant. Having considered it with that solemn regard to the principles of the Constitution which the day was calculated to inspire, and come to the conclusion that it ought not to become a law, I herewith return it to the Senate, in which it originated, with my objections.

A bank of the United States is in many respects convenient for the Government and useful to the people. Entertaining this opinion, and deeply impressed with the belief that some of the powers and privileges possessed by the existing bank are unauthorized by the Constitution, subversive of the rights of the States, and dangerous to the liberties of the people, I felt it my duty at an early period of my Administration to call the attention of Congress to the practicability of organizing an institution combining all its advantages and obviating these objections. I sincerely regret that in the act before me I can perceive none of those modifications of the bank charter which are necessary, in my opinion, to make it compatible with justice, with sound policy, or with the Constitution of our country.

The present corporate body, denominated the president, directors, and company of the Bank of the United States, will have existed at the time this act is intended to take effect twenty years. It enjoys an exclusive privilege of banking under the authority of the General Government, a monopoly of its favor and support, and, as a necessary consequence, almost a monopoly of the foreign and domestic exchange. The powers, privileges, and favors bestowed upon it in the original charter, by increasing the value of the stock far above its par value, operated as a gratuity of many millions to the stockholders.

[*Here Jackson argued that the profits paid to the Bank's stockholders "must come directly or indirectly out of the earnings of the American people, and that, therefore, the people should share in the profits."*]

It is not conceivable how the present stockholders can have any claim to the special favor of the Government. The present corporation has enjoyed its monopoly during the period stipulated in the original contract. If we must have such a corporation, why should not the Government sell out the whole stock and thus secure to the people the full market value of the privileges granted? Why should not Congress create and sell twenty-eight millions of stock, incorporating the purchasers with all the powers and privileges secured in this act and putting the premium upon the sales into the Treasury?

But this act does not permit competition in the purchase of this monopoly. It seems to be predicated on the erroneous idea that the present stockholders have a prescriptive right not only to the favor but to the bounty of Government. It appears that more than a fourth part of the stock is held by foreigners and the residue is held by a few hundred of our own citizens, chiefly of the richest class. For their benefit does this act exclude the whole American people from competition in the purchase of this monopoly and dispose of it for many millions less than it is worth. This seems the less excusable because some of our citizens not

Chapter 5
The Clash of
Political and
Economic
Philosophies:
Jackson's Veto
of the Bank
Recharter

now stockholders petitioned that the door of competition might be opened, and offered to take a charter on terms much more favorable to the Government and country. . . .

Of the twenty-five directors of this bank five are chosen by the Government and twenty by the citizen stockholders. From all voice in these elections the foreign stockholders are excluded by the charter. In proportion, therefore, as the stock is transferred to foreign holders the extent of suffrage in the choice of directors is curtailed. Already is almost a third of the stock in foreign hands and not represented in elections. It is constantly passing out of the country, and this act will accelerate its departure. The entire control of the institution would necessarily fall into the hands of a few citizen stockholders, and the ease with which the object would be accomplished would be a temptation to designing men to secure that control in their own hands by monopolizing the remaining stock. There is danger that a president and directors would then be able to elect themselves from year to year, and without responsibility or control manage the whole concerns of the bank during the existence of its charter. It is easy to conceive that great evils to our country and its institutions might flow from such a concentration of power in the hands of a few men irresponsible to the people.

Is there no danger to our liberty and independence in a bank that in its nature has so little to bind it to our country? The president of the bank has told us that most of the State banks exist by its forbearance. Should its influence become concentrated, as it may under the operation of such an act as this, in the hands of a self-elected directory whose interests are identified with those of the foreign stockholders, will there not be cause to tremble for the purity of our elections in peace and for the independence of our country in war? Their power would be great whenever they might choose to exert it; but if this monopoly were regularly renewed every fifteen or twenty years on terms proposed by themselves, they might seldom in peace put forth their strength to influence elections or control the affairs of the nation. But if any private citizen or public functionary should interpose to curtail its powers or prevent a renewal of its privileges, it can not be doubted that he would be made to feel its influence.

Should the stock of the bank principally pass into the hands of the subjects of a foreign country, and we should unfortunately become involved in a war with that country, what would be our condition? Of the course which would be pursued by a bank almost wholly owned by the subjects of a foreign power, and managed by those whose interests, if not affections, would run in the same direction there can be no doubt. All its operations within would be in aid of the hostile fleets and armies without. Controlling our currency, receiving our public moneys, and holding thousands of our citizens in dependence, it would be more formidable and dangerous than the naval and military power of the enemy.

If we must have a bank with private stockholders, every consideration of sound policy and every impulse of American feeling admonishes that it should be *purely American.* Its stockholders should be composed exclusively of our own citizens, who at least ought to be friendly to our Government and willing to support it in times of difficulty and danger. So abundant is domestic capital that competition in subscribing for the stock of local banks has recently led almost to riots. To a bank exclusively of American stockholders, possessing the powers and privileges granted by this act, subscriptions for $200,000,000 could be readily obtained. Instead of sending abroad the stock of the bank in which the Government must deposit its funds and on which it must rely to sustain its credit in times of emergency, it would rather seem to be expedient to prohibit its sale to aliens under penalty of absolute forfeiture.

It is maintained by the advocates of the bank that its constitutionality in all its features ought to be considered as settled by precedent and by the decision of the Supreme Court. To this conclusion I can not assent. Mere precedent is a dangerous source of authority, and should not be regarded as deciding questions of constitutional power except where the acquiescence of the people and the States can be considered as well settled. So far from this being the case on this subject, an argument against the bank might be based on precedent. One Congress, in 1791, decided in favor of a bank; another, in 1811, decided against it. One Congress, in 1815, decided against a bank; another, in 1816, decided in its favor. Prior to the present Congress, therefore, the precedents drawn from that source were equal. . . . There is nothing in precedent, therefore, which, if its authority were admitted, ought to weigh in favor of the act before me.

If the opinion of the Supreme Court covered the whole ground of this act, it ought not to control the coordinate authorities of this Government. The Congress, the Executive, and the Court must each for itself be guided by its own opinion of the Constitution. Each public officer who takes an oath to support the Constitution swears that he will support it as he understands it, and not as it is understood by others. It is as much the duty of the House of Representatives, of the Senate, and of the President to decide upon the constitutionality of any bill or resolution which may be presented to them for passage or approval as it is of the supreme judges when it may be brought before them for judicial decision. The opinion of the judges has no more authority over Congress than the

Chapter 5
The Clash of
Political and
Economic
Philosophies:
Jackson's Veto
of the Bank
Recharter

opinion of Congress has over the judges, and on that point the President is independent of both. The authority of the Supreme Court must not, therefore, be permitted to control the Congress or the Executive when acting in their legislative capacities, but to have only such influence as the force of their reasoning may deserve. . . .

Suspicions are entertained and charges are made of gross abuse and violation of its charter. An investigation unwillingly conceded and so restricted in time as necessarily to make it incomplete and unsatisfactory discloses enough to excite suspicion and alarm. In the practices of the principal bank partially unveiled, in the absence of important witnesses, and in numerous charges confidently made and as yet wholly uninvestigated there was enough to induce a majority of the committee of investigation — a committee which was selected from the most able and honorable members of the House of Representatives — to recommend a suspension of further action upon the bill and a prosecution of the inquiry. As the charter had yet four years to run, and as a renewal now was not necessary to the successful prosecution of its business, it was to have been expected that the bank itself, conscious of its purity and proud of its character, would have withdrawn its application for the present, and demanded the severest scrutiny into all its transactions. In their declining to do so there seems to be an additional reason why the functionaries of the Government should proceed with less haste and more caution in the renewal of their monopoly.

The bank is professedly established as an agent of the executive branch of the Government, and its constitutionality is maintained on that ground. Neither upon the propriety of present action nor upon the provisions of this act was the Executive consulted. It has had no opportunity to say that it neither needs nor wants an agent clothed with such powers and favored by such exemptions. There is nothing in its legitimate functions which makes it necessary or proper. Whatever interest or influence, whether public or private, has given birth to this act, it can not be found either in the wishes or necessities of the executive department, by which present action is deemed premature, and the powers conferred upon its agent not only unnecessary, but dangerous to the Government and country.

It is to be regretted that the rich and powerful too often bend the acts of government to their selfish purposes. Distinctions in society will always exist under every just government. Equality of talents, of education, or of wealth can not be produced by human institutions. In the full enjoyment of the gifts of Heaven and the fruits of superior industry, economy, and virtue, every man is equally entitled to protection by law; but when the laws undertake to add to these natural and just advantages artificial distinctions, to grant titles, gratuities, and exclusive privileges, to make the rich richer and the potent more powerful, the humble members of society — the farmers, mechanics, and laborers — who have neither the time nor the means of securing like favors to themselves, have a right to complain of the injustice of their Government. There are no necessary evils in government. Its evils exist only in its abuses. If it would confine itself to equal protection, and, as Heaven does its rain, shower its favors alike on the high and the low, the rich and the poor, it would be an unqualified blessing. In the act before me there seems to be a wide and unnecessary departure from these just principles.

Nor is our Government to be maintained or our Union preserved by invasions of the rights and powers of the several States. In thus attempting to make our General Government strong we make it weak. Its true strength consists in leaving individuals and States as much as possible to themselves — in making itself felt, not in its power, but in its beneficence; not in its control, but in its protection; not in binding the States more closely to the center, but leaving each to move unobstructed in its proper orbit.

Experience should teach us wisdom. Most of the difficulties our Government now encounters and most of the dangers which impend over our Union have sprung from an abandonment of the legitimate objects of Government by our national legislation, and the adoption of such principles as are embodied in this act. Many of our rich men have not been content with equal protection and equal benefits, but have besought us to make them richer by act of Congress. By attempting to gratify their desires we have in the results of our legislation arrayed section against section, interest against interest, and man against man, in a fearful commotion which threatens to shake the foundations of our Union. It is time to pause in our career to review our principles, and if possible revive that devoted patriotism and spirit of compromise which distinguished the sages of the Revolution and the fathers of our Union. If we can not at once, in justice to interests vested under improvident legislation, make our Government what it ought to be, we can at least take a stand against all new grants of monopolies and exclusive privileges, against any prostitution of our Government to the advancement of the few at the expense of the many, and in favor of compromise and gradual reform in our code of laws and system of political economy.

I have now done my duty to my country. If sustained by my fellow-citizens, I shall be grateful and happy; if not, I shall find in the motives which impel me

*Chapter 5
The Clash of
Political and
Economic
Philosophies:
Jackson's Veto
of the Bank
Recharter*

ample grounds for contentment and peace. In the difficulties which surround us and the dangers which threaten our institutions there is cause for neither dismay nor alarm. For relief and deliverance let us firmly rely on that kind Providence which I am sure watches with peculiar care over the destinies of our Republic, and on the intelligence and wisdom of our countrymen. Through *His* abundant goodness and *their* patriotic devotion our liberty and Union will be preserved.

REACTIONS OF MEMBERS
OF CONGRESS

From Calvin Colton, ed., The Works of Henry Clay, *Vol. 7 (New York: G. P. Putnam's Sons, 1904), pp. 524–527, 533–534.*

HENRY CLAY

. . . The veto is an extraordinary power, which, though tolerated by the Constitution, was not expected, by the convention, to be used in ordinary cases. It was designed for instances of precipitate legislation, in unguarded moments. Thus restricted, and it has been thus restricted by all former presidents, it might not be mischievous. During Mr. Madison's administration of eight years, there occurred but two or three cases of its exercise. During the last administration, I do not now recollect that it was once. In a period little upward of three years, the present chief magistrate has employed the veto four times. We now hear quite frequently, in the progress of measures through Congress, the statement that the president will veto them, urged as an objection to their passage.

The veto is hardly reconcilable with the genius of representative government. It is totally irreconcilable with it, if it is to be frequently employed in respect to the expediency of measures, as well as their constitutionality. It is a feature of our government, borrowed from a prerogative of the British king. And it is remarkable, that in England it has grown obsolete, not having been used for upward of a century. . . .

No question has been more generally discussed, within the last two years, by the people at large, and in State Legislatures, than that of the bank. And this consideration of it has been prompted by the president himself. In the first message to Congress (in December, 1829) he brought the subject to the view of that body and the nation, and expressly declared, that it could not, for the interest of all concerned, be "too soon" settled. In each of his subsequent annual messages, in 1830, and 1831, he again invited the attention of Congress to the subject. Thus, after an interval of two years, and after the intervention of the election of a new Congress, the president deliberately renews the chartering of the bank of the United States. And yet his friends now declare the agitation of the question to be premature! It was not premature, in 1829, to present the question, but it is premature in 1832 to consider and decide it! . . .

The friends of the president, who have been for nearly three years agitating this question, now turn round upon their opponents, who have supposed the president quite serious and in earnest, in presenting it for public consideration, and charge them with prematurely agitating it. And that for electioneering purposes! The other side understands perfectly, the policy of preferring an unjust charge, in order to avoid a well-founded accusation.

If there be an electioneering motive in the matter, who have been actuated by it? . . .

I voted, in 1811, against the old bank of the United States, and I delivered, on that occasion, a speech, in which, among other reasons, I assigned that of its being unconstitutional. My speech has been read to the Senate, during the progress of this bill, but the reading of it excited no other regret than that it was read in such a wretched, bungling, mangling manner. During a long public life (I mention the fact not as claiming any merit for it), the only great question on which I have ever changed my opinion, is that of the bank of the United States. If the researches of the senator had carried him a little further, he would, by turning over a few more leaves of the same book from which he read my speech, have found that which I made in 1816, in support of the present bank. By the reasons assigned in it for the change of my opinion, I am ready to abide in the judgment of the present generation and of posterity. In 1816, being Speaker of the House of Representatives, it was perfectly in my power to have said nothing and done nothing, and thus have concealed the change of opinion my mind had undergone. But I did not choose to remain silent and escape responsibility. I chose publicly to avow my actual conversion. The war and the fatal experience of its disastrous events had changed me. Mr. Madison, Governor Pleasants, and almost all the public men around me, my political friends, had changed their opinions from the same causes. . . .

There are some parts of this message that ought to excite deep alarm; and that especially in which the president announces, that each public officer may interpret the Constitution as he pleases. His language is, "Each public officer, who takes an oath to support the Constitution, swears that he will support it as

Chapter 5
The Clash of
Political and
Economic
Philosophies:
Jackson's Veto
of the Bank
Recharter

he understands it, and not as it is understood by others." . . . "The opinion of the judges has no more authority over Congress than the opinion of Congress has over the judges; and on that point the president is independent of both." Now, Mr. President, I conceive, with great deference, that the president has mistaken the purport of the oath to support the Constitution of the United States. No one swears to support it as he understands it, but to support it simply as it is in truth. . . .

From The Writings and Speeches of Daniel Webster, *Vol. 6 (Boston: Little, Brown and Co., 1903), pp. 157, 179–180.*

DANIEL WEBSTER

. . . [The Bank] bill was not passed for the purpose of benefiting the present stockholders. Their benefit, if any, is incidental and collateral. Nor was it passed on any idea that they had a *right* to a renewed charter, although the message argues against such right, as if it had been somewhere set up and asserted. No such right has been asserted by any body. Congress passed the bill, not as a bounty or a favor to the present stockholders, nor to comply with any demand of right on their part; but to promote great public interest, for great public objects. . . .

Sir, the object aimed at by such institutions is to connect the public safety and convenience with private interests. It has been found by experience, that banks are safest under private management, and that government banks are among the most dangerous of all inventions. Now, Sir, the whole drift of the message is to reverse the settled judgment of all the civilized world, and to set up government banks, independent of private interest or private control. For this purpose the message labors, even beyond the measure of all its other labors, to create jealousies and prejudices, on the ground of the alleged benefit which individuals will derive from the renewal of this charter. Much less effort is made to show that government, or the public, will be injured by the bill, than that individuals will profit by it. . . .

Mr. President, we have arrived at a new epoch. We are entering on experiments, with the government and the Constitution of the country, hitherto untried, and of fearful and appalling aspect. This message calls us to the contemplation of a future which little resembles the past. Its principles are at war with all that public opinion has sustained, and all which the experience of the government has sanctioned. It denies first principles; it contradicts truths, heretofore received as indisputable. It denies to the judiciary the interpretation of law, and claims to divide with Congress the power of originating statutes. It extends the grasp of executive pretension over every power of the government. But this is not all. It presents the chief magistrate of the Union in the attitude of arguing away the powers of that government over which he has been chosen to preside; and adopting for this purpose modes of reasoning which, even under the influence of all proper feeling towards high official station, it is difficult to regard as respectable. It appeals to every prejudice which may betray men into a mistaken view of their own interests, and to every passion which may lead them to disobey the impulses of their understanding. It urges all the specious topics of State rights and national encroachment against that which a great majority of the States have affirmed to be rightful, and in which all of them have acquiesced. It sows, in an unsparing manner, the seeds of jealousy and ill-will against that government of which its author is the official head. It raises a cry, that liberty is in danger, at the very moment when it puts forth claims to powers heretofore unknown and unheard of. It affects alarm for the public freedom, when nothing endangers that freedom so much as its own unparalleled pretences. This, even, is not all. It manifestly seeks to inflame the poor against the rich; it wantonly attacks whole classes of the people, for the purpose of turning against them the prejudices and the resentments of other classes. It is a state paper which finds no topic too exciting for its use, no passion too inflammable for its address and its solicitation.

Such is this message. It remains now for the people of the United States to choose between the principles here avowed and their government. These cannot subsist together. The one or the other must be rejected. If the sentiments of the message shall receive general approbation, the Constitution will have perished even earlier than the moment which its enemies originally allowed for the termination of its existence. It will not have survived to its fiftieth year.

REACTIONS OF
THE PRESS

Daily National Intelligencer (Washington, D.C.), August 9, 1832, quoting from a Boston newspaper. From Thomas A. Bailey and David M. Kennedy, The American Spirit: United States History as Seen by Contemporaries, *Vol. I (Lexington, Mass.: D.C. Heath, 1984), p. 244.*

It impudently asserts that Congress have acted prematurely, blindly, and without sufficient examination.

Chapter 5
The Clash of
Political and
Economic
Philosophies:
Jackson's Veto
of the Bank
Recharter

It falsely and wickedly alleges that the rich and powerful throughout the country are waging a war of oppression against the poor and the weak; and attempts to justify the President on the ground of its being his duty thus to protect the humble when so assailed.

Finally, it unblushingly denies that the Supreme Court is the proper tribunal to decide upon the constitutionality of the laws!

The whole paper is a most thoroughgoing electioneering missile, intended to secure the madcaps of the South, and as such deserves the execration of all who love their country or its welfare.

This veto seems to be the production of the whole Kitchen Cabinet — of hypocrisy and arrogance; of imbecility and talent; of cunning, falsehood, and corruption — a very firebrand, intended to destroy their opponents, but which now, thanks to Him who can bring good out of evil, bids fair to light up a flame that shall consume its vile authors.

If the doctrines avowed in this document do not arouse the nation, we shall despair that anything will, until the iron hand of despotism has swept our fair land, and this glorious Republic, if not wholly annihilated, shall have been fiercely shaken to its very foundations.

Boston Daily Advertisor and Patriot, *September 26, 1832. From Richard W. Leopold, Arthur S. Link, and Stanley Coben,* Problems in American History, *Vol. I, 4th ed. (Englewood Cliffs, N.J.: Prentice-Hall, 1972), pp. 275–277.*

The national bank, though not properly a *political* institution, is one of the most important and valuable instruments that are used in the practical administration of the government. . . . As the fiscal agent of the executive, it has exhibited a remarkable intelligence, efficiency, energy, and above all, INDEPENDENCE. This — as we shall presently see — has been its real crime. As the regulator of the currency, it has furnished the country with a safe, convenient, and copious circulating medium, and prevented the mischiefs that would otherwise result from the insecurity of the local banks. As a mere institution for loaning money, it has been, as it were, the Providence of the less wealthy sections of the Union. It has distributed with unsparing hand almost the whole of its vast capital throughout the western states, where capital, at any moderate rate of interest, would be otherwise almost inaccessible. The extent of the benefit conferred in this way, not on the west only, but on the whole country, will never be fully appreciated except, should that unfortunately happen, by its loss. Through its dealings in exchange at home and abroad, the bank has materially facilitated the operations of our foreign and domestic trade. What would be the effect of its destruction? It would unsettle the currency and carry desolation and bankruptcy through the whole Western country. The debt of thirty millions due from that section to the Bank CANNOT BE PAID. The attempt to enforce it would ruin thousands of our most industrious and valuable citizens, and arrest for years the prosperity of the whole West. Will the people consent to this for the mere purpose of securing to the military chieftain and his partizans the SPOILS OF VICTORY for another term! THEY WILL NOT.

Washington Globe, *July 23, 1832. From Robert V. Remini, ed.,* The Age of Jackson *(New York: Harper & Row, 1972), pp. 85–86.*

The name of Daniel Webster appears on the list of stockholders; but he declared, in his speech against the veto, that he held no stock, having probably transferred it after the Bank applied for a new charter, lest he should appear to vote for giving money directly to himself. But Daniel Webster's chief interest was not in the stock which he held. It was discovered by the Committee of Investigation that he had received from the principal Bank, as lawyer's fees, upwards of EIGHT THOUSAND DOLLARS. What he has received from the Branches, they did not ascertain. In one case disclosed by the Committee, the Bank gave him *one hundred dollars* for writing *eight words*, being at the rate of *twelve dollars fifty cents per word!* — Had not Mr. Webster an interest in a vote which was to preserve such a *valuable client?*

Mr. Clay, in 1811, voted and spoke against the old Bank of the United States on the ground that it was both inexpedient and unconstitutional. At a subsequent time, having suffered great losses, he quitted public life and re-commenced the practice of law. He was employed to attend to all the law business of the Branches in Kentucky and Ohio; but what he received for those services, has never been disclosed. The Committee, however, ascertained, that he had received from the principal Bank "for professional services," upwards of SEVENTEEN THOUSAND DOLLARS. This much is *certain;* and it is probable, he has received enough from the Branches to make it THIRTY THOUSAND! Had Mr. Clay no *interest* in his vote for this Bank? Had he not a *motive* to be liberal to the Stockholders of an institution which had been so liberal to him?

But he had another interest. The Bank has undertaken *to make him President!* He himself avows, that the object of the Bank in coming forward now, was to ascertain whether Gen. Jackson would consent to re-charter it or not, that all those interested might go against him, if he would not, in the coming election.

*Chapter 5
The Clash of
Political and
Economic
Philosophies:
Jackson's Veto
of the Bank
Recharter*

And whom will they go *for,* if they go *against* General Jackson? For the opposing candidate, *Mr. Clay.* The object of the Bank, therefore, as Mr. Clay well understood, was to support him for President in case Gen. Jackson refused to award to them a new charter. That he would refuse, Mr. Clay never had a doubt.

In voting to recharter the Bank, therefore, Mr. Clay had both a pecuniary and political interest. It was to him a most valuable client, and it had resolved to put forth all its money and power *to make him President.*

In these interests of leading men in Congress, the people may find the reason why that body was deluded into giving to the titled Aristocracy in England and the moneyed Aristocracy of America, *seven or eight millions of dollars.* They will know how far the Bank Candidate for the Presidency deserves the support of those whose interests he has thus endeavored to sacrifice; and they will duly appreciate the firmness and patriotism of that man who dares to set all these corrupt influences at defiance and rely for support on the virtue and intelligence of his countrymen.

Questions to Consider

The evidence contains Jackson's veto message, two speeches and two newspaper editorials opposing the message, and one editorial supporting the president.

Obviously Jackson's message is the key piece of evidence. To assist you in following Jackson's reasoning, consider the following questions as you think about his message:

1. The president does not deny that the Bank could be "convenient for the Government and useful to the people." Why, then, did he object to its monopolistic features?

2. The purchase of Bank stock by non-Americans brought millions of dollars into the Bank's coffers. What does Jackson feel is wrong with that? (The president noted three objections.)

3. In 1819 the Supreme Court ruled that the Bank was constitutional (in *McCulloch v. Maryland,* decision by Chief Justice John Marshall). Did Jackson agree with that ruling? How did he propose to get around it? How valid were his arguments?

4. The House of Representatives had cleared the Bank of accusations that it had abused its charter. Did Jackson agree?

5. Jackson claimed that there were other reasons why the Bank sought rechartering four years early. To what was he referring?

6. The president claimed that the Bank was injurious to states' rights. How? He also claimed that it injured the Union. How?

7. How does the message provide clues to Jackson's economic and social philosophy? What, in his opinion, was the proper role of the government in its relations with the private economic sector?

8. Reviewing the message, how does Jackson's uses of the words *monopoly* and *competition* help to clarify his general philosophy?

Both Henry Clay and Daniel Webster attacked the veto message. What were the main points each opponent made? Both warned of the dangers of the president's philosophy of government. What were these dangers, according to Clay and Webster? How does Clay's speech show the shift in thinking of many Democratic-Republicans after the War of 1812?

Two Boston newspapers also criticized the decision. How does each article show the political ramifications of the veto message? What did Clay have to say on that subject? Did the *Washington Globe* also see the message in a political light?

Now put all the evidence together. What does it collectively say about the political and social climate in the 1830s?

Epilogue

Although many people expected Jackson's veto of the Bank recharter bill to be a major issue in the 1832 presidential election, which pitted the president against Henry Clay, it was probably of only minor concern to most voters. As in 1828, Andrew Jackson's political image and general popularity were the chief factors that carried him to victory. Clay received only 37.5 percent of the popular vote and only 49 of the 268 electoral votes. Indeed, Jackson's triumph was almost complete.

Convinced, however, that the election had been a popular mandate for him to move against the Bank, Jackson devised a plan by which he could kill the institution even before its charter expired in 1836. Simply put, Jackson withdrew all federal government funds from the Bank of the United States, placing them in a number of smaller state banks, nicknamed "pet banks" because they were chosen by the president and his advisers to receive federal funds. That decision in effect killed the Bank that Jackson had once referred to as "a monster, a hydra-headed monster." The Bank went under in 1841.

Chapter 5
The Clash of
Political and
Economic
Philosophies:
Jackson's Veto
of the Bank
Recharter

Jacksonians rejoiced about the restoration of free competition in the banking community. To his supporters, the president's victory over the Bank of the United States made him even more a man of the people, a true hero of the democratic nation. Although we can recognize now that this period of American history was considerably less democratic than Jacksonians claimed, it is nevertheless important to understand that most Americans *believed* that political, economic, and social life was becoming more egalitarian and that in the future the United States would be a democratic utopia that all the world would admire.

That belief, the changes occurring in American political institutions, and the sharp political battles of the Jackson years were responsible for the reemergence of the two-party system in the 1830s. Followers of Andrew Jackson dropped the "Republican" designation from Democratic-Republicans and became simply "Democrats." Those who sided with Clay and Webster ultimately adopted the name "Whigs." Political battles were vicious and bitter, and the uses of modern campaign tactics and symbols became more widespread. Indeed, in the presidential election of 1840, over 80 percent of the eligible voters actually cast ballots, a percentage that has been exceeded only twice in American history (in 1860 and 1876 — since 1908 no election has attracted more than 65 percent of the eligible voters).

President Jackson's 1832 veto of the Bank recharter bill, however, did not end the debate over the proper relationship between the federal government and the private economic sector. Rather, debate over that question has become an almost regular feature of American presidential elections in the twentieth century. Nor is the discussion likely to cease in a society that venerates individual economic progress, private property, and the sanctity of competition while at the same time recognizes the federal government's power to oversee banking practices, control the circulation of currency, and set economic and financial priorities for the collective society. Since 1832 this has been recognized as one of the dilemmas of American life.

Chapter 6

Away from Home: The Working Girls of Lowell

The Problem

By the end of the eighteenth century, the American economy had begun to undergo a process that historians call modernization. This process involves a number of changes, including the rapid expansion of markets, commercial specialization, improved transportation networks, the growth of credit transactions, the proliferation of towns and cities, and the rise of manufacturing and the factory system. Quite obviously all of these factors are interrelated. Furthermore, such changes always have profound effects on people's life-styles as well as on the pace of life itself.

While the frontier moved steadily westward and the South remained primarily agrarian — tied to cash crops like cotton and tobacco — New England's economy quickly became modernized. Although agriculture was never completely abandoned in

New England, by the early 1800s it was increasingly difficult to obtain land, and many small New England farms suffered from soil exhaustion. Young men, of course, could go West — in fact, so many of them left New England that soon there was a "surplus" of young women in the area. What were these farmers' daughters supposed to do? What were their options?

At the same time that these economic developments were occurring, ideas about white middle-class women and their place in society were also changing. Historian Barbara Welter has described this phenomenon as "the cult of true womanhood,"[1] the emergence of the belief that every

1. Barbara Welter, "The Cult of True Womanhood, 1820–1860," *American Quarterly*, 18 (Summer 1966), 151–174.

(true) woman was "a lady" who behaved in certain ways because of her female nature. True women possessed four virtues: piety, purity, submissiveness, and domesticity. These characteristics, it was thought, were not so much learned as they were biologically natural, simply an inherent part of being born female. Women's magazines, etiquette books for young ladies, sermons and religious tracts, popular short stories and novels — all these sources told women what they were like and how they should feel about themselves. Such sources are called "prescriptive literature" because they literally prescribe how people should — and should not — behave.

What, then, was expected of New England farmers' daughters and other respectable (white) women? They were supposed to be pious, more naturally religious than men (real men might occasionally swear, but real women never did!). Because they were naturally logical and rational, men might pursue education, but true women should not because they might be led into error if they strayed from the Bible. As daughters, wives, or even sisters, women had the important responsibility of being the spiritual uplifters to whom men could turn when necessary.

Just as important as piety was the true woman's purity. This purity was absolute, for while a man might "sow his wild oats" and then be saved by the love of a good woman, a "fallen woman" could never be saved. In the popular fiction of the period, a woman who had been seduced usually became insane, died, or both. If she had a baby, it also came to a bad end. Only on her wedding night did a true woman surrender her virginity, and then out of duty rather than passion, since it was widely believed that pure women were not sexually responsive. In fact, many young women of this era knew nothing at all about their own bodies or the nature of sexual intercourse until they married.

Submission and domesticity were perhaps not as vital as piety and purity. Although women who did not submit to men's leadership were destined to be unhappy (according to the thought of the day), they could correct their mistaken behavior. Men were, after all, stronger and more intelligent, the natural protectors of women. A true woman, wrote then-popular author Grace Greenwood, should be like a "perpetual child," who is always "timid, doubtful, and clingingly dependent." Such pious, pure, submissive women were particularly well-suited to the important task of creating a pleasant, cheerful home — a place where men could escape from their worldly struggles and be fed, clothed, comforted, and nursed if they were ill. Even a woman who did not have very much money could create such a haven, people believed, simply by using her natural talents of sewing, cooking, cleaning, and flower arranging.

Simultaneously, then, two important trends were occurring in the early 1800s. At the same time that the northern economy was modernizing, sexual stereotypes were developing that assigned very different roles to men and women. While a man should be out in the world of education, work, and politics, a woman's place was in the home, a sphere where she could be sheltered. But what would happen if the economic need for an increased supply of labor clashed with the new ideas about the women's place in society? If a young unmarried woman went to work in a factory far away from her parents' farm, would she still be respectable? Where would she live? Who would protect her? Perhaps the experience of factory work itself would destroy those special feminine characteristics all true women possessed. All these fears and more would have to be confronted in the course of the development of the New England textile industry during the 1830s and 1840s.

Although the first American textile mill using water-powered spinning machines was built in 1790, it and the countless other mills that sprung up throughout New England during the next thirty years depended heavily on the "putting out" system. The mills made only the yarn, which was then distributed ("put out") to women who wove the cloth in their own homes and returned the finished products to the mills. In 1820 two-thirds of all American cloth was still being produced by women working at home. But the pace of modernization accelerated sharply with the formation of the Boston Manufacturing Company, a heavily capitalized firm that purchased a large tract of rural land in the Merrimack River Valley. The Boston Associates adopted the latest technology and, more importantly, concentrated all aspects of cloth production inside their factories. Since they no longer "put out" work, they had to attract large numbers of workers, especially young women from New England farms, to their mills. Lowell, Massachusetts (the "City of Spindles"), and the Lowell mills became a kind of model, an experiment that received a good deal of attention in both Europe and America.

The great majority of the Lowell mill girls were between fifteen and thirty years old, unmarried, and from farm families that were neither the richest nor the poorest in their area. Although some of the Lowell girls occasionally sent small amounts of money back to their families, most used their wages for new clothes, education, and dowries. These wages were significantly higher than those for teaching, farm labor, or domestic services, the three other major occupations open to women.

The factory girls were required to live and eat in boardinghouses run according to company rules and supervised by respectable landladies. The company partially subsidized the cost of room-and-board, and also encouraged the numerous lecture series, evening schools, and church-related activities in Lowell. Girls worked together in the mills, filling the unskilled and semiskilled positions, while men (about one-fourth of the work force) performed the skilled jobs and served as overseers (foremen). Work in the mills was also characterized by strict regulations and an elaborate system of bells that signaled meal times and work times. During the 1840s factory girls occasionally published their own magazines, the most famous of which was the *Lowell Offering.*

In this chapter you will be looking at the description and rules of Lowell mills and boardinghouses as well as some selections from the *Lowell Offering* and other sources. The conflict between economic modernization and the cult of true womanhood was indirectly recognized by many New Englanders and directly experienced by the Lowell mill girls. What forms did this conflict take? What kind of fears and anxieties did it reveal? How did the mill girls attempt to cope with this tension?

The Method

When historians use prescriptive literature as evidence, they ask (1) what message is being conveyed, (2) who is sending the message, (3) why is it being sent, and (4) for whom is it intended? All of the evidence you are using in this chapter is in some ways prescriptive — that is, it tells women how they *should* behave. The evidence includes excerpts from a brief, popular book about Lowell, written by the Reverend Henry Mills in 1845. The Reverend Mills was a local Protestant minister who was asked by the textile company owners to conduct surveys into the workers' habits, health, and moral character. Depending heavily on information provided by company officials, overseers and landladies, the Reverend Mills published *Lowell, As It Was, and As It Is.* Also excerpted is a book written by Lucy Larcom, one of the few children (under age fifteen) employed in the Lowell mills in the late 1830s. She was a factory girl for more than ten years, after which she went West and obtained a college education. She became a well-known teacher and author when she returned to New England. Larcom published the book about her New England girlhood when she was sixty-five years old. The final set of evidence, the *Lowell Offering* selections, was written by factory girls during the years 1840–1843.

First read through the evidence, looking for elements of the cult of true womanhood in the factory girls' writings and in the Lowell system itself. Be sure to consider all four questions listed above. This will tell you a great deal, not only about the social standards for respectable young white women, but also about the fears and anxieties aroused by a factory system that employed women away from their homes.

Reading about how people *should* behave, however, does not tell us how people actually behaved. Remember that the central question of this problem involves a clash — a conflict between ideas (the cult) and reality (the factory system). Go through the evidence again, this time trying to reconstruct what it was really like for the young women who lived and worked in Lowell. Ask yourself to what degree and in what ways they might have deviated from the ideal of "true" women. Also ask whether they could have achieved this ideal goal — and whether they really wanted to — while working and living in Lowell. In other words, try to clarify in your own mind the forms of the conflict and the reactions (both of society and of the young women) to that conflict.

The Evidence

From the Reverend Henry A. Mills, Lowell, As It Was, and As It Is *(Lowell, Mass.: Powers, Bagley, and Dayton, 1845).*

A Lowell Boardinghouse

[*Reverend Mills began by describing the long blocks of boardinghouses, each three stories high, which were built in a style reminiscent of country farm houses. Clean, well-painted, and neat, these houses contained common eating rooms, parlors, and sleeping rooms for two to six boarders. The boarders, Reverend Mills observed, were sometimes a bit crowded but actually lived under better conditions than seamstresses and milliners in other towns.*]

As one important feature in the management of these houses, it deserves to be named that male operatives and female operatives do not board in the same tenement; and the following Regulations, printed by one of the companies, and given to each keeper of their houses, are here subjoined, as a simple statement of the rules generally observed by all the Corporations.

REGULATIONS to be observed by persons occupying the Boarding-houses belonging to the Merrimack Manufacturing company.

They must not board any persons not employed by the company, unless by special permission.

No disorderly or improper conduct must be allowed in the houses.

The doors must be closed at 10 o'clock in the evening; and no person admitted after that time, unless a sufficient excuse can be given.

Those who keep the houses, when required, must give an account of the number, names, and employment of their boarders; also with regard to their general conduct and whether they are in the habit of attending public worship.

The buildings, both inside and out, and the yards about them, must be kept clean, and in good order. If the buildings or fences are injured, they will be repaired and charged to the occupant.

No one will be allowed to keep swine.

The hours of taking meals in these houses are uniform throughout all the Corporations in the city, and are as follows: Dinner — always at half-past twelve o'clock. Breakfast — from November 1 to February 28, before going to work, and so early as to begin work as soon as it is light; through March at half-past seven o'clock; from April 1 to September 19, at seven o'clock; and from September 20 to October 31, at half-past seven o'clock. Supper — always after work at night, that is, after seven o'clock, from March 20 to September 19; after half-past seven o'clock, from September 20 to March 19. The time allowed for each meal is thirty minutes for breakfast, when that meal is taken after beginning work; for dinner, thirty minutes, from September 1 to April 30; and forty-five minutes from May 1 to August 31.

[*The meals might seem rushed, Mills noted, but that was common among all Americans, particularly businesspeople. Working girls could choose whichever boardinghouses they preferred, rents were very low, and the living arrangements were very respectable.*]

No tenant is admitted who has not hitherto borne a good character, and who does not continue to sustain it. In many cases the tenant has long been keeper of the house, for six, eight, or twelve years, and is well known to hundreds of her girls as their adviser and friend and second mother. . . .

The influence which this system of boarding-houses has exerted upon the good order and good morals of the place, has been vast and beneficent. It is this system to which we especially referred in our previous chapter on Waltham. By it the care and influence of the superintendent are extended over his operatives, while they are out of the mill, as well as while they are in it. Employing chiefly those who have no permanent residence in Lowell, but are only temporary boarders, upon any embarrassment of affairs they return to their country homes, and do not sink down here a helpless caste, clamouring for work, starving unless employed, and hence ready for a riot, for the destruction of property, and repeating here the scenes enacted in the manufacturing villages of England. To a very great degree the future condition of Lowell is dependent upon a faithful adhesion to this system; and it will deserve the serious consideration of those old towns which are now introducing steam mills, whether, if they do not provide boarding-houses, and employ chiefly other operatives than resident ones, they be not bringing in the seeds of future and alarming evil. . . .

To obtain this constant importation of female hands from the country, it is necessary to secure *the moral protection of their characters while they are resident in Lowell.* This, therefore, is the chief object of that moral police referred to, some details of which will now be given.

It should be stated, in the outset, that no persons are employed on the Corporations who are addicted to intemperance, or who are known to be guilty of any immoralities of conduct. As the parent of all other vices, intemperance is most carefully excluded. Absolute freedom from intoxicating liquors is understood, throughout the city, to be a prerequisite to obtaining employment in the mills, and any person known to be addicted to their use is at once dismissed. This point has not received the attention, from writers upon the moral conditions of Lowell, which it deserves; and we are surprised that the English traveller and divine, Dr. Scoresby, in his recent book upon Lowell, has given no more notice to this subject. A more strictly and universally temperate class of persons cannot be found, than the nine thousand operatives of this city; and the fact is as well known to all others living here, as it is of some honest pride among themselves. In relation to other immoralities, it may be stated, that the suspicion of criminal conduct, association with suspected persons, and general and habitual light behavior and conversation, are regarded as sufficient reasons for dismissions, and for which delinquent operatives are discharged.

[*Reverend Mills also described the discharge system at the factories. For those girls whose conduct was satisfactory and who had worked at least a year, honorable discharges were issued. Discharge letters could be used as a recommendations for another job. Those who received dishonorable discharges for such things as stealing, lying, leaving the job without permission, or other "improper conduct," however, would have difficulty finding other employment.*]

So much for honorable discharges. Those dishonorable have another treatment. The names of all persons dismissed for bad conduct, or who leave the mill irregularly, are also entered in a book kept for that purpose, and these names are sent to all the counting-rooms of the city, and are there entered on *their* books. *Such persons obtain no more employment throughout the city.* The question is put to each applicant, "Have you worked before in the city, and if so, where is your discharge?" If no discharge be presented, an inquiry of the applicant's name will enable the superintendent to know whether that name stands on his book of dishonorable discharges, and he is thus saved from taking in a corrupt or unworthy hand. This system, which has been in operation in Lowell from the beginning, is of great and important effect in driving unworthy persons from our city, and in preserving the high character of our operatives.

[*Male overseers, or foremen, were also closely screened and had to possess good moral character. In response to the Reverend's questions about male overseers, one factory owner responded as follows.*]

Lowell, May 10, 1841

Dear Sir: —

I employ in our mills, and in the various departments connected with them, thirty overseers, and as many second overseers. My overseers are married men, with families, with a single exception, and even he has engaged a tenement, and is to be married soon. Our second overseers are younger men, but upwards of twenty of them are married, and several others are soon to be married. Sixteen of our overseers are members of some regular church, and four of them are deacons. Ten of our second overseers are also members of the church, and one of them is the Superintendent of a Sunday School. I have no hesitation in saying that in all the sterling requisites of character, in native intelligence, and practical good sense, in sound morality, and as active, useful, and exemplary citizens, they may, as a class, safely challenge comparison with any class in our community. I know not, among them all, an intemperate man, nor, at this time, even what is called a moderate drinker.

[*Furthermore, the girls were expected to obey numerous rules.*]

Still another source of trust which a Corporation has, for the good character of its operatives, is the moral control which they have over one another. Of course this control would be nothing among a generally corrupt and degraded class. But among virtuous and high-minded young women, who feel that they have the keeping of their characters, and that any stain upon their associates brings reproach upon themselves, the power of opinion becomes an ever-present, and ever-active restraint. A girl, *suspected* of immoralities, or serious improprieties of conduct, at once loses caste. Her fellow-boarders will at once leave the house, if the keeper does not dismiss the offender. In self-protection, therefore, the matron is obliged to put the offender away. Nor will her former companions walk with, or work with her; till at length, finding herself every-where talked about, and pointed at, and shunned, she is obliged to relieve her fellow-operatives of a presence which they feel brings disgrace. From this power of opinion, there is no appeal; and as long as it is exerted in favor of pro-priety of behavior and purity of life, it is one of the most active and effectual safeguards of character.

It may not be out of place to present here the regulations, which are ob-served alike on all the Corporations, which are given to the operatives when they are first employed, and are posted up conspicuously in all the mills. They are as follows: —

Regulations to be observed by all persons employed by the _____ Manu-facturing Company, in the Factories.

Every overseer is required to be punctual himself, and to see that those em-ployed under him are so.

The overseers may, at their discretion, grant leave of absence to those em-ployed under them, when there are sufficient spare hands to supply their place; but when there are not sufficient spare hands, they are not allowed to grant leave of absence unless in cases of absolute necessity.

All persons are required to observe the regulations of the room in which they are employed. They are not allowed to be absent from their work without the consent of their overseer, except in case of sickness, and then they are required to send him word of the cause of their absence.

All persons are required to board in one of the boarding-houses belonging to the company, and conform to the regulations of the house in which they board.

All persons are required to be constant in attendance on public worship, at one of the regular places of worship in this place.

Persons who do not comply with the above regulations will not be employed by the company.

Persons entering the employment of the company are considered as engaging to work one year.

All persons intending to leave the employment of the company, are required to give notice of the same to their overseer, at least two weeks previous to the time of leaving.

Any one who shall take from the mills, or the yard, any yarn, cloth, or other article belonging to the company, will be considered guilty of STEALING — and prosecuted accordingly.

The above regulations are considered part of the contract with all persons entering the employment of the _____ MANUFACTURING COMPANY. All persons who shall have complied with them, on leaving the employment of the company, shall be entitled to an honorable discharge, which will serve as a recommendation to any of the factories in Lowell. No one who shall not have complied with them will be entitled to such a discharge.

_____ _____ , Agent

FIGURE 1   Time Table of the Lowell Mills. *(Courtesy Merrimack Valley Textile Museum.)*

TIME TABLE OF THE LOWELL MILLS,

Arranged to make the working time throughout the year average 11 hours per day.

TO TAKE EFFECT SEPTEMBER 21st., 1853.

The Standard time being that of the meridian of Lowell, as shown by the Regulator Clock of AMOS SANBORN, Post Office Corner, Central Street.

From March 20th to September 19th, inclusive.

COMMENCE WORK, at 6.30 A. M.   LEAVE OFF WORK, at 6.30 P. M., except on Saturday Evenings.
BREAKFAST at 6 A. M.   DINNER, at 12 M.   Commence Work, after dinner, 12.45 P. M.

From September 20th to March 19th, inclusive.

COMMENCE WORK at 7.00 A. M.   LEAVE OFF WORK, at 7.00 P. M., except on Saturday Evenings.
BREAKFAST at 6.30 A. M.   DINNER, at 12.30 P.M.   Commence Work, after dinner, 1.15 P. M.

BELLS.

From March 20th to September 19th, inclusive.

Morning Bells.	Dinner Bells.	Evening Bells.
First bell,..........4.30 A. M.	Ring out,.............12.00 M.	Ring out,............6.30 P. M.
Second, 5.30 A. M.; Third, 6.20.	Ring in,............12.35 P. M.	Except on Saturday Evenings.

From September 20th to March 19th, inclusive.

Morning Bells.	Dinner Bells.	Evening Bells.
First bell,..........5.00 A. M.	Ring out,.............12.30 P. M.	Ring out at............7.00 P. M.
Second, 6.00 A. M.; Third, 6.50.	Ring in,............1.05 P. M.	Except on Saturday Evenings.

SATURDAY EVENING BELLS.

During APRIL, MAY, JUNE, JULY, and AUGUST, Ring Out, at 6.00 P. M.
The remaining Saturday Evenings in the year, ring out as follows :

SEPTEMBER.
First Saturday, ring out 6.00 P. M.
Second   "   "   5.45   "
Third   "   "   5.30   "
Fourth   "   "   5.20   "

OCTOBER.
First Saturday, ring out 5.05 P. M.
Second   "   "   4.55   "
Third   "   "   4.45   "
Fourth   "   "   4.35   "
Fifth   "   "   4.25   "

NOVEMBER.
First Saturday, ring out 4.15 P. M.
Second   ".   "   4.05   "

NOVEMBER.
Third Saturday ring out 4.00 P. M.
Fourth   "   "   3.55   "

DECEMBER.
First Saturday, ring out 3.50 P. M.
Second   "   "   3.55   "
Third   "   "   3.55   "
Fourth   "   "   4.00   "
Fifth   "   "   4.00   "

JANUARY.
First Saturday, ring out 4.10 P. M.
Second   "   "   4.15   "

JANUARY.
Third Saturday, ring out 4.25 P. M.
Fourth   "   "   4.35   "

FEBRUARY.
First Saturday ring out 4.45 P. M.
Second   "   "   4.55   "
Third   "   "   5.00   "
Fourth   "   "   5.10   "

MARCH.
First Saturday, ring out 5.25 P. M.
Second   "   "   5.30   "
Third   "   "   5.35   "
Fourth   "   "   5.45   "

YARD GATES will be opened at the first stroke of the bells for entering or leaving the Mills.

SPEED GATES commence hoisting three minutes before commencing work.

Penhallow, Printer, Wyman's Exchange, 28 Merrimack St.

SELECTION FROM
A NEW ENGLAND GIRLHOOD

From Lucy Larcom, A New England Girlhood *(Boston: Houghton Mifflin, 1889).*

During my father's life, a few years before my birth, his thoughts had been turned towards the new manufacturing town growing up on the banks of the Merrimack. He had once taken a journey there, with the possibility in his mind of making the place his home, his limited income furnishing no adequate promise of a maintenance for his large family of daughters. From the beginning, Lowell had a high reputation for good order, morality, piety, and all that was dear to the old-fashioned New Englander's heart.

After his death, my mother's thoughts naturally followed the direction his had taken; and seeing no other opening for herself, she sold her small estate, and moved to Lowell, with the intention of taking a corporation-house for mill-girl boarders. Some of the family objected, for the Old World traditions about factory life were anything but attractive; and they were current in New England until the experiment at Lowell had shown that independent and intelligent workers invariably give their own character to their occupation. My mother had visited Lowell, and she was willing and glad, knowing all about the place, to make it our home. . . .

[*Because her mother could not earn enough to support the family, Lucy (age eleven) and her sister went to work in the mills.*]

So I went to my first day's work in the mill with a light heart. The novelty of it made it seem easy, and it really was not hard, just to change the bobbins on the spinning-frames every three quarters of an hour or so, with half a dozen other little girls who were doing the same thing. When I came back at night, the family began to pity me for my long, tiresome day's work, but I laughed, and said, —

"Why, it is nothing but fun. It is just like play."

And for a little while it was only a new amusement; I liked it better than going to school and "making believe" I was learning when I was not. And there was a great deal of play mixed with it. We were not occupied more than half the time. The intervals were spent frolicking around among the spinning-frames, teasing and talking to the older girls, or entertaining ourselves with games and stories in a corner, or exploring, with the overseer's permission, the mysteries of the carding-room, the dressing-room, and the weaving-room. . . .

There were compensations for being shut in to daily toil so early. The mill itself had its lessons for us. But it was not, and could not be, the right sort of life for a child, and we were happy in the knowledge that, at the longest, our employment was only to be temporary.

When I took my next three months at the grammar school, everything there was changed, and I too was changed. The teachers were kind, and thorough in their instruction; and my mind seemed to have been ploughed up during that year of work, so that knowledge took root in it easily. It was a great delight to me to study, and at the end of the three months the master told me that I was prepared for the high school.

But alas! I could not go. The little money I could earn — one dollar a week, besides the price of my board — was needed in the family, and I must return to the mill. It was a severe disappointment to me, though I did not say so at home. . . .

In the older times it was seldom said to little girls, as it always has been said to boys, that they ought to have some definite plan, while they were children, what to be and do when they were grown up. There was usually but one path open before them, to become good wives and housekeepers. And the ambition of most girls was to follow their mothers' footsteps in this direction; a natural and laudable ambition. But girls, as well as boys, must often have been conscious of their own peculiar capabilities, — must have desired to cultivate and make use of their individual powers. When I was growing up, they had already begun to be encouraged to do so. We were often told that it was our duty to develop any talent we might possess, or at least learn how to do some one thing which the world needed, or which would make it a pleasanter world. . . .

At this time I had learned to do a spinner's work, and I obtained permission to tend some frames that stood directly in front of the river-windows, with only them and the wall behind me, extending half the length of the mill, — and one young woman beside me, at the farther end of the row. She was a sober, mature person, who scarcely thought it worth her while to speak often to a child like me; and I was, when with strangers, rather a reserved girl; so I kept myself occupied with the river, my work, and my thoughts. . . .

The printed regulations forbade us to bring books into the mill, so I made my window-seat into a small library of poetry, pasting its side all over with newspaper clippings. In those days we had only weekly papers, and they had always a "poet's corner," where standard writers were well represented, with anonymous ones, also. I was not, of course, much of a critic. I chose my verses for their sentiment, and because I wanted to commit them to memory; sometimes it was a long poem, sometimes a hymn, sometimes only a stray verse. . . .

Some of the girls could not believe that the Bible was meant to be counted among forbidden books. We all thought that the Scriptures had a right to go wherever we went, and that if we needed them anywhere, it was at our work. I evaded the law by carrying some leaves from a torn Testament in my pocket.

The overseer, caring more for law than gospel, confiscated all he found. He had his desk full of Bibles. It sounded oddly to hear him say to the most religious girl in the room, when he took hers away, "I did think you had more conscience than to bring that book here." But we had some close ethical questions to settle in those days. It was a rigid code of morality under which we lived. Nobody complained of it, however, and we were doubtless better off for its strictness, in the end.

The last window in the row behind me was filled with flourishing house plants — fragrant-leaved geraniums, the overseer's pets. They gave that corner a bowery look; the perfume and freshness tempted me there often. Standing before that window, I could look across the room and see girls moving backwards and forwards among the spinning-frames, sometimes stooping, sometimes reaching up their arms, as their work required, with easy and not ungraceful movements. On the whole, it was far from being a disagreeable place to stay in. The girls were bright-looking and neat, and everything was kept clean and shining. The effect of the whole was rather attractive to strangers. . . .

One great advantage which came to these many stranger girls through being brought together, away from their own homes, was that it taught them to go out of themselves, and enter into the lives of others. Home-life, when one always stays at home, is necessarily narrowing. That is one reason why so many women are petty and unthoughtful of any except their own family's interests. We have hardly begun to live until we can take in the idea of the whole human family as the one to which we truly belong. To me, it was an incalculable help to find myself among so many working-girls, all of us thrown upon our own resources, but thrown much more upon each others' sympathies. . . .

My grandfather came to see my mother once at about this time and visited the mills. When he had entered the room, and looked around for a moment, he took off his hat and made a low bow to the girls, first toward the right, and then toward the left. We were familiar with his courteous habits, partly due to his French descent; but we had never seen anybody bow to a room full of mill girls in that polite way, and some one of the family afterwards asked him why he did so. He looked a little surprised at the question, but answered promptly and with dignity, "I always take off my hat to ladies."

His courtesy was genuine. Still, we did not call ourselves ladies. We did not forget that we were working-girls, wearing coarse aprons suitable to our work, and that there was some danger of our becoming drudges. I know that sometimes the confinement of the mill became very wearisome to me. In the sweet June weather I would lean far out of the window, and try not to hear the unceasing clash of sound inside. Looking away to the hills, my whole stifled being would cry out

"Oh, that I had wings!"
Still I was there from choice, and
"The prison unto which we doom ourselves,
No prison is."

FIGURE 2 Title page of *Lowell Offering*. *(From Series I, 1840. Courtesy Merrimack Valley Textile Museum.)*

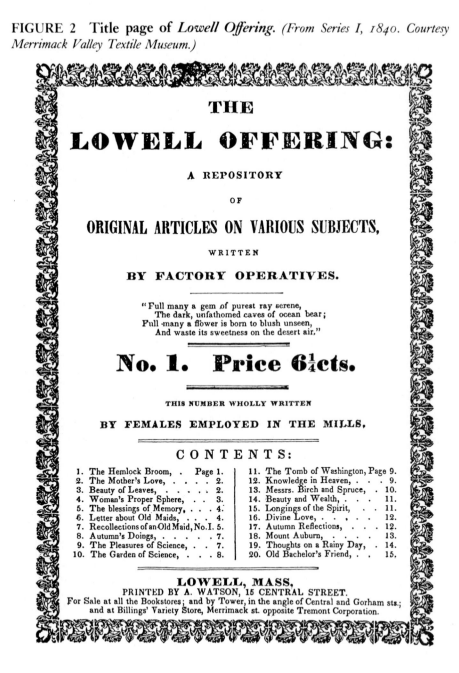

THE
LOWELL OFFERING:

A REPOSITORY

OF

ORIGINAL ARTICLES ON VARIOUS SUBJECTS,

WRITTEN

BY FACTORY OPERATIVES.

"Full many a gem of purest ray serene,
The dark, unfathomed caves of ocean bear;
Full many a flower is born to blush unseen,
And waste its sweetness on the desert air."

No. 1. Price 6¼cts.

THIS NUMBER WHOLLY WRITTEN

BY FEMALES EMPLOYED IN THE MILLS,

CONTENTS:

LOWELL, MASS,
PRINTED BY A. WATSON, 15 CENTRAL STREET.
For Sale at all the Bookstores; and by Tower, in the angle of Central and Gorham sts.;
and at Billings' Variety Store, Merrimack st. opposite Tremont Corporation.

SELECTIONS FROM
LOWELL OFFERING

From Lowell Offering, *Series I (1840), p. 16.*

Editorial Corner

The Lowell Offering is strictly what it purports to be, a "Repository of original articles on various subjects, written by Factory Operatives." — The objects of the publication are, to encourage the cultivation of talent; to preserve such articles as are deemed most worthy of preservation; and to correct an erroneous idea which generally prevails in relation to the intelligence of persons employed in the Mills. This number is wholly the offering of Females. . . .

We are persuaded that the citizens generally, and those engaged in the Mills particularly, will feel and manifest a lively interest in the prosperity of the Lowell Offering. That it is faultless — that the severe and captious critic will find no room for his vocation, is not to be expected. Nevertheless, while the work makes no noisy pretensions to superior excellency, it would claim no unusual indulgences. It asks only that, all the circumstances incident to its peculiar character being duly weighed, it shall be fairly and candidly judged. The Editors do not hesitate to say, that they anticipate for a favorable reception at the hands of those who have at heart the interests of that important and interesting portion of our population, whose intellectual elevation and moral welfare it aims to promote. . . .

The critical reader will doubtless discover, in many of the articles making this number of the Offering, words and phrases for which better might be substituted; and also sentences that want the freedom and smoothness of perfect composition. In explanation, the Editors have to say, that, in preparing the articles for the press, while they claimed to exercise the rights usually granted to the editorial fraternity, they resolved carefully to avoid any alteration which might affect the sentiment or style of the several writers. In consequence of this resolution a few expressions and sentences have been allowed to pass, which a less scrupulous regard for strict originality would have rejected. Nevertheless they are quite sure the rule adopted will be approved by all who shall look to the articles of the Offering as evidence of the intellectual and literary power of the writers.

An opinion extensively prevails, not merely beyond the limits of Massachusetts, that the Manufacturing city of Lowell is a nucleus of depravity and ignorance.

Confessedly, wherever there exists *any* depravity or ignorance, there is *too much* of it. We have this to testify however, that they who know least of the people of Lowell, including the Factory Operatives, entertain the most unworthy and unjust opinions of them. Close personal observations has satisfied us, that in respect of morality and intelligence, they will not suffer in comparison with the inhabitants of any part of moral and enlightened New England. We shall have occasion to speak of this subject at considerable length hereafter. We shall note the unsurpassed (if not unequaled) advantages of education enjoyed by our population; and the extensive means of information and piety furnished by popular lectures and religious institutions. We shall note the absence of theatres and kindred abominations; the care taken to exclude unworthy persons from the Corporations, &c.

And as to the intelligence of our people, we may safely present the pages of the Offering as a testimony against all revilers "who know not whereof they affirm." Editors who think proper to copy any thing therefrom, are requested to give due credit, and thus assist in the correction of an unwarranted and injurious error.

From Lowell Offering, *Series II, Vol. II (1842), p. 192.*

Dignity of Labor

From whence originated the idea, that it was derogatory to a lady's dignity, or a blot upon the female character, to labor? and who was the first to say, sneeringly, 'Oh, she *works* for a living'? Surely, such ideas and expressions ought not to grow on republican soil. The time has been, when ladies of the first rank were accustomed to busy themselves in domestic employment.

Homer tells us of princesses who used to draw water from the springs, and wash with their own hands the finest of the linen of their respective families. The famous Lucretia used to spin in the midst of her attendants; and the wife of Ulysses, after the siege of Troy, employed herself in weaving, until her husband returned to Ithaca. And in later times, the wife of George the Third of England, has been represented as spending a whole evening in hemming pocket-handkerchiefs, while her daughter Mary sat in the corner, darning stockings.

Few American fortunes will support a woman who is above the calls of her family; and a man of sense, in choosing a companion to jog with him through all the up-hills and down-hills of life, would sooner choose one who *had* to work for a living, than one who thought it beneath her to soil her pretty hands with manual labor, although she possessed her thousands. To be able to earn one's own living by laboring with the hands, should be reckoned among female accomplishments; and I hope the time is not far distant when none of my countrywomen will be ashamed to have it known that they are better versed in useful, than they are in ornamental accomplishments.

C. B.

From Lowell Offering, *Series II, Vol. III (1842), pp. 69–70.*

Editorial
Home in a Boarding-House

[*Factory boardinghouses were not really like homes, the editor pointed out. A place to eat and lodge, the boardinghouses often seemed crowded and impersonal.*]

But these are all trifles, compared with the perplexities to which we are subjected in other ways; and some of these things might be remedied by the girls themselves. We now allude to the importunities of evening visitors, such as peddlers, candy and newspaper boys, shoe-dealers, book-sellers, &c., &c., breaking in upon the only hours of leisure we can call our own, and proffering their articles with a pertinacity which will admit of no denial. That these evening salesmen are always unwelcome we will not assert, but they are too often inclined to remain where they know they are considered a nuisance. And then they often forget, if they ever knew, the rules of politeness which should regulate all transient visitors. They deal about their hints, inuendoes, and low cunning, as though a factory boarding-house was what no boarding-house should ever be.

The remedy is entirely with the girls. Treat all of these comers with a politeness truly lady-like, when they appear as gentlemen, but let your manners change to stern formality when they forget that they are in the company of respectable females. . . .

From Lowell Offering, *Series I (1840), pp. 17–19.*

Factory Girls

"SHE HAS WORKED IN A FACTORY, *is sufficient to damn to infamy the most worthy and virtuous girl.*"

So says Mr. Orestes A. Brownson; and either this horrible assertion is true, or Mr. Brownson is a slanderer. I assert that it is *not* true, and Mr. B. may consider himself called upon to prove his words, if he can.

This gentleman has read of an Israelitish boy who, with nothing but a stone and sling, once entered into a contest with a Philistine giant, arrayed in brass, whose spear was like a weaver's beam; and he may now see what will probably appear to him quite as marvellous; and that is, that a *factory girl* is not afraid to oppose herself to the *Editor of the Boston Quarterly Review.* True, he has upon his side fame, learning, and great talent; but I have what is better than either of these, or all combined, and that is *truth.* Mr. Brownson has not said that this thing should be so; or that he is glad it is so; or that he deeply regrets such a state of affairs; but he has said it *is* so; and *I* affirm that it is *not.*

And whom has Mr. Brownson slandered? A class of girls who in this city alone are numbered by thousands, and who collect in many of our smaller towns by hundreds; girls who generally come from quiet country homes, where their minds and manners have been formed under the eyes of the worthy sons of the Pilgrims, and their virtuous partners, and who return again to become the wives of the free intelligent yeomanry of New England and the mothers of quite a portion of our future republicans. Think, for a moment, how many of the next generation are to spring from mothers doomed to infamy! "Ah," it may be replied, "Mr. Brownson acknowledges that you may still be worthy and virtuous." Then we must be a set of worthy and virtuous idiots, for no virtuous girl of common sense would choose for an occupation one that would consign her to infamy. . . .

That there has been prejudice against us, we know; but it is wearing away, and has never been so deep nor universal as Mr. B's statement will lead many to believe. Even now it may be that "the mushroom aristocracy" and "would-be fashionables" of Boston, turn up their eyes in horror at the sound of those vulgar words, *factory girls;* but *they* form but a small part of the community, and theirs are not the opinions which Mr. Brownson intended to represent. . . .

[The prejudice against factory girls was connected to the degraded and exploited conditions of European workers, the angry letter writer asserted. "Yankee girls," she said, are independent, and although the work is hard, the wages are better than those in other kinds of employment. It is no wonder, she concluded, that so many intelligent, worthy, and virtuous young women have been drawn to Lowell.]

The erroneous idea, wherever it exists, must be done away, that there is in factories but one sort of girls, and *that* the baser and degraded sort. There are among us *all sorts* of girls. I believe that there are few occupations which can exhibit so many gradations of piety and intelligence; but the majority may at least lay claim to as much of the former as females in other stations of life. . . . The Improvement Circles, the Lyceum and Institute, the social religious meetings, the Circulating and other libraries, can bear testimony that the little time they have is spent in a better manner. Our well filled churches and lecture halls and the high character of our clergymen and lecturers, will testify that the state of morals and intelligence is not low.

Mr. Brownson, I suppose, would not judge of our moral characters by our church-going tendencies; but as many do, a word on this subject may not be amiss. That there are many in Lowell who do not regularly attend any meeting, is as true as the correspondent of the Boston Times once represented it; but for this there are various reasons. . . .

There have also been nice calculations made, as to the small proportion which the amount of money deposited in the Savings Bank bears to that earned in the city; but this is not all that is saved. Some is deposited in Banks at other places, and some is put into the hands of personal friends. Still, much that is earned is immediately, though not foolishly, spent. Much that none but the parties concerned will ever know of, goes to procure comforts and necessaries for some lowly home, and a great deal is spent for public benevolent purposes. . . .

And now, if Mr. Brownson is a *man,* he will endeavor to retrieve the injury he has done; he will resolve that "the dark shall be light, and the wrong made right," and the assertion he has publicly made will be as publicly retracted. If he still doubts upon the subject let him come among us: let him make himself as well acquainted with us as our pastors and superintendents are; and though he will find error, ignorance, and folly among us, (and where would he find them not?) yet he would not see worthy and virtuous girls consigned to infamy, because they work in a factory.

A FACTORY GIRL

From Lowell Offering, *Series I (1840), p. 61.*

A Familiar Letter

Friends and Associates: —

With indescribable emotions of pleasure, mingled with feelings of deepest gratitude to Him who is the Author of every good and perfect gift, I have perused the second and third numbers of the Lowell Offering.

As a laborer among you, (tho' least of all) I rejoice that the time has arrived when a class of laboring females (who have long been made a reproach and by-word, by those whom fortune or pride has placed above the avocation by which we have subjected ourselves to the sneers and scoffs of the idle, ignorant and envious part of community,) are bursting asunder the captive chains of prejudice. . . .

I know it has been affirmed, to the sorrow of many a would-be lady, that factory girls and ladies could not be distinguished by their apparel. What a lamentable evil! and no doubt it would be a source of much gratitude to such, if the awful name of "factory girl!" were branded on the forehead of every female who is, or ever was, employed in the Mills. Appalling as the name may sound in the delicate ears of a sensitive lady, as she contrasts the music of her piano with the rumblings of the factory machinery, we would not shrink from such a token of our calling, could the treasures of the mind be there displayed, and merit, in her own unbiased form be stamped there also. . . .

Yours, in the bonds of affection,

DOROTHEA

From Lowell Offering, *Series I (1840), pp. 44–46.*

Gold Watches

It is now nearly a year since an article appeared in the Ladies' Book, in the form of a tale, though it partakes more of the character of an essay. It was written by Mrs. Hale, and exhibits her usual judgment and talent. Her object evidently was to correct the many erroneous impressions which exist in society, with regard to the folly of extravagance in dress, and all outward show. I was much pleased with all of it, with the exception of a single sentence. Speaking of the impossibility of considering dress a mark of distinction, she observed, — (addressing herself, I presume, to the *ladies* of New England,) — "How stands the difference now? Many of the factory girls wear gold watches, and an imitation, at least, of all the ornaments which grace the daughters of our most opulent citizens."

O the times! O the manners! Alas! how very sadly the world has changed! The time was when the *lady* could be distinguished from the *no-lady* by her dress, as far as the eye could reach; but now, you might stand in the same room, and judging by their outward appearance, you could not tell "which was which." Even gold watches are now no *sure* indication — for they have been worn by the lowest, even by "many of the factory girls." No *lady* need carry one now, for any other than the simple purpose of easily ascertaining the time of day, or night, if she so please! . . .

Those who do not labor for their living, have more time for the improvement of their minds, for the cultivation of conversational powers, and graceful manners; but if, with these advantages, they still need richer dress to distinguish them from *us,* the fault must be their own, and they should at least learn to honor merit, and acknowledge talent wherever they see it. . . .

And now I will address myself to my sister operatives in the Lowell factories. Good advice should be taken, from whatever quarter it may come, whether from friend or foe; and part of the advice which Mrs. Hale has given to the readers of the Ladies' Book, may be of advantage to us. Is there not among us, as a class, too much of this striving for distinction in dress? Is it not the only aim and object of too many of us, to wear something a little better than others can obtain? Do we not sometimes see the girl who has half a dozen silk gowns, toss her head, as if she felt herself six times better than her neighbor who has none?. . .

We all have many opportunities for the exercise of the kindly affections, and more than most females. We should look upon one another something as a band of orphans should do. We are fatherless and motherless: we are alone, and surrounded by temptation. Let us caution each other; let us watch over and endeavor to improve each other; and both at our boarding-houses and in the Mill, let us strive to promote each other's comfort and happiness. Above all, let us endeavor to improve ourselves by making good use of the many advantages we here possess. I say let us at least strive to do this; and if we succeed, it will finally be acknowledged that Factory Girls shine forth in ornaments far more valuable than *Gold Watches.*

A FACTORY GIRL

FIGURE 3 Song of the Spinners. *(From Lowell Offering, Series II, Vol. I,*
1841, p. 32. Courtesy Merrimack Valley Textile Museum.)

SONG OF THE SPINNERS.

Questions to Consider

What are the major advantages Reverend Mills observes in the Lowell system? In what important ways did the system (both the factories and the boardinghouses) regulate the girls' lives? How did it protect the morals of its female employees? Of course, not all girls lived up to these standards. What did they do? How were they punished? Do you think Reverend Mills has presented a relatively unbiased view? Why or why not?

Why did Lucy Larcom have to go to work in the mills when she was so young? How did she feel about the work when she was a child? What contrast does she draw between young boys' and young girls' upbringings in the early nineteenth century? Did she and the other girls always obey the factory rules? What advantages did she discover in her factory experience? What were the disadvantages?

Look carefully at the table of contents and the first editorial of the *Lowell Offering.* What do they tell you about the factory girls, their interests, and their concerns? Was C. B. upholding the cult of true womanhood in her article about the dignity of labor? How did "home" in the boardinghouse differ from the girls' real homes? From what you read earlier (Reverend Mills's account), in what ways might a boardinghouse also be similar to the girls' real homes?

The next three letters are written by girls who were rather angry. What had the reformer Orestes Brownson said? How did "a factory girl" try to disprove his view? What fears and anxieties are revealed by this letter and the one from Dorothea? What were these two girls trying to prove? The third letter writer retained her sense of humor, but she too was upset. In this case, the offensive remark to which she referred appeared in *Godey's Lady's Book,* the most popular American women's magazine of the period, and was written by the highly respected Sarah Josepha Hale (the magazine's editor and author of "Mary Had a Little Lamb"). What had Mrs. Hale written? What was the factory girl's response? What advice did she give her co-workers about fashion? About being a true woman? Even the "Song of the Spinners," the last piece of evidence, contains a message. What do the lyrics tell you about the spinners' values and attitudes toward work?

Now that you are thoroughly familiar with the ideas about how the working girls of Lowell were supposed to behave and the realities of the system under which they lived, you are ready to frame an answer to the central question: how did people react when the needs of a modernizing economy came into conflict with the ideas about the women's place in society?

Epilogue

Although several major strikes (or "turnouts," as they were called) occurred in the Lowell mills in the mid-1830s, it was not until the mid-1840s that Lowell began to experience serious labor problems. In order to remain competitive yet at the same time maximize profits, companies introduced the "speed up" (a much faster pace of work) and the "stretch out" (where one worker was put in charge of more machinery — sometimes as many as four looms). The mills also cut wages in spite of the fact that boardinghouse rents were rising. In Lowell, workers first tried to have the length of the working day reduced and, like many other American workers, united in support of the Ten-Hour Movement. When women workers joined such protests, they further challenged the ideas embodied in the cult of true womanhood — especially that of submissiveness.

Even before the strikes, the Lowell system was breaking down as more and more mills were built, far larger than their predecessors. Construction of private housing (especially tenements) expanded and a much smaller proportion of mill hands lived in boardinghouses. Both housing and neighborhoods became badly overcrowded. By 1850 mill owners were looking for still other ways (in addition to the speed up and stretch out) to reduce the cost of labor. They found their answer in the waves of Irish immigrants coming to America to escape the economic hardships so widespread in their own country. Fewer and fewer "Yankee girls" were recruited for work in the textile mills. At one Lowell company, for example, the number of native-born girls declined from 737 in 1836 to 324 in 1860, although the total number of female workers remained constant. Irish men, women, and increasing numbers of children filled the gap, for as wages declined, a family income became a necessity.

By 1860 what Reverend Mills had characterized as "the moral and intellectual advantages" of the Lowell system had come to an end. Indeed, many Americans could see little or no difference between our own factory towns and those of Europe.

Chapter 7

The "Peculiar Institution": Slaves Tell Their Own Story

The Problem

In his first draft of the Declaration of Independence, Thomas Jefferson accused George III of England of having

> waged cruel war against human nature itself, violating its most sacred rights of life and liberty in the persons of a distant people who never offended him, captivating and carrying them into slavery in another hemisphere, or to incur miserable death in their transportation thither. . . . Determined to keep open a market where MEN should be bought and sold, he has prostituted his negative for suppressing every legislative attempt to prohibit or to restrain this execrable commerce. . . .

The Continental Congress, however, voted to remove the entire passage.

Many of Jefferson's fellow southerners found it too antislavery in tone, while some northerners probably were embarrassed by the flagrant discrepancy between Jefferson's words and actual fact. Too, some northerners made considerable fortunes in that very slave trade. For by the time of the American Revolution, what had begun in 1619 as a trickle of Africans intended to supplement the farm labor of indentured servants from England had swelled to a slave population of approximately 500,000 people, the vast majority of them concentrated on tobacco, rice, and cotton plantations in the South. Moreover, as the black population grew, what apparently had been a fairly loose and unregimented labor system gradually evolved into an increasingly harsh, rigid, and complete system of chattel slavery that tried to control nearly every aspect of the slaves' lives. Whatever Jefferson may have thought and written, by 1775 black slavery had become a significant (some would have said indispensable) part of southern life.

Nor did the American Revolution reverse those trends. Although northern states in which black slavery was not so deeply rooted began to institute gradual emancipation, after the Revolution, the slave system — as well as its harshness — appears to have increased in the South. The invention of the cotton gin, which made possible the removal of seeds from the easily grown short staple cotton, permitted southerners to cultivate cotton on the uplands, thereby spurring the westward movement of the plantation system and of slavery. As a result slavery expanded along with settlement into nearly every area of the South — the Gulf region, Tennessee, Kentucky, and ultimately Texas. Simultaneously, the slave population burgeoned, roughly doubling every thirty years (from approximately 700,000 in 1790 to 1.5 million in 1820 to over 3.2 million in 1850). Since importation of slaves from Africa was banned in 1808 (although there was some illegal slave smuggling), most further gains in the slave population were due to natural increase.

But as the slave population grew, the fears and anxieties of southern whites grew correspondingly. In 1793 a slave rebellion in the Caribbean caused tremendous consternation in the white South. Rumors of uprisings plotted by slaves were numerous. And the actual rebellion of Nat Turner in Virginia in 1831 (in which fifty-five whites were killed, many of them while asleep) only increased white insecurities and dread. In response, southern states passed a series of laws that served to make the system of slavery even more restrictive. Toward the end of his life, Thomas Jefferson (who did not live to see Nat Turner's uprising) agonized:

> But as it is, we have the wolf by the ears, and we can neither hold him, nor safely let him go. Justice is in one scale, and self-preservation in the other. . . . I regret that I am now to die in the belief, that the useless sacrifice of themselves by the generation of 1776, to acquire self-government and happiness to their country, is to be thrown away by the unwise and unworthy passions of their sons. . . .

By this time, however, Jefferson was nearly alone among white southerners. Most did not question the assertions that slavery was a necessity, that it was good for the slave as well as for the owner, and that it must be preserved at any cost.

It has often been pointed out that the majority of white southerners did not own slaves. In fact, the proportion of white southern families that did own slaves was actually declining in the nineteenth century, from one-third in 1830 to roughly one-fourth by 1860. Moreover, nearly three-fourths of these slaveholders owned fewer than ten slaves. Slaveholders, then, were a distinct minority of the white southern population, and those slaveholders with large plantations and hundreds of slaves were an exceedingly small group.

How, then, did the "peculiar institution" of slavery, as one southerner called it, become so imbedded in the Old South? To begin with, even though only a minority of southern whites owned slaves, nearly all were somehow touched by the institution of slavery. Fear of black uprisings prompted many non-slaveholders to support an increasingly rigid slave system that included night patrols, written passes for slaves away from plantations, supervised religious services for slaves, a law prohibiting teaching slaves to read or write, and other measures to keep slaves ignorant, dependent, and always under the eyes of whites. Too, many non-slave-owners were afraid that emancipation would bring them into direct economic competition with blacks who, it was assumed, would drive down wages. Finally, although large planters represented only a fraction of the white population, they virtually controlled the economic, social, and political institutions and were not about to injure either themselves or their status by doing away with the slave system that essentially supported them.

To defend their "peculiar institution," white southerners constructed a remarkably complete and diverse set of arguments. Slavery, they maintained, was actually a far more humane system than northern capitalism. After all, slaves were fed, clothed, sheltered, cared for when they were ill, and supported in their old age, while northern factory workers were paid pitifully low wages, were used, and were then discarded when no longer useful. Furthermore, many white southerners maintained that slavery was a positive good, for it had introduced the "barbarous" Africans to civilized American ways and, more importantly, to Christianity. Other southern whites stressed what they believed was the childlike, dependent nature of Afro-Americans, insisting that they could never cope with life outside the paternalistic and "benevolent" institution of slavery. In such an atmosphere, in which many of the white southern intellectual efforts went into the defense of slavery, dissent and freedom of thought were not welcome. Hence, those white southerners who disagreed and might have challenged the South's dependence on slavery either remained silent, were hushed up, or decided to leave the section. In many ways, then, the enslavement of blacks partly rested on the limitation of rights and freedoms for southern whites as well.

But how did the slaves react to an economic and social system that meant that neither they nor their children would ever experience freedom? Most white southerners assumed that slaves were happy and content. Northern abolitionists (to be sure, a minority of the white population) believed that slaves continually yearned for freedom. Both groups used oceans of ink to justify and support their claims. But evidence of how the slaves felt and thought is woefully sparse. And, given the restrictive nature of the slave system (which included enforced illiteracy among slaves), this pitiful lack of evidence is hardly surprising.

How, then, can we learn how slaves felt and thought about the "peculiar institution"? Slave uprisings were almost nonexistent, but does that mean the vast majority were happy with their lot? Runaways were common, and some, like Frederick Douglass, actually reached the North and wrote about their experiences as slaves. Yet how typical were Douglass's experiences? In sum, the vast majority of slaves were born, lived, and died in servitude, did not participate in organized revolts, and did not run away. How did they feel about the system of slavery?

While most slaves did not read or write, did not participate in organized revolts, and did not attempt to run away, they did leave a remarkable amount of evidence that can help us understand their thoughts and feelings. Yet we must be imaginative in how we approach and use that evidence.

In an earlier chapter, you discovered that statistical information (of births, deaths, age at marriage, farm size, inheritance, tax rolls, and so forth) can reveal a great deal about ordinary people like the New Englanders on the eve of the American Revolution. Such demographic evidence can aid the historian in forming a picture of who these people were and of the socioeconomic trends of the time, even if the people themselves were not aware of those trends. In this exercise, you will be using another kind of evidence and asking different questions. Your evidence will not come from white southerners (whose stake in maintaining slavery was enormous), from foreign travelers (whose own cultural biases often influenced what they reported), nor even from white or black abolitionists in the North (whose urgent need to eradicate the "sin" of slavery sometimes led them to gross exaggerations for propaganda purposes). Rather you will use anecdotes, stories, and songs from the rich oral tradition of the Afro-American slaves to investigate the human dimensions of the "peculiar institution."

Some of this evidence was collected and transcribed by people soon after emancipation. However, much of the evidence did not come to light until many years later, when the former slaves who were still alive were very old men and women. In fact, it was not until the 1920s that concerted efforts began to preserve the reminiscences of these people. In the 1920s Fisk University collected a good deal of evidence. In the 1930s the government-financed Federal Writers' Project accumulated over two thousand narratives from ex-slaves in every southern state except Louisiana and deposited them in the Library of Congress in Washington, D.C.

Much of the evidence, however, is in the form of slave songs and stories that slaves created and told to one another. Like the narratives of former slaves, these sources also must be used with imagination and with care.

The central question you are to answer is: how did the slaves themselves view the "peculiar institution"? How did they endure under a labor system that, at its very best, was still based on the total ownership of one human being by another?

The Method

Historians must always try to be aware of the limitations of their evidence. In the Federal Writers' Project, most of the former slaves were in their eighties or nineties (quite a few were over one hundred years old!) at the time they were interviewed. It is also important to know that while some of the interviewers were black, the overwhelming majority were white. Lastly, although many of the former slaves had moved to another location or a different state after the Civil War, many others were still living in the same county (sometimes even on the same land) where they had been slaves. In what ways might the age of the former slave, the race of the interviewer, or the place where the former slave was living affect the narratives?

Nevertheless, these narratives do reveal much about these people's thoughts and feelings about slavery. What direct reactions did the ex-slaves give? Why did many of them choose to be indirect? Some chose to answer questions by telling stories. Why? And remember, although some of the stories or anecdotes may not actually be true, they can be taken as representative of what the former slaves wished had actually happened or what they really thought about an incident. Therefore, often you must pull the true meaning from a narrative, inferring what the interviewee meant as well as what he or she said.

As to slaves' songs and other contemporary evidence, the vast majority of slaves could never have spoken their thoughts or vented their feelings directly. Instead they often hid their true meanings through the use of symbols, metaphors, and allegories. Here again you must be able to read between the lines, extracting thoughts, attitudes, and feelings that were purposely hidden or concealed from all but other slaves.

Included in the evidence are three *Uncle Remus* stories, which were written down by Joel Chandler Harris, a white man. Harris tried to remain faithful to the stories as he heard them. For this reason, he chose to transcribe them in Afro-American dialect. You will find it extremely helpful to read these stories aloud.

As you examine each piece of evidence, jot down enough notes to allow you to recall that piece of evidence later. But also (perhaps in a separate column) write down what you consider to be the *attitude* each piece of evidence communicates about the "peculiar institution" of slavery. What is the hidden message?

After you have examined each piece of evidence, look back over the notes you have made. What attitudes about slavery stand out? What did the slaves think about the slave system?

The Evidence

REMINISCENCES

Reminiscences I–XVI from B. A. Botkin, Federal Writers' Project, Lay My Burden Down: A Folk History of Slavery *(Chicago: University of Chicago Press, 1945). Reminiscences XVII and XVIII from Gilbert Osofsky, compiler,* Puttin' on Ole Massa *(New York: Harper and Row, 1969), p. 22.*

I

. . . I remember Mammy told me about one master who almost starved his slaves. Mighty stingy, I reckon he was.

Some of them slaves was so poorly thin they ribs would kinda rustle against each other like corn stalks a-drying in the hot winds. But they gets even one hog-killing time, and it was funny, too, Mammy said.

They was seven hogs, fat and ready for fall hog-killing time. Just the day before Old Master told off they was to be killed, something happened to all them porkers. One of the field boys found them and come a-telling the master: "The hogs is all died, now they won't be any meats for the winter."

When the master gets to where at the hogs is laying, they's a lot of Negroes standing round looking sorrow-eyed at the wasted meat. The master asks: "What's the illness with 'em?"

"Malitis," they tells him, and they acts like they don't want to touch the hogs. Master says to dress them anyway for they ain't no more meat on the place.

He says to keep all the meat for the slave families, but that's because he's afraid to eat it hisself account of the hogs' got malitis.

"Don't you all know what is malitis?" Mammy would ask the children when she was telling of the seven fat hogs and seventy lean slaves. And she would laugh, remembering how they fooled Old Master so's to get all them good meats.

"One of the strongest Negroes got up early in the morning," Mammy would explain, "long 'fore the rising horn called the slaves from their cabins. He skitted to the hog pen with a heavy mallet in his hand. When he tapped Mister Hog 'tween the eyes with the mallet, 'malitis' set in mighty quick, but it was a uncommon 'disease,' even with hungry Negroes around all the time."

II

The mistress had an old parrot, and one day I was in the kitchen making cookies, and I decided I wanted some of them, so I tooks me out some and put them on a chair; and when I did this the mistress entered the door. I picks up a cushion and throws [it] over the pile of cookies on the chair, and Mistress came near the chair and the old parrot cries out, "Mistress burn, Mistress burn." Then the mistress looks under the cushion, and she had me whupped, but the next day I killed the parrot, and she often wondered who or what killed the bird.

III

Every time I think of slavery and if it done the race any good, I think of the story of the coon and dog who met. The coon said to the dog, "Why is it you're so fat and I am so poor, and we is both animals?" The dog said: "I lay round Master's house and let him kick me and he gives me a piece of bread right on." Said the coon to the dog: "Better, then, that I stay poor." Them's my sentiment. I'm like the coon, I don't believe in 'buse.

IV

. . . A partridge and a fox 'greed to kill a beef. They kilt and skinned it. Before they divide it, the fox said, "My wife says send her some beef for soup." So he took a piece of it and carried it down the hill, then come back and said, "My wife wants more beef for soup." He kept this up till all the beef was gone 'cept the liver. The fox come back, and the partridge says, "Now let's cook this liver and both of us eat it." The partridge cooked the liver, et its parts right quick, and then fell over like it was sick. The fox got scared and said that beef is pizen, and he ran down the hill and started bringing the beef back. And when he brought it all back, he left, and the partridge had all the beef.

[121]

V

I want to tell you one story 'bout the rabbit. The rabbit and the tortoise had a race. The tortoise git a lot of tortoises and put 'em 'long the way. Ever' now and then a tortoise crawl 'long the way, and the rabbit say, "How you now, Br'er Tortoise?" And he say, "Slow and sure, but my legs very short." When they git tired, the tortoise win 'cause he there, but he never run the race, 'cause he had tortoises strowed out all 'long the way. The tortoise had other tortoises help him.

VI

The niggers didn't go to the church building; the preacher came and preached to them in their quarters. He'd just say, "Serve your masters. Don't steal your master's turkey. Don't steal your master's chickens. Don't steal your master's hogs. Don't steal your master's meat. Do whatsomever your master tells you to do." Same old thing all the time.

VII

I been preaching the gospel and farming since slavery time. I jined the church 'most 83 years ago when I was Major Gaud's slave, and they baptizes me in the spring branch close to where I finds the Lord. When I starts preaching I couldn't read or write and had to preach what Master told me, and he say tell them niggers iffen they obeys the master they goes to Heaven; but I knowed there's something better for them, but daren't tell them 'cept on the sly. That I done lots. I tells 'em iffen they keeps praying, the Lord will set 'em free.

VIII

My master used to ask us children, "Do your folks pray at night?" We said "No," 'cause our folks had told us what to say. But the Lord have mercy, there was plenty of that going on. They'd pray, "Lord, deliver us from under bondage."

IX

My wife was sick, down, couldn't do nothing. Someone got to telling her about Cain Robertson. Cain Robertson was a hoodoo doctor in Georgia. They [say] there wasn't nothing Cain couldn't do. She says, "Go and see Cain and have him come up here."

I says, "There ain't no use to send for Cain. Cain ain't coming up here because they say he is a 'two-head' nigger." (They called all them hoodoo men "two-head" niggers; I don't know why they called them two-head). "And you know he knows the white folks will put him in jail if he comes to town."

But she says, "You go and get him."

So I went.

I left him at the house, and when I came back in, he said, "I looked at your wife and she had one of them spells while I was there. I'm afraid to tackle this thing because she has been poisoned, and it's been going on a long time. And if she dies, they'll say I killed her, and they already don't like me and looking for an excuse to do something to me."

My wife overheard him and says, "You go on, you got to do something."

So he made me go to town and get a pint of corn whiskey. When I brought it back he drunk a half of it at one gulp, and I started to knock him down. I'd thought he'd get drunk with my wife lying there sick.

Then he said, "I'll have to see your wife's stomach." Then he scratched it, and put three little horns on the place he scratched. Then he took another drink of whiskey and waited about ten minutes. When he took them off her stomach, they were full of blood. He put them in the basin in some water and sprinkled some powder on them, and in about ten minutes more he made me get them and they were full of clear water and there was a lot of little things that looked like wiggle tails swimming around it.

He told me when my wife got well to walk in a certain direction a certain distance, and the woman that caused all the trouble would come to my house and start a fuss with me.

I said, "Can't you put this same thing back on her?"

He said, "Yes, but it would kill my hand." He meant that he had a curing hand and that if he made anybody sick or killed them, all his power to cure would go from him.

I showed the stuff he took out of my wife's stomach to old Doc Matthews, and he said, "You can get anything into a person by putting it in them." He asked me how I found out about it, and how it was taken out, and who did it.

I told him all about it, and he said, "I'm going to see that that nigger practices anywhere in this town he wants to and nobody bothers him." And he did.

X

They was pretty good to us, but old Mr. Buck Brasefield, what had a plantation 'jining us'n, was so mean to his'n that 'twa'n't nothing for 'em to run away.

One nigger, Rich Parker, runned off one time, and whilst he gone he seed a hoodoo man, so when he got back Mr. Brasefield took sick and stayed sick two or three weeks. Some of the darkies told him, "Rich been to the hoodoo doctor." So Mr. Brasefield go tup outen that bed and come a-yelling in the field, "You thought you had old Buck, but by God he rose again." Them niggers was so scared they squatted in the field just like partridges, and some of 'em whispered, "I wish to God he had-a died."

XI

Now I'll tell you another incident. This was in slave times. My mother was a great hand for nice quilts. There was a white lady had died, and they were going to have a sale. Now this is true stuff. They had the sale, and Mother went and bought two quilts. And let me tell you, we couldn't sleep under 'em. What happened? Well, they'd pinch your toes till you couldn't stand it. I was just a boy and I was sleeping with my mother when it happened. Now that's straight stuff. What do I think was the cause? Well, I think that white lady didn't want no nigger to have them quilts. I don't know what Mother did with 'em, but that white lady just wouldn't let her have 'em.

XII

My papa was strong. He never had a licking in his life. He helped the master, but one day the master says, "Si, you got to have a whopping," and my poppa says, "I never had a whopping and you can't whop me." And the master says, "But I can kill you," and he shot my papa down. My mama took him in the cabin and put him on a pallet. He died.

XIII

None of us was 'lowed to see a book or try to learn. They say we git smarter than they was if we learn anything, but we slips around and gits hold of that Webster's old blue-back speller and we hides it till 'way in the night and then we lights a little pine torch, and studies that spelling book. We learn it too. I can read some now and write a little too.

They wasn't no church for the slaves, but we goes to the white folks' arbor on Sunday evening, and a white man he gits up there to preach to the niggers. He say, "Now I takes my text, which is, Nigger obey your master and your mistress, 'cause what you git from them here in this world am all you ever going to git, 'cause you just like the hogs and the other animals — when you dies you ain't no more, after you been throwed in that hole." I guess we be-

[124]

lieved that for a while 'cause we didn't have no way finding out different. We didn't see no Bibles.

XIV

I seen children sold off and the mammy not sold, and sometimes the mammy sold and a little baby kept on the place and give to another woman to raise. Them white folks didn't care nothing 'bout how the slaves grieved when they tore up a family.

XV

We was scared of Solomon and his whip, though, and he didn't like frolicking. He didn't like for us niggers to pray, either. We never heared of no church, but us have praying in the cabins. We'd set on the floor and pray with our heads down low and sing low, but if Solomon heared he'd come and beat on the wall with the stock of his whip. He'd say, "I'll come in there and tear the hide off you backs." But some the old niggers tell us we got to pray to God that He don't think different of the blacks and the whites. I know that Solomon is burning in hell today, and it pleasures me to know it.

XVI

After while I taken a notion to marry and Massa and Missy marries us same as all the niggers. They stands inside the house with a broom held crosswise of the door and we stands outside. Missy puts a little wreath on my head they kept there, and we steps over the broom into the house. Now, that's all they was to the marrying. After freedom I gits married and has it put in the book by a preacher.

XVII

Pompey, how do I look?
O, massa, mighty.
What do you mean "mighty," Pompey?
Why, massa, you look noble.
What do you mean by "noble"?
Why, sar, you just look like one *lion*.
Why, Pompey, where have you ever seen a lion?
I see one down in yonder field the other day, massa.
Pompey, you foolish fellow, that was a *jackass*.
Was it, massa? Well you look just like him.

XVIII

Two slaves were sent out to dig a grave for old master. They dug it very deep. As I passed by I asked Jess and Bob what in the world they dug it so deep for. It was down six or seven feet. I told them there would be a fuss about it, and they had better fill it up some. Jess said it suited him exactly. Bob said he would not fill it up; he wanted to get the old man as near *home* as possible. When we got a stone to put on his grave, we hauled the largest we could find, so as to fasten him down as strong as possible.

SONGS

Songs I–III from Lawrence W. Levine, "Slave Songs and Slave Consciousness: An Exploration in Neglected Sources," in Anonymous Americans: Explorations in Nineteenth Century Social History, *edited by Tamara K. Hareven (Englewood Cliffs, N.J.: Prentice-Hall, 1971). Songs IV and V from Sterling Stuckey, "Through the Prism of Folklore: The Black Ethos in Slavery,"* Massachusetts Review *(1968).*

I

We raise de wheat,
Dey gib us de corn;
We bake de bread,
Dey gib us de crust;
We sif de meal,
Dey gib us de huss;
We [peel] de meat,
Dey gib us de skin;
And dat's de way
Dey take us in;
We skim de pot,
Dey gib us de liquor,
And say dat's good enough for nigger.

II

My ole Mistiss promise me,
W'en she died, she'd set me free,
She lived so long dat 'er head got bal',
An' she give out'n de notion a dyin' at all.

III

He delivered Daniel from the lion's den,
Jonah from de belly ob de whale,
And de Hebrew children from de fiery furnace,
And why not every man?

IV

When I get to heaven, gwine be at ease,
Me and my God gonna do as we please.
Gonna chatter with the Father, argue with the Son,
Tell um 'bout the world I just come from.

V

[*a song about Samson and Delilah*]

He said, 'An' if I had-'n my way,'
He said, 'An' if I had-'n my way,'
He said, 'An' if I had-'n my way,
I'd tear the build-in' down!'

STORIES

Story I, "The Wonderful Tar-Baby Story," Story II, "How Mr. Rabbit Was Too Sharp for Mr. Fox," and Story III, "Mr. Rabbit and Mr. Bear," from Robert Chase, ed., Complete Tales of Uncle Remus *(Boston: Houghton Mifflin, 1955).*

I

"DIDN'T THE FOX *never* catch the rabbit, Uncle Remus?" asked the little boy the next evening.

"He come mighty nigh it, honey, sho's you born — Brer Fox did. One day atter Brer Rabbit fool 'im wid dat calamus root, Brer Fox went ter wuk en got 'im some tar, en mix it wid some turkentime, en fix up a contrapshun w'at he call a Tar-Baby, en he tuck dish yer Tar-Baby en he sot 'er in de big road, en

[127]

den he lay off in de bushes fer to see what de news wuz gwine ter be. En he didn't hatter wait long, nudder, kaze bimeby here come Brer Rabbit pacin' down de road — lippity-clippity, clippity-lippity — dez ez sassy ez a jay-bird. Brer Fox, he lay low. Brer Rabbit come prancin' 'long twel he spy de Tar-Baby, en den he fotch up on his behime legs like he wuz 'stonished. De Tar-Baby, she sot dar, she did, en Brer Fox, he lay low.

"'Mawnin'!' sez Brer Rabbit, sezee — 'nice wedder dis mawnin',' sezee.

"Tar-Baby ain't saying' nothing', en Brer Fox, he lay low.

"'How duz yo' sym'tums seem ter segashuate?' sez Brer Rabbit, sezee.

"Brer Fox, he wink his eye slow, en lay low, en de Tar-Baby, she ain't sayin' nothin'.

"'How you come on, den? Is you deaf?' sez Brer Rabbit, sezee. 'Kaze if you is, I kin holler louder,' sezee.

"Tar-Baby stay still, en Brer Fox, he lay low.

"'You er stuck up, dat's w'at you is,' says Brer Rabbit, sezee, 'en I'm gwine ter kyore you, dat's w'at I'm a gwine ter do,' sezee.

"Brer Fox, he sorter chuckle in his stummick, he did, but Tar-Baby ain't sayin' nothin'.

"'I'm gwine ter larn you how ter talk ter 'spectubble folks ef hit's de las' ack,' sez Brer Rabbit, sezee. 'Ef you don't take off dat hat en tell me howdy, I'm gwine ter bus' you wide open,' sezee.

"Tar-Baby stay still, en Brer Fox, he lay low.

"Brer Rabbit keep on axin' 'im, en de Tar-Baby, she keep on sayin' nothin', twel present'y Brer Rabbit draw back wid his fis', he did, en blip he tuck 'er side er de head. Right dar's whar he broke his merlasses jug. His fis' stuck, en he can't pull loose. De tar hilt 'im. But Tar-Baby, she stay still, en Brer Fox, he lay low.

"'Ef you don't lemme loose, I'll knock you agin,' sez Brer Rabbit, sezee, en wid dat he fotch 'er a wipe wid de udder han', en dat stuck. Tar-Baby, she ain't sayin' nothin', en Brer Fox, he lay low.

"'Tu'n me loose, fo' I kick de natchul stuffin' out'n you,' sez Brer Rabbit, sezee, but de Tar-Baby, she ain't sayin' nothin'. She des hilt on, en den Brer Rabbit lose de use er his feet in de same way. Brer Fox, he lay low. Den Brer Rabbit squall out dat ef de Tar-Baby don't tu'n 'im loose he butt 'er cranksided. En den he butted, en his head got stuck. Den Brer Fox, he sa'ntered fort', lookin' des ez innercent ez one er yo' mammy's mockin'-birds.

[128]

"'Howdy, Brer Rabbit,' sez Brer Fox, sezee. 'You look sorter stuck up dis mawnin',' sezee, en den he rolled on de groun', en laughed en laughed twel he couldn't laugh no mo'. 'I speck you'll take dinner wid me dis time, Brer Rabbit. I done laid in some calamus root, en I ain't gwine ter take no skuse,' sez Brer Fox, sezee."

Here Uncle Remus paused, and drew a two-pound yam out of the ashes.

"Did the Fox eat the Rabbit?" asked the little boy to whom the story had been told.

"Dat's all de fur de tale goes," replied the old man. "He mought, en den again he moughtent. Some say Jedge B'ar come long en loosed 'im — some say he didn't. I hear Miss Sally callin'. You better run 'long."

II

"UNCLE REMUS," said the little boy one evening, when he had found the old man with little or nothing to do, "did the Fox kill and eat the Rabbit when he caught him with the Tar-Baby?"

"Law, honey, ain't I tell you 'bout dat?" replied the old darkey, chuckling slyly. "I 'clar ter gracious I ought er tole you dat, but old man Nod wuz ridin' on my eyeleds twel a leetle mo'n I'd a dis'member'd my own name, en den on to dat here come yo' mammy hollerin' atter you.

"W'at I tell you w'en I fus' begin? I tole you Brer Rabbit wuz a monstus soon creetur; leas'ways dat's w'at I laid out fer ter tell you. Well, den, honey, don't you go en make no udder calkalashuns, kaze in dem days Brer Rabbit en his fambly wuz at de head er de gang w'en enny racket wuz on han', en dar dey stayed. 'Fo' you begins fer ter wipe yo' eyes 'bout Brer Rabbit, you wait en see whar'bouts Brer Rabbit gwine ter fetch up at. But dat's needer yer ner dar.

"W'en Brer Fox fin' Brer Rabbit mixt up wid de Tar-Baby, he feel mighty good, en he roll on de groun' en laugh. Bimeby he up'n say, sezee:

"'Well, I speck I got you dis time,' Brer Rabbit, sezee; 'maybe I ain't, but I speck I is. You bin runnin' roun' here sassin' atter me a mighty long time, but I speck you done come ter de een' er de row. You bin cuttin' up yo' capers en bouncin' 'roun' in dis neighborhood ontwel you come ter b'lief yo'se'f de boss er de whole gang. En den you er allers somers whar you got no bizness,' sez Brer Fox, sezee. 'Who ax you fer ter come en strike up a 'quaintance wid dish yer Tar-Baby? En who stuck you up dar whar you iz? Nobody in de roun' worl'. You des tuck en jam yo'se'f on dat Tar-Baby widout waitin' fer enny invite,' sez

Brer Fox, sezee, 'en dar you is, en dar you'll stay twel I fixes up a bresh-pile and fiers her up, kaze I'm gwine ter bobbycue you dis day, sho,' sez Brer Fox, sezee.

"Den Brer Rabbit talk mighty 'umble.

"'I don't keer w'at you do wid me, Brer Fox,' sezee, 'so you don't fling me in dat brier-patch. Roas' me, Brer Fox,' sezee, 'but don't fling me in dat brier-patch,' sezee.

"'Hit's so much trouble fer ter kindle a fier,' sez Brer Fox, sezee, 'dat I speck I'll hatter hang you,' sezee.

"'Hang me des ez high as you please, Brer Fox,' sez Brer Rabbit, sezee, 'but do fer de Lord's sake don't fling me in dat brier-patch,' sezee.

"'I ain't got no string,' sez Brer Fox, sezee, 'en now I speck I'll hatter drown you,' sezee.

"'Drown me des ez deep ez you please, Brer Fox,' sez Brer Rabbit, sezee, 'but don't fling me in dat brier-patch,' sezee.

"'Dey ain't no water nigh,' sez Brer Fox, sezee, 'en now I speck I'll hatter skin you,' sezee.

"'Skin me, Brer Fox,' sez Brer Rabbit, sezee, 'snatch out my eye-balls, t'ar out my years by de roots, en cut off my legs,' sezee, 'but do please, Brer Fox, don't fling me in dat brier-patch,' sezee.

"Co'se Brer Fox wanter hurt Brer Rabbit bad ez he kin, so he cotch 'im by de behime legs en slung 'im right in de middle er de brier-patch. Dar wuz a considerabul flutter whar Brer Rabbit struck de bushes, en Brer Fox sorter hang 'roun' fer ter see w'at wuz gwine ter happen. Bimeby he hear somebody call 'im, en way up de hill he see Brer Rabbit settin' cross-legged on a chinkapin log koamin' de pitch out'n his ha'r wid a chip. Den Brer Fox know dat he bin swop off mighty bad. Brer Rabbit wuz bleedzd fer ter fling back some er his sass, en he holler out:

"'Bred en bawn in a brier-patch, Brer Fox — bred en bawn in a brier-patch!' en wid dat he skip out des ez lively ez a cricket in de embers."

III

"DAR WUZ one season," said Uncle Remus, pulling thoughtfully at his whiskers, "w'en Brer Fox say to hisse'f dat he speck he better whirl in en plant a goober-patch, en in dem days, mon, hit wuz tech en go. De wud weren't mo'n out'n his mouf 'fo' de groun' 'uz brok'd up en de goobers 'uz planted. Ole Brer

Rabbit, he sot off en watch de motions, he did, en he sorter shet one eye en sing to his chilluns:

Ti-yi! Tungalee!
I eat um pea, I pick um pea.
Hit grow in de groun', hit grow so free;
Ti-yi! dem goober pea.

"Sho nuff w'en de goobers 'gun ter ripen up, eve'y time Brer Fox go down ter his patch, he fin' whar somebody bin grabblin' 'mongst de vines, en he git mighty mad. He sorter speck who de somebody is, but ole Brer Rabbit he cover his tracks so cute dat Brer Fox dunner how ter ketch 'im. Bimeby, one day Brer Fox take a walk all 'roun' de groun'-pea patch, en 'twa'n't long 'fo' he fin' a crack in de fence whar de rail done bin rub right smoove, en right dar he sot 'im a trap. He tuck'n ben' down a hick'ry saplin', growin' in de fence-cornder, en tie one een' un a plow-line on de top, en in de udder een' he fix a loop-knot, en dat he fasten wid a trigger right in de crack. Nex' mawnin' w'en ole Brer Rabbit come slippin' 'long en crope thoo de crack, de loop-knot cotch 'im behime de fo'legs, en de saplin' flew'd up, en dar he wuz 'twix' de heavens en de yeth. Dar he swung, en he fear'd he gwine ter fall, en he fear'd he weren't gwine ter fall. W'ile he wuz a fixin' up a tale fer Brer Fox, he hear a lumberin' down de road, en present'y yer cum ole Brer B'ar amblin' 'long fum whar he bin takin' a bee-tree. Brer Rabbit, he hail 'im:

"'Howdy, Brer B'ar!'

"Brer B'ar, he look 'roun' en bimeby he see Brer Rabbit swingin' fum de saplin', en he holler out:

"'Heyo, Brer Rabbit! How you come on dis mawnin'?'

"'Much oblije, I'm middlin', Brer B'ar,' sez Brer Rabbit, sezee.

"Den Brer B'ar, he ax Brer Rabbit w'at he doin' up dar in de elements, en Brer Rabbit, he up'n say he makin' dollar minnit. Brer B'ar, he say how. Brer Rabbit say he keepin' crows out'n Brer Fox's groun'-pea patch, en den he ax Brer B'ar ef he don't wanter make dollar minnit, kaze he got big fambly er chilluns fer to take keer un, en den he make sech nice skeer-crow. Brer B'ar 'low dat he take de job, en den Brer Rabbit show 'im how ter ben' down de saplin', en 'twa'n't long 'fo' Brer B'ar wuz swingin' up dar in Brer Rabbit place. Den Brer Rabbit, he put out fer Brer Fox house, en w'en he got dar he sing out:

"'Brer Fox! Oh, Brer Fox! Come out yer, Brer Fox, en I'll show you de man w'at bin stealin' yo' goobers.'

"Brer Fox, he grab up his walkin'-stick, en bofe un um went runnin' back down ter der goober-patch, en w'en dey got dar, sho nuff, dar wuz ole Brer B'ar.

"'Oh, yes! you er cotch, is you?' sez Brer Fox, en 'fo' Brer B'ar could 'splain, Brer Rabbit he jump up en down, en holler out:

"'Hit 'im in de mouf, Brer Fox; hit 'im on de mouf;' en Brer Fox, he draw back wid de walkin'-cane, en blip he tuck 'im, en eve'y time Brer B'ar'd try ter 'splain, Brer Fox'd shower down on him.

"W'iles all dis 'uz gwine on, Brer Rabbit, he slip off en git in a mud-hole en des lef' his eyes stickin' out, kaze he know'd dat Brer B'ar'd be a comin' atter 'im. Sho nuff, bimeby here come Brer B'ar down de road, en w'en he git ter de mud-hole, he say:

"'Howdy, Brer Frog; is you seed Brer Rabbit go by yer?'

"'He des gone by,' sez Brer Rabbit, en ole man B'ar tuck off down de road like a skeer'd mule, en Brer Rabbit, he come out en dry hisse'f in de sun, en go home ter his fambly same ez enny udder man."

"The Bear didn't catch the Rabbit, then?" inquired the little boy, sleepily.

"Jump up fum dar, honey!" exclaimed Uncle Remus, by way of reply. "I ain't got no time fer ter be settin' yer proppin' yo' eyelids open."

Questions to Consider

For the sake of convenience, the evidence has been divided into three categories: reminiscences from former slaves, from interviews done in the 1930s; songs either transcribed soon after the Civil War, recalled by runaway slaves, or remembered years after; and stories collected and edited by white journalist Joel Chandler Harris, the first of which appeared in 1880. These categories are artificial at best, and you might want to rearrange the evidence in a way that may suit your purpose better.

But how best to rearrange the evidence? The evidence contains a number of subtopics, and arrangement into those subtopics may be profitable. For example:

1. How did slaves feel about their masters and/or mistresses?

2. How did slaves feel about their work? Their families? Their religion?

3. How did they feel about freedom?

4. How did slaves feel about themselves?

By regrouping the evidence into subtopics and then using each piece of evidence to answer the question for that subtopic, you should be able to answer the central question: what did slaves (or former slaves) think and feel about the "peculiar institution" of slavery?

As mentioned earlier, some of the slaves and former slaves chose to be direct in their messages (see for example, Song I). But many more chose to communicate their thoughts and feelings more indirectly or obliquely. Some of the symbols and metaphors used are easy to figure out (see Song V). Others, however, will take considerably more care. But the messages are there.

Joel Chandler Harris transcribed the *Uncle Remus* stories and purposely tried to put them in what he considered to be black dialect. Most of his readers (he published eight *Uncle Remus* books) were whites, many of whom delighted both in the stories and in Harris's method of presentation. The originators of these stories, however, were blacks whom Harris overheard or with whom he conversed. Although Harris may have altered the stories somewhat, we can assume that the majority of the material was left fairly intact. Would white readers in the 1880s appreciate the full meanings of the stories? What might they have missed? What points do you think the *original* storytellers wanted to make?

One last point you might want to consider: why have historians neglected this evidence for so long?

Epilogue

Even before the Civil War formally ended, thousands of blacks began to cast off the shackles of slavery. Some ran away to meet the advancing Union armies (where they were often treated no better than they were by their former masters and mistresses). Others drifted into cities where they hoped to find work and opportunities for themselves and their families. Still others stayed on the land, perhaps hoping to become free farmers. At the end of the war, blacks were quick to establish their own churches and enrolled in schools established by the Freedmen's Bureau. For most former slaves, the impulse seems to have been to look forward and not backward into the agonizing past of slavery.

Yet memories of slavery were not forgotten and often were passed down orally, from generation to generation. In 1976 Alex Haley's book *Roots* stunned an American public that had assumed that blacks' memories of their origins and of slavery had been for the most part either forgotten or obliterated.[1] Although much of Haley's work showed the author's artistic license, the skeleton of the book was the oral tradition transmitted by his family since the capture of his ancestor Kunta Kinte in West Africa in the late eighteenth century. Not only had Haley's family remembered its African origins, but stories about slavery had not been lost — they'd been passed down through the generations.

While Haley was engaged in his twelve years of research and writing, historian Henry Irving Tragle proposed to compile a documentary history of the Nat Turner Rebellion of 1831. Talking to black people in 1968 and 1969 in Southampton County where the rebellion took place, Tragle discovered that in spite of numerous attempts to obliterate Turner from the area's historical memory, Turner's action had become part of the oral history of the region. As the surprised Tragle wrote, "I believe it possible to say with certainty that Nat Turner did exist as a folk-hero to several generations of black men and women who have lived and died in Southampton County since 1831."[2] Again, oral history had persisted and triumphed over time, and professional historians began to look with a new eye on what in the past many had dismissed as unworthy of their attention.

So too with folk music, customs, religious practices, stories, and artifacts. Increasingly, students of history have been able to reconstruct the lives, thoughts, and feelings of people once thought to have been inarticulate. Of course, they were no such thing. But it took imagination to let their evidence speak.

Many people have argued over the impact that slavery left on blacks and whites alike, and that question may never fully be answered. What we *do* know is that an enormous amount of historical evidence about slavery exists, from the perspectives of both blacks and whites. And the memory of that institution lingers. It is part of what one southern white and professional historian calls the "burden of southern history," a burden to be overcome but never completely forgotten.

1. A condensed version of *Roots* had appeared in 1974 in *Reader's Digest*.

2. Henry Irving Tragle, *The Southampton Slave Revolt of 1831: A Compilation of Source Material* (Amherst, Mass.: University of Massachusetts Press, 1971), p. 12.

Chapter 8

War and Manifest Destiny: A Problem in Causation

For days the city of Washington had been abuzz with rumors that the long-expected hostilities had broken out between United States and Mexican troops stationed along the Texas border. On Friday, May 9, 1846, news finally arrived that fighting actually had taken place, and with the aid of some of his cabinet members, President James K. Polk began rapidly drafting a war message. On Monday, May 11, the president's message requesting a declaration of war against the Republic of Mexico was delivered to Congress and read to both Houses. That same day the House of Representatives, by a vote of 174 to 14, approved the war message, and the Senate, by a vote of 40 to 2, concurred the next day. On Wednesday, May 13, 1846, Polk signed the war bill, and the Mexican War had officially begun.

Polk's war message (reproduced in the Evidence section) summarized his justifications for declaring war against Mexico — a war he felt was both just and necessary. In brief, the president listed two principal causes of the war: (1) Mexico had refused to receive United States envoy John Slidell, who had been sent to Mexico City "to adjust every existing difference" between the two nations, and (2) Mexican soldiers "have at last invaded our territory and shed the blood of our fellow-citizens on our own soil." Although the United States, Polk asserted, had made every effort to reach a peaceful agreement with the Republic of Mexico, at last the "cup of for-bearance had been exhausted," and war was the only alternative.

Polk's war message, however, poses an intriguing problem. Were the causes of the war as simple as those Polk addressed? History has proven that the causes of wars, as of other important events in history, are considerably more complex than those either seen by casual observers or claimed by the combatants. In almost all cases, one must also look for long-range and underlying causes, some of which might stretch back for years prior to the outbreak of the war. And, further, secret decisions or moves may have been made, helping to precipitate hostilities. Indeed, assessing what caused the Mexican War can be considerably more difficult than the task at first appears.

Ever since colonial times, Americans had seen the West as the key to both their individual and collective futures. To land companies and investors, the West held out the promise of great riches, fortunes made either in land speculation or in trade. To southern planters who often exhausted the soil growing cash crops like tobacco, it offered the chance to repeat their successes on rich, virgin land. To European immigrants and to people from the overpopulated northeastern farming communities, the West was seen as a Garden of Eden where they could make a new start. Later, to Thomas Jefferson, it represented an "Empire of Liberty" that

would prevent the rise of unwholesome cities and social conflict in the young Republic. Hence, it is easy to see why most Americans came to equate national progress with western expansion. In this atmosphere, the ceding of western lands by the new states to the national government in the 1780s and the Louisiana Purchase of 1803 were seen as the insurors of national greatness. And in a society in which private property was venerated and the acquisition of land had become for many almost a cultural imperative, expansion westward was very nearly inevitable.

Although there were a number of obstacles to westward expansion, at most they proved temporary. The Indian nations offered brisk opposition, but they could fight only a holding action against the more numerous and technologically superior Caucasians. When the United States put its mind to it, the Indians were quickly, and sometimes mercilessly, eradicated or gathered onto reservations where they were forced to become dependent on the United States government for their existence. For their part, the Spanish (in the Floridas), French (in the Louisiana Territory), and British (in the Northwest) could not bring sufficient military power to bear so far from home, and ultimately preferred either to sell or to give up through treaty their territorial claims. Even the Republic of Mexico, which did choose to fight, was no match for its expansion-minded neighbor.

The demographic, economic, and cultural imperatives to expand and the absence of powerful opposition gradually convinced many Americans that westward expansion was both a right and a duty, approved by God for "His people." As one editor explained, it was America's "manifest destiny to overspread the continent allotted by Providence for the free development of our yearly multiplying millions." Another contemporary envisaged a time when the American eagle would have its beak in Canada, its talons in Mexico, and its wings flapping in the two oceans. While one can detect in both statements more than a trace of arrogance and feelings of superiority, it is important to note that a vast number of American Caucasians sincerely believed in those claims, much as many white southerners in the same era sincerely believed that most slaves were happy with their collective lot.

By the 1830s the westward expansion of Americans had gone beyond the Louisiana Territory into Texas (owned by the Republic of Mexico) and Oregon (claimed by Great Britain). In Texas, settlers from the United States ignored Mexican laws and officials with regularity. For example, Mexico's prohibition of slavery did not stop settlers from bringing slaves into Texas. Mexican law, which required that all settlers convert to Roman Catholicism, was scoffed at and almost universally broken. When the Mexican government attempted to enforce these and other laws in 1836, American migrants to Texas (numbering approximately 35,000) rebelled.

Mexico attempted to crush the rebellion harshly. At the Alamo, Mexican general Santa Anna killed all the defenders (he spared women and children and, according to legend, at least one male native Mexican) and then stacked their bodies like cordwood and burned them. Later, Mexicans shot every defender at Goliad, despite the fact that a formal surrender had been arranged with an agreement that survivors would be spared. Still, the Texans under General Sam Houston prevailed, and by the end of 1836 Texas was an independent nation.

Whether to annex Texas to the United States was an issue that divided Americans for the next eight years. Some people in the North and Midwest opposed the annexation of Texas, fearing that it would tip the political balance in Congress in favor of the slave states. Presidents Jackson and Van Buren cautiously avoided the issue, and Tyler (1841–1845) was rebuffed by the United States Senate when he proposed annexation in 1844. Finally on March 1, 1845, three days before Polk's inauguration as president, a joint congressional resolution approved the inclusion of Texas in the United States. Mexico promptly broke off diplomatic relations.

There is little doubt that Polk sided firmly with the expansionists. During the presidential campaign of 1844, he had made it clear that he approved of his party's pro-expansion platform and that he would move aggressively to fulfill it. Indeed, it is likely that Polk's and the Democrats' stand on westward expansion was in part responsible for their 1844 victory. The presidential election was a surprisingly close one, with Polk winning 50 percent of the popular vote and 170 electoral votes to Henry Clay's 48 percent of the popular vote and 105 electoral votes. Expansionism could well have made the difference.

In spite of his party's pro-expansion platform and its rather bellicose rhetoric, once in office Polk worked diligently to acquire territory by negotiation rather than by war. On the Oregon question, the president privately informed the British ambassador that he would accept a compromise that would set the Oregon-Canadian boundary at the forty-ninth parallel.[1] Troubled by difficulties at home, Great Britain also was eager to compromise, and an agreement was reached between the two nations in 1846.

Polk's efforts to acquire California and the Southwest from Mexico did not end so amicably. Even before his inauguration, Polk had his eyes on California. Unstable political conditions in Mexico City had prevented Mexico from exercising much power

in the area, and by 1841 most semblances of Mexican authority in California had vanished. Such a power vacuum made it likely that another nation would try to acquire California. Many Americans — including Polk — believed that both England and France were anxious to establish footholds in the region. If either nation were to acquire California (which in 1845 contained only a few hundred United States citizens), the United States' "manifest destiny" would be thwarted. With European nations showing increasing interest and with Mexico so internally unstable, Polk was determined to move swiftly.

As with the Oregon question, Polk would have preferred to acquire California by negotiation. Yet war with Mexico broke out in May 1846. Your task in this chapter is to explain the causes of the Mexican War. You must do this by assessing the role of long-range and underlying causes and analyzing the below-the-surface events and decisions. Then, by combining those with Polk's announced causes, you will be able to emerge with a more complete understanding of the causes of the Mexican War.

The Method

Your supplementary reading and the introduction to this chapter should be helpful in determining the long-range causes of the Mexican War (the drive

---

1. The original American claim was considerably north of that, at 54°40′, thus leading to the popular American slogan "Fifty-four forty or fight!"

for westward expansion, the Texas war for independence, and so forth). Be sure to note the political considerations (such as the presidential election of 1844), the instability in Mexico, Mexico's feelings about the United States, and the situations in Oregon and California. Also remember the long-held attitudes of United States citizens on the subject of expansion.

Several pieces of evidence have been provided to enable you to assess the below-the-surface events and decisions that may have contributed to the Mexican War. This evidence has been drawn from official and private correspondence, diaries and recollections, newspapers, diplomatic dispatches, and congressional proceedings. The evidence has been arranged chronologically. Keep in mind that wars often have many causes, although one particular cause is often central to the war's occurrence. Is there a central cause here? How can the available evidence be pieced together to discover the cause (or causes)?

The problem of causation is a primary concern of historians. Yet unlike the natural sciences where an experiment in causation can be observed and reproduced (allowing for altitude, water *always* boils at a certain temperature), the study of people — and especially people in the past — is not an exact discipline. For instance, while wars have been an almost constant feature throughout history, they have been caused by a variety of factors and knowing what caused one war cannot really explain what caused another. Too, while psychologists, sociologists, and cultural anthropologists have discovered certain patterns of human behavior, few if any of these patterns are valid for all times and all cultures. Therefore, historians and social scientists cannot approach the problem of causation in the same way that natural scientists (such as biologists, physicists, chemists, and geologists) can.

What historians can do, however, is look for *probable* cause, an explanation of the evidence that is likely and reasonable. It is not scientific, nor is it verifiable by laboratory experiment. But by closely examining and analyzing the evidence and by knowing something of the background and people involved, the historian can offer a cause that is reasonable, supported by evidence (and not strongly contradicted by other evidence), and probably the best explanation available.

As in earlier chapters, be willing to read between the lines. After examining some of the evidence, you may have a notion as to what caused the Mexican War. Historians call these early notions "working hypotheses." Using that working hypothesis, see if all the evidence can be arranged to support it. If it can, that working hypothesis then becomes your *thesis* (a statement of opinion supported by the evidence). State your thesis and show how all the evidence supports it. If, however, later evidence disproves your working hypothesis, you must begin again.

Lastly, you have already come to realize that certain pieces of evidence have more weight than others. For example, lawyers prefer eyewitnesses to people who have only heard about an event (indeed, "hearsay evidence" is usually inadmissable in American courts). In this exercise, are there pieces of evidence that are more important than others? What are they? Are there pieces of evidence that are more likely to be true? (False evidence is always a problem.) Weigh each piece of evidence carefully. In the chain of explanation, some links are stronger than others.

The Evidence

CHARACTERS

James Knox Polk, *president, 1845–1849*
George Bancroft, *secretary of the navy, 1846*
John Slidell, *minister to Mexico, 1845–1846*
Robert Field Stockton, *commodore, U.S. Navy*
Anson Jones, *president of Texas*
John C. Fremont, *captain, U.S. Army*
Charles Elliot, *British minister to Texas*
Charles Bankhead, *British minister to Mexico*
Zachary Taylor, *general, U.S. Army*
William L. Marcy, *secretary of war, 1845–1849*

March 1, 1845

Joint congressional resolution offering annexation to Texas

March 4, 1845

Inauguration of Polk

Soon after inauguration — Private conversation between Polk and Bancroft, recalled by Bancroft to historian James Schouler, 1887

From James Schouler, History of the United States Under the Constitution, *Vol. IV (New York: Dodd, Mead & Co., 1889), p. 498.*

In a private conversation with one of his chosen cabinet which is still preserved, Polk announced his purpose soon after he had taken the oath of office. "There are four great measures," said he, with emphasis, striking his thigh forcibly as he spoke, "which are to be the measures of my administration: one, a reduction of the tariff; another, the independent treasury; a third, the settlement of the Oregon boundary question; and, lastly, the acquisition of California."

March 6, 1845

Slidell asks for passport (breaking diplomatic relations)

April 22, 1845 — Bancroft to Stockton

From Glenn W. Price, Origins of the War with Mexico: The Polk-Stockton Intrigue *(Austin: University of Texas Press, 1967), p. 48.*

You will proceed with the vessels that have been placed under your command to the vicinity of Galveston, Texas, and lay as close to the shore as security will permit. You will take one of the vessels into the port of Galveston, and there display the American flag; or more if the bar will permit.

You will yourself go on shore, and make yourself acquainted with the dispositions of the people of Texas, and their relations with Mexico, of which you will make report to this Department.

After remaining at or off Galveston as long as in your judgment may seem necessary, you will proceed to join the squadron of Commodore Conner, off Vera Cruz.

Memoirs, 1859 — Jones memoirs

From Price, Origins of the War with Mexico: The Polk-Stockton Intrigue, *pp. 11–12.*

In May, 1845, Commodore Stockton, with a fleet of four or five vessels, arrived at Galveston, and with him Hon. C. A. Wickliffe, ex-Postmaster General of the United States. These gentlemen had various interviews with Major Gen. Sherman, the chief officer of the militia of Texas, the character of which is not precisely known to me; but the result of which was active preparations at Galveston for organizing volunteer forces, the ostensible (and no doubt real) object of which was an invasion of Mexico. A party [Jones thus seems to refer to President Polk], it appears, was anxious that the expedition should be set on foot, under the auspices of the Major-General and Com. Stockton; but these gentlemen, it appears, were unwilling to take so great a responsibility: it was therefore resolved that the plan should be submitted to me and my sanction obtained — (quere [*sic*], forced?) — indeed such, as afterwards became apparent, were the Commodore's instructions; and the organizing, &c, had been gone into for the purpose of forcing my assent to the proposed scheme. On the 28th May, Gen. Sherman for himself and associates in the militia, and Dr. Wright, surgeon of the steamer Princeton, and secretary of the Commodore, (as he informed me) took three days in unfolding to me the object of their visit. Dr. Wright stated that he was sent by Com. Stockton to propose that I should authorize Major Gen. Sherman to raise a force of two thousand men, or as many as might be necessary, and make a descent upon the Mexican town of Matamoras, and capture and hold it; that Com. Stockton would give assistance with the fleet under his command, under the pretext of giving the protection promised by the United States to Texas by Gen. Murphy; that he would undertake to supply the necessary provisions, arms and munitions of war for the expedition, would land them at convenient points on our coast, and would agree to pay the men and officers to be engaged; that he had consulted Gen. Sherman, who approved the plan, and was present to say so; and, besides that, the people generally from Galveston to Washington [the city in Texas] had been spoken to about it, that it met their unanimous approval; and all that was now wanting was the sanction of the Government to the scheme. Gen. Sherman confirmed what Dr. Wright stated, said he had had various interviews with Com. Stockton, and hoped I would approve the expedition.

May 1845

Fremont ordered to take sixty men on expedition to visit both Oregon and California

May 26–August 16, 1845 — Fremont memoirs

From Mary Lee Spence and Donald Jackson, eds., The Expeditions of John Charles Fremont, *Vol. II (Urbana: University of Illinois Press, 1973), pp. 3–4.*

Concurrently with the Report upon the second expedition the plans and scope of a third one had been matured. It was decided that it should be directed to that section of the Rocky Mountains which gives rise to the Arkansas River, the Rio Grande del Norte of the Gulf of Mexico, and the Rio Colorado of the Gulf of California; to complete the examination of the Great Salt Lake and its interesting region; and to extend the survey west and southwest to the examination of the great ranges of the Cascade Mountains and the Sierra Nevada, so as to ascertain the lines of communication through the mountains to the ocean in that latitude. And in arranging this expedition, the eventualities of war were taken into consideration.

Mexico, at war with the United States, would inevitably favor English protection for California. English citizens were claiming payment for loans and indemnity for losses. Our relations with England were already clouded, and in the event of war with Mexico, if not anticipated by us, an English fleet would certainly take possession of the Bay of San Francisco.

For use in such a contingency the only available force was our squadron in the North Pacific, and the measures for carrying out the design of the President fell to the Navy Department. During the year such precautionary measures as were practicable were taken, especially by the vigilant Secretary of the Navy, Mr. [George] Bancroft, whose orders continuously evince comprehending foresight and insistence. Imbued with the philosophy of history, his mind was alive to the bearing of the actual conditions, and he knew how sometimes skill and sometimes bold action determine the advantages of a political situation; and in this his great desire was to secure for the United States the important one that hung in the balance. In the government at Washington he was the active principle [*sic*], having the activity of brain and keen perception that the occasion demanded. With him Mr. Benton[2] had friendly personal relations of long standing.

As affairs resolved themselves, California stood out as the chief subject in the impending war; and with Mr. Benton and other governing men at Washington it became a firm resolve to hold it for the United States. To them it seemed reasonably sure that California would eventually fall to England or to the United States and that the eventuality was near. This was talked over fully during the time of preparation for the third expedition, and the contingencies anticipated and weighed. The relations between the three countries made a chief subject of interest about which our thoughts settled as the probability of war grew into certainty. For me, no distinct course or definite instruction could be laid down, but the probabilities were made known to me as well as what to do when they became facts. The distance was too great for timely communication; but failing this I was given discretion to act.

2. Thomas Hart Benton was senator of Missouri, an influential Democrat, confidant of Polk, and father-in-law of Captain John C. Fremont.

May 21, 1845 — Stockton to Bancroft

From Price, Origins of the War with Mexico: The Polk-Stockton Intrigue, *p. 118.*

War now exists and as any & every man here fights on his "own hook," the Texans ought therefore in my opinion to take possession and drive the Mexicans over the other side of the river before the meeting of Congress.

May 22, 1845 — Stockton to Bancroft

From Price, Origins of the War with Mexico: The Polk-Stockton Intrigue, *p. 119.*

I will want more provisions and powder, that [*sic*] I expected when I left the United States. I will send to Pensacola for them, and if not there to New Orleans. Please to send the necessary orders to let me have what I shall deem necessary for the Squadron under my command.

[*These were granted by Bancroft on June 2, 1845.*]

May 27, 1845 — Stockton to Bancroft

From Price, Origins of the War with Mexico: The Polk-Stockton Intrigue, *p. 122.*

My Dear Sir

Since my last letter I have seen Mr. Mayfield late Secretary of State — who says that if the people here did not feel assured that the Boundary line would be the Rio Grande three fourths and himself amongst the number would oppose the annexation — But I need hardly say another word on that subject; its importance is apparent — But it may perhaps be as well for me *in this way* to let you know how I propose to settle the matter without committing the U. States — The Major Genl will call out three thousand men & "R. F. Stockton Esq" will supply them in a private way with provisions & ammunition —

June 4, 1845 — Stockton to Bancroft

From Price, Origins of the War with Mexico: The Polk-Stockton Intrigue, *pp. 129–130.*

I am informed that there are seven thousand Mexican troops on the Rio Grande del Norte ready for invasion. No provision has been made to meet such an exigency, but that which I am & have been since my arrival here endeavoring to get the authorities of Texas to adopt.

The Government and people of Texas do most unfortunately entertain the expectation that the Government of the United States can and will protect them from any and all Mexican aggression, from the moment that the Congress of Texas shall accept the resolutions of the congress of the United States. This has caused among the people an apathy on the subject of the necessary defences which ought to be in my judgment alarming.

The Mexicans are ready to inflict a blow on the Territory of Texas as soon as they shall hear the result of Capt. Elliots [*sic*] mission. The United States troops cannot (if it were right to do so) be here to resist them. The Texans must be aroused to a proper sense of their own danger and my advice to this Government has been to call the Texan volunteer army into the field, to defend themselves from aggression, to regulate the Boundary and to be prepared to hand over to the United States and [*sic*] undisturbed and undisputed territory when the U.S. may be (of right) ready to occupy it.

June 11, 1845 — Charles Elliot to Charles Bankhead

From Price, Origins of the War with Mexico: The Polk-Stockton Intrigue, *pp. 131–132.*

I should tell you that I learnt as soon as I landed from a source of information entirely to be depended upon that Commodore Stockton was using every effort to induce the President to issue a Proclamation calling out Volunteers for the purpose of occupying the Country *to the Rio Grande at once.*

The President frankly admitted to me that such was the case, and told me (I use his own words as nearly as I can remember them) that he said to those parties "I see not one single motive for Annexation if it is not for security and protection, or if we are *to do our own fighting,* and I tell you plainly that I will not be made the scape goat in such an affair as you have proposed to me. The United States Government must take all the responsibility, and all the expense and all the labour of hostile movements upon Mexico. I will issue no Proclamation of the kind you wish, and authorize no movement unless Mexico makes a movement upon us. Somebody else must break up the state of peace. It shall not be me."

August 9, 1845 — Polk to William H. Hayward (U.S. Senator from North Carolina)

From David M. Pletcher, The Diplomacy of Annexation: Texas, Oregon, and the Mexican War *(Columbia, Mo.: University of Missouri, 1973), p. 270.*

Care has been taken — that all our military and naval movements shall be strictly defensive. — We will not be the aggressor upon Mexico; — but if her army shall cross the Del Norte[3] and invade Texas, we will if we can drive her army — to her own territory. Less than this — in good faith to Texas, I think this government could not have done. We invite Texas to unite her destinies with our own. She has accepted the invitation, upon the terms proposed, . . . and if because she has done so, she is invaded by the Mexican Army — surely we are bound to give her our aid in her own defence.

August 12, 1845 — T. J. Green (former member of Texas Congress) to Robert Walker

From Price, Origins of the War with Mexico: The Polk-Stockton Intrigue, *p. 163.*

. . . that your troops advance west to the Rio Grande. Let one division strike that river at Laredo 140 miles south west from San Antonio, making the latter place head quarters. Let another division strike lower down the river. . . . *These* movements may be strictly defensive as the President please, but they will certainly *provoke offence* from the Mexicans. The bandit soldiery of Mexico will *commence* the game by plundering your commisariat [*sic*], stealing your cavalry horses, and murdering small parties. In such case, even the "National Intelligencer," will say to you "play the game out."

August 15, 1845

General Zachary Taylor ordered to move his 3,900 troops to Texas

August 29, 1845 — Polk diary

All Polk diary entries from Allan Nevins, ed., Polk: The Diary of a President, *1845–1849 (London & New York: Longmans, Green, 1952), pp. 5–84.*

---

3. Polk always referred to the Rio Grande as the Del Norte. Its full name was the Rio Grande del Norte.

The President called a special meeting of the Cabinet at twelve o'clock, all the members present except Mr. Mason. The President brought up for consideration our relations with Mexico, and the threatened invasion of Texas with that power. He submitted the following propositions which were unanimously agreed to as follows, *viz.,* If Mexico should declare war or actual hostilities should be commenced by that power, orders to be issued to General Taylor to attack and drive her back across the Del Norte. General Taylor shall be instructed that the crossing [of] the Del Norte by a Mexican army in force shall be regarded as an act of war on her part, and in that event General Taylor to be ordered, if he shall deem it advisable, not to wait to be attacked but to attack her army first. General Taylor in case of invasion by Mexico to be ordered not only to drive the invading army back to the west of the Del Norte, but to dislodge and drive back in like manner the Mexican post now stationed at Santiago. General Taylor to be vested with discretionary authority to pursue the Mexican army to the west of the Del Norte, and take Matamoras or any other Spanish post west of that river but not to penetrate any great distance into the interior of the Mexican territory.

September 1, 1845 — Polk diary

Senator Bagby of Alabama called today and held a long conversation with the President. The President asked his opinion as to the necessity or propriety of calling Congress, in the event of a declaration of war or an invasion of Texas by Mexico. Mr. Bagby gave it as his clear opinion that Congress should not be called, and assigned his reasons at some length. . . . Mr. Senator Archer of Virginia called the same day and paid his respects to the President in his office. The subject of the existing relations with Mexico was spoken of. Mr. Archer expressed the opinion that Mexico would neither declare war nor invade Texas. The military and naval preparations which had been made by the Administration were spoken of, and Mr. Archer concurred in an opinion, expressed by the President, that the appearance of our land and naval forces on the borders of Mexico and in the Gulf would probably deter and prevent Mexico from either declaring war or invading Texas.

September 16, 1845 — Polk diary

The Cabinet met today, all the members present. Despatches were read from Dr. Parrott, the confidential agent of the United States in Mexico, giving an account of another threatened revolution, etc., and of the refusal of Paredes to march his army to Texas. Dr. Parrott's latest despatch was of date 29th August, 1845. He gives it as his opinion that there will be no declaration of war against the United States and no invasion of Texas; that the government will be kept employed to keep down another revolution which was threatened. He is also of opinion that the government is desirous to re-establish diplomatic relations with the United States, and that a Minister from the United States would be received. In these opinions Mr. Black, the United States consul at Mexico, of date 23d August, and Mr. Dimond, United States consul at Vera Cruz, of date 30th August, concurred. After much consultation it was agreed unanimously that it was expedient to reopen diplomatic relations with Mexico; but that it was to be kept a profound secret that such a step was contemplated, for the reason mainly that if it was known in advance in the United States that a Minister had been sent to Mexico, it would, of course, be known to the British, French, and other foreign Ministers at Washington, who might take measures to thwart or defeat the objects of the mission. The President, in consultation with the Cabinet, agreed that the Hon. John Slidell of New Orleans, who spoke the Spanish language and was otherwise well qualified, should be tendered the mission. It was agreed that Mr. Slidell, if he accepted, should leave Pensacola in a national armed vessel and proceed to Vera Cruz, without disclosing or making known his official character. One great object of the mission, as stated by the President, would be to adjust a permanent boundary between Mexico and the United States, and that in doing this the Minister would be instructed to purchase for a pecuniary consideration Upper California and New Mexico. He said that a better boundary would be the Del Norte from its mouth to the Passo, in latitude about 32° north, and thence west to the Pacific Ocean, Mexico ceding to the United States all the country east and north of these lines.[4] The President said that for such a boundary the amount of pecuniary consideration to be paid would be of small importance. He supposed it might be had for fifteen or twenty millions, but he was ready to pay forty millions for it, if it could not be had for less. In these views the Cabinet agreed with the President unanimously.

October 24, 1845 — Polk diary

The conversation then turned on California, on which I remarked that Great Britain had her eye on that country and intended to possess it if she could, but

4. That would be the approximate present boundary of the United States, less the 1853 Gadsden Purchase.

that the people of the United States would not willingly permit California to
pass into the possession of any new colony planted by Great Britain or any foreign monarchy, and that in reasserting Mr. Monroe's doctrine I had California
and the fine bay of San Francisco as much in view as Oregon. Col. Benton
agreed that no foreign power ought to be permitted to colonize California, any
more than they would be to colonize Cuba. As long as Cuba remained in the
possession of the present government we would not object, but if a powerful
foreign power was about to possess it, we would not permit it. On the same
footing we would place California. . . .

Some conversation occurred concerning Capt. Fremont's expedition, and his
intention to visit California before his return. Col. Benton expressed the opinion
that Americans would settle on the Sacramento River and ultimately hold the
country.

November 10, 1845 — Polk diary

Saw and had a full conversation with Dr. Parrott, who had been in Mexico as a
confidential agent of the United States for some months, and who arrived at
Washington last night. He confirmed the opinion I had entertained that Mexico was anxious to settle the pending difficulties between the two countries, including those of boundary. I informed Dr. Parrott that I wished him to return
to Mexico as secretary of legation to the Minister whom I intended to appoint
this day, and told him the Hon. John Slidell of New Orleans was the person I
intended to appoint as Minister. He was not anxious to accept the office of secretary of legation, but agreed to do so, and said he would be ready to leave in
about ten days. At ten o'clock P.M., the instructions and all the documents referred to being copied, I signed the commission of the Hon. John Slidell as
Envoy Extraordinary and Minister Plenipotentiary to Mexico.

January 12, 1846

Washington learns of Slidell's initial rejection

January 13, 1846

Marcy orders Taylor into the disputed territory between the Nueces River and
the Rio Grande

March 5, 1846 — Manuel de Jesus Castro to Fremont (Castro was in Monterey)

From Spence and Jackson, eds., The Expeditions of John Charles Fremont, *p. 75.*

I have learnt with surprise that you against the laws of the authorities of Mexico have introduced yourself into the towns of this Departmental district under my charge with an armed force under a commission which must have been given you by your government only to survey its own proper lands.

In consequence this Prefectura now orders that you will immediately on receipt of this without any pretext return with your people out of the limits of this territory. If not this office will take the necessary measures to cause respect to this determination.

I have the honor to transcribe this to you for your intelligence that you may act in the case as belongs to your office and that he may comply with the expressed order. God & Liberty. Monterey March 5th 1846.

(Signed) MANUEL CASTRO

March 28, 1846 — Polk diary

The government of General Paredes, having recently overthrown that of President Herrera, was a military government and depended for its continuance in power upon the allegiance of the army under his command, and by which he had been enabled to effect the late revolution. It was known that the government of Paredes was in great need of money, and that in consequence of the deficiencies in the treasury and the deranged state of the finances, the army upon whose support General Paredes depended to uphold him in power, being badly fed and clothed and without pay, might and probably would soon desert him, unless money could be obtained to supply their wants. I stated that if our Minister could be authorized upon the *signing* of the treaty to pay down a half a million or a million of dollars, it would enable General Paredes to pay, feed, and clothe the army, and maintain himself in power until the treaty could be ratified by the United States and the subsequent instalments which might be stipulated in the treaty be paid. Indeed, I thought that the prompt payment of such a sum might induce him to make a treaty, which he would not otherwise venture to make. In these views there seemed to be a concurrence. The question followed how an appropriation could be obtained from Congress without exposing to the public and to foreign governments its object.

May 8, 1846 — Polk diary

Saw company until twelve o'clock today. Among others the Hon. John Slidell, late United States Minister to Mexico, called in company with the Secretary of State. Mr. Buchanan retired after a few minutes, and Mr. Slidell remained about an hour in conversation concerning his mission and the state of our relations with Mexico. Mr. Slidell's opinion was that but one course towards Mexico was left to the United States, and that was to take the redress of the wrongs and injuries which we had so long borne from Mexico into our own hands, and to act with promptness and energy. In this I agreed with him, and told him it was only a matter of time when I would make a communication to Congress on the subject, and that I had made up my mind to do so very soon.

May 9, 1846 — Polk diary

The Cabinet held a regular meeting today; all the members present. I brought up the Mexican question, and the question of what was the duty of the administration in the present state of our relations with that country. The subject was very fully discussed. All agreed that if the Mexican forces at Matamoras committed any act of hostility on General Taylor's forces I should immediately send a message to Congress recommending an immediate declaration of war. I stated to the Cabinet that up to this time, as we knew, we had heard of no open act of aggression by the Mexican army, but that the danger was imminent that such acts would be committed. I said that in my opinion we had ample cause of war, and that it was impossible that we could stand in *status quo*, or that I could remain silent much longer; that I thought it was my duty to send a message to Congress very soon and recommend definite measures. I told them that I thought I ought to make such a message by Tuesday next, that the country was excited and impatient on the subject, and if I failed to do so I would not be doing my duty. I then propounded the distinct question to the Cabinet, and took their opinions individually, whether I should make a message to Congress on Tuesday, and whether in that message I should recommend a declaration of war against Mexico. All except the Secretary of the Navy gave their advice in the affirmative. Mr. Bancroft dissented but said if any act of hostility should be committed by the Mexican forces he was then in favour of immediate war. Mr. Buchanan said he would feel better satisfied in his course if the Mexican forces had or should commit any act of hostility, but that as matters stood we had ample cause of war against Mexico, and he gave his assent to the measure. It was agreed that the message should be prepared and submitted to the Cabinet in their meeting on Tuesday. A history of our causes of complaint against Mexico had been at my request previously drawn up by Mr. Buchanan. I stated that what was said in my annual message in December gave that history as succinctly and satisfactorily as Mr. Buchanan's statement, that in truth it was the same history in both, expressed in different language, and that if I repeated that history in a message to Congress now I had better employ the precise language used in my message of December last. Without deciding this point the Cabinet passed to the consideration of some other subjects of minor importance. . . .

About six o'clock P.M. General R. Jones, the Adjutant-General of the army, called and handed to me despatches received from General Taylor by the Southern mail which had just arrived, giving information that a part of the Mexican army had crossed the Del Norte and attacked and killed and captured two companies of dragoons of General Taylor's army consisting of 63 officers and men. The despatch also stated that he had on that day (26th April) made a requisition on the Governors of Texas and Louisiana for four regiments each, to be sent to his relief at the earliest practicable period. Before I had finished reading the despatch, the Secretary of War called. I immediately summoned the Cabinet to meet at half past seven o'clock this evening. The Cabinet accordingly assembled at that hour; all the members present. The subject of the despatch received this evening from General Taylor, as well as the state of our relations with Mexico, were fully considered. The Cabinet were unanimously of opinion, and it was so agreed, that a message should be sent to Congress on Monday laying all the information in my possession before them and recommending vigorous and prompt measures to enable the executive to prosecute the war. The Secretary of War and Secretary of State agreed to put their clerks to work to copy the correspondence between Mr. Slidell and the Mexican Government and Secretary of State and the correspondence between the War Department and General Taylor, to the end that these documents should be transmitted to Congress with my message on Monday. The other members of the Cabinet tendered the services of their clerks to aid in preparing these copies.

Mr. Senator Houston, Hon. Barclay Martin, and several other members of

Congress called in the course of the evening, and were greatly excited at the news brought by the Southern mail from the army. They all approved the steps which had been taken by the administration, and were all of opinion that war with Mexico should now be prosecuted with vigor.

The Cabinet adjourned about ten o'clock and I commenced my message; Mr. Bancroft and Mr. Buchanan, the latter of whom had prepared a history of our causes of complaint against Mexico, agreed to assist me in preparing the message.

May 11, 1846 — Polk's war message

From James D. Richardson, ed., Messages and Papers of the Presidents, *Vol. IV (Washington, D.C.: U.S. Government Printing Office, 1897), pp. 437–442.*

THE STRONG desire to establish peace with Mexico on liberal and honorable terms, and the readiness of this Government to regulate and adjust our boundary and other causes of difference with that power on such fair and equitable principles as would lead to permanent relations of the most friendly nature, induced me in September last to seek the reopening of diplomatic relations between the two countries. Every measure adopted on our part had for its object the furtherance of these desired results. In communicating to Congress a succinct statement of the injuries which we had suffered from Mexico, and which have been accumulating during a period of more than twenty years, every expression that could tend to inflame the people of Mexico or defeat or delay a pacific result was carefully avoided. An envoy of the United States repaired to Mexico with full powers to adjust every existing difference. But though present on the Mexican soil by agreement between the two Governments, invested with full powers, and bearing evidence of the most friendly dispositions, his mission has been unavailing. The Mexican Government not only refused to receive him or listen to his propositions, but after a long-continued series of menaces have at last invaded our territory and shed the blood of our fellow-citizens on our own soil.

It now becomes my duty to state more in detail the origin, progress, and failure of that mission. In pursuance of the instructions given in September last, an inquiry was made on the 13th of October, 1845, in the most friendly terms, through our consul in Mexico, of the minister for foreign affairs, whether the Mexican Government "would receive an envoy from the United States intrusted with full powers to adjust all the questions in dispute between the two

Governments," with the assurance that "should the answer be in the affirmative such an envoy would be immediately dispatched to Mexico." The Mexican minister on the 15th of October gave an affirmative answer to this inquiry, requesting at the same time that our naval force at Vera Cruz might be withdrawn, lest its continued presence might assume the appearance of menace and coercion pending the negotiations. This force was immediately withdrawn. On the 10th of November, 1845, Mr. John Slidell, of Louisiana, was commissioned by me as envoy extraordinary and minister plenipotentiary of the United States to Mexico, and was intrusted with full powers to adjust both the questions of the Texas boundary and of indemnification to our citizens. The redress of the wrongs of our citizens naturally and inseparably blended itself with the question of boundary. The settlement of the one question in any correct view of the subject involves that of the other. I could not for a moment entertain the idea that the claims of our much-injured and long-suffering citizens, many of which had existed for more than twenty years, should be postponed or separated from the settlement of the boundary question.

Mr. Slidell arrived at Vera Cruz on the 30th of November, and was courteously received by the authorities of that city. But the Government of General Herrera was then tottering to its fall. The revolutionary party had seized upon the Texas question to effect or hasten its overthrow. Its determination to restore friendly relations with the United States, and to receive our minister to negotiate for the settlement of this question, was violently assailed, and was made the great theme of denunciation against it. The Government of General Herrera, there is good reason to believe, was sincerely desirous to receive our minister; but it yielded to the storm raised by its enemies, and on the 21st of December refused to accredit Mr. Slidell upon the most frivolous pretexts. These are so fully and ably exposed in the note of Mr. Slidell of the 24th of December last to the Mexican minister of foreign relations, herewith transmitted, that I deem it unnecessary to enter into further detail on this portion of the subject.

Five days after the date of Mr. Slidell's note General Herrera yielded the Government to General Paredes without a struggle, and on the 30th of December resigned the Presidency. This revolution was accomplished solely by the army, the people having taken little part in the contest; and thus the supreme power in Mexico passed into the hands of a military leader.

Determined to leave no effort untried to effect an amicable adjustment with Mexico, I directed Mr. Slidell to present his credentials to the Government of General Paredes and ask to be officially received by him. . . .

[154]

Under these circumstances, Mr. Slidell, in obedience to my direction, addressed a note to the Mexican minister of foreign relations, under date of the 1st of March last, asking to be received by that Government in the diplomatic character to which he had been appointed. This minister in his reply, under date of the 12th of March, reiterated the arguments of his predecessor, and in terms that may be considered as giving just grounds of offense to the Government and people of the United States denied the application of Mr. Slidell. Nothing therefore remained for our envoy but to demand his passports and return to his own country.

Thus the Government of Mexico, though solemnly pledged by official acts in October last to receive and accredit an American envoy, violated their plighted faith and refused the offer of a peaceful adjustment of our difficulties. Not only was the offer rejected, but the indignity of its rejection was enhanced by the manifest breach of faith in refusing to admit the envoy who came because they had bound themselves to receive him. . . .

In my message at the commencement of the present session I informed you that upon the earnest appeal both of the Congress and convention of Texas I had ordered an efficient military force to take a position "between the Nueces and the Del Norte." This had become necessary to meet a threatened invasion of Texas by the Mexican forces, for which extensive military preparations had been made. The invasion was threatened solely because Texas had determined, in accordance with a solemn resolution of the Congress of the United States, to annex herself to our Union, and under these circumstances it was plainly our duty to extend our protection over her citizens and soil. . . .

Meantime Texas, by the final action of our Congress, had become an integral part of our Union. The Congress of Texas, by its act of December 19, 1836, had declared the Rio del Norte to be the boundary of that Republic. Its jurisdiction had been extended and exercised beyond the Nueces. The country between that river and the Del Norte had been represented in the Congress and in the convention of Texas, had thus taken part in the act of annexation itself, and is now included within one of our Congressional districts. Our own Congress had, moreover, with great unanimity, by the act approved December 31, 1845, recognized the country beyond the Nueces as a part of our territory by including it within our own revenue system, and a revenue officer to reside within that district has been appointed by and with the advice and consent of the Senate. It became, therefore, of urgent necessity to provide for the defense of that portion of our country. Accordingly, on the 13th of January last instructions were issued to the general in command of these troops to occupy the left bank of the Del Norte. This river, which is the southwestern boundary of the State of Texas, is an exposed frontier. From this quarter invasion was threatened; upon it and in its immediate vicinity, in the judgment of high military experience, are the proper stations for the protecting forces of the Government. . . .

The movement of the troops to the Del Norte was made by the commanding general under positive instructions to abstain from all aggressive acts toward Mexico or Mexican citizens and to regard the relations between that Republic and the United States as peaceful unless she should declare war or commit acts of hostility indicative of a state of war. He was specially directed to protect private property and respect personal rights.

The Army moved from Corpus Christi on the 11th of March, and on the 28th of that month arrived on the left bank of the Del Norte opposite to Matamoras, where it encamped on a commanding position, which has since been strengthened by the erection of fieldworks. A depot has also been established at Point Isabel, near the Brazos Santiago, 30 miles in rear of the encampment. The selection of his position was necessarily confided to the judgment of the general in command.

The Mexican forces at Matamoras assumed a belligerent attitude, and on the 12th of April General Ampudia, then in command, notified General Taylor to break up his camp within twenty-four hours and to retire beyond the Nueces River, and in the event of his failure to comply with these demands announced that arms, and arms alone, must decide the question. But no open act of hostility was committed until the 24th of April. On that day General Arista, who had succeeded to the command of the Mexican forces, communicated to General Taylor that "he considered hostilities commenced and should prosecute them." A party of dragoons of 63 men and officers were on the same day dispatched from the American camp up the Rio del Norte, on its left bank, to ascertain whether the Mexican troops had crossed or were preparing to cross the river, "became engaged with a large body of these troops, and after a short affair, in which some 16 were killed and wounded, appear to have been surrounded and compelled to surrender."

The grievous wrongs perpetrated by Mexico upon our citizens throughout a long period of years remain unredressed, and solemn treaties pledging her public faith for this redress have been disregarded. A government either unable or unwilling to enforce the execution of such treaties fails to perform one of its plainest duties.

[156]

Our commerce with Mexico has been almost annihilated. It was formerly highly beneficial to both nations, but our merchants have been deterred from prosecuting it by the system of outrage and extortion which the Mexican authorities have pursued against them, whilst their appeals through their own Government for indemnity have been made in vain. Our forbearance has gone to such an extreme as to be mistaken in its character. Had we acted with vigor in repelling the insults and redressing the injuries inflicted by Mexico at the commencement, we should doubtless have escaped all the difficulties in which we are now involved.

Instead of this, however, we have been exerting our best efforts to propitiate her good will. Upon the pretext that Texas, a nation as independent as herself, thought proper to unite its destinies with our own, she has affected to believe that we have severed her rightful territory, and in official proclamations and manifestoes has repeatedly threatened to make war upon us for the purpose of reconquering Texas. In the meantime we have tried every effort at reconciliation. The cup of forbearance had been exhausted even before the recent information from the frontier of the Del Norte. But now, after reiterated menaces, Mexico has passed the boundary of the United States, has invaded our territory and shed American blood upon the American soil. She has proclaimed that hostilities have commenced, and that the two nations are now at war.

As war exists, and, notwithstanding all our efforts to avoid it, exists by the act of Mexico herself, we are called upon by every consideration of duty and patriotism to vindicate with decision the honor, the rights, and the interests of our country. . . .

Questions to Consider

When examining a problem of this sort, historians first arrange the evidence chronologically and then see whether it can be grouped into major categories. In this case, the chronological groups are the period from Polk's election to approximately August 1845, in which Commodore Robert Field Stockton plays a major role; the nearly six months from August 1845 to mid-January 1846, in which the central character becomes special minister John Slidell; and the time from mid-January to May 1846, in which General Zachary Taylor plays a prominent part. Not all the pieces of evidence fit neatly into those categories; those that do not fit will have to be dealt with in a separate step.

You will find it necessary to read through the evidence twice. In the first reading, take each chronological group (see above) and read through it carefully. Ask questions of the evidence as you go along. For the first group,

1. What was Stockton's mission? What did Jones think Stockton's mission was? Is there evidence to corroborate Jones? What is the significance of "R. F. Stockton Esq." in the May 27 letter?

2. What was Fremont's mission? What do his memoirs reveal?

3. What did Stockton want the Texans to do? Why Texans, and not United States troops?

4. How can Polk's letter to Haywood of August 9, 1845, be interpreted? Does other evidence help with this interpretation?

5. Why was Taylor ordered to Texas on August 15, 1845?

Now put all the evidence in the first chronological group together. What does it tell you?

Having done this, move on to the second chronological group, the six months from August 1845 to mid-January 1846. Ask the following questions of the evidence:

1. Bagby and Archer had one explanation for why United States troops were sent to Texas. What was it?

How does this explanation fit with the other pieces of evidence?

2. Why was Slidell sent to Mexico? What were his chances of success? (Remember Stockton and Fremont.)

3. What was the general feeling in Polk's cabinet about California? What about Benton's opinion?

4. Why did Secretary of War William Marcy order Taylor into the disputed territory? How does the timing fit with Slidell's mission? What was Slidell's fate?

Now repeat the process you used in the first group. What does the evidence collectively tell you? Are there pieces that don't seem to fit? How can you explain them?

Then go to the third chronological group, repeating the process.

1. Manuel de Jesus Castro was a Mexican official. What is the gist of his letter to Fremont? Was he justified in writing to Fremont?

2. A revolution had taken place in Mexico. How did Polk seek to take advantage of it?

3. What was Polk's frame of mind on May 8–9, 1846?

4. The May 9 cabinet meetings (remember there were two of them on the same day) are crucial. In the first meeting, what had Polk made up his mind to do?

5. President Polk's war message has been reproduced almost in its entirety. How does it fit with the other evidence? What is *not* mentioned in the message? How important are these omissions?

Now you are ready to put the three groups together. But before you do that, read the introduction to this exercise to review the long-range causal factors. Once you have done that, you will be ready to form a thesis as to the causes of the Mexican War. Are there pieces of evidence that do not fit your thesis? If so, you will have to explain them. When most of the evidence does fit, however, and you can explain the pieces that do not fit (your instructor can be very helpful here), then you will be ready to offer your explanation for the causes of the Mexican War.

Epilogue

From the point of view of the United States, the Mexican War was won with a minimum of effort, for Mexico was badly overmatched. Troops under General Zachary Taylor moved across the Rio Grande, winning important battles at Monterey and Buena Vista. Simultaneously, General Winfield Scott landed at Vera Cruz and marched inland to Mexico City. In California a combined force of army and navy easily scattered the weak Mexican resistance. In all, the war lasted less than twenty-one months and cost the United States only thirteen thousand men.

Several people benefited from the war. Taylor and Scott became war heroes. Indeed, Taylor won the presidency in 1848 almost on the sole basis of being a military hero. He had never even voted, and it has been said that he refused to accept the notification of his nomination for the presidency because the letter had postage due on it. Many younger men also made their military reputations during the Mexican War and gained valuable combat experience. For example, most of the generals on both sides of the Civil War (including Ulysses S. Grant and Robert E. Lee) saw action in that conflict.

Yet at home the Mexican War was the subject of bitter debate. Some northeasterners charged that it was a "slaveholders' war," designed to add slave territory to the United States. For his part, Henry David Thoreau refused to pay taxes to support the conflict (he spent one night in jail) and wrote his famous essay "On Civil Disobedience," which posed the timeless question of what people should do when their own moral convictions clash with the will and laws of their government. Writing from far-off Europe, American author, journalist, and feminist Margaret Fuller mourned her country's involvement in what she called an "unjust war." Under this strain, the unity of America's political parties was noticeably weakened.

The extent to which the issue of slavery had intruded itself into American life can be seen in the debate over the future of the territory taken from Mexico. How these territories were to be organized and whether slavery would be permitted in them were subjects of intense discussion that the Compromise of 1850 only partially alleviated. As Americans would come to realize, the linking of the issues of slavery and territorial expansion proved tragic. Ultimately, only the Civil War — and the loss of over 600,000 lives — would settle the question.

The Mexican War also left a residue of bad feelings between the United States and Mexico, which has never really been overcome. The southwesterners' treatment of Mexicans as inferiors was not much different from the white southerners' treatment of blacks and the far westerners' of orientals. President Woodrow Wilson's brief invasion of Mexico hardly furthered better relations, and President Jimmy Carter's offhand comment about the purity of Mexican water was at the very least an unfortunate quip that many Mexicans viewed as offensive. Equally offensive to many is the habit people of the United States have (and, if you look back, you will see that we have been guilty too) of referring to themselves as "Americans," as if no one else in the Western Hemisphere deserves the title. In all, the relationship between the two nations has been less than harmonious.

Perhaps most important from our point of view, however, is the fact that the Mexican War added significantly (over 529,000 square miles) to the size of the United States, thus further assuring United States power and world influence. Untold billions of dollars of natural resources, beginning with the discovery of gold in California one month before the end of the Mexican War, have been tapped. In search of gold or land or opportunity, millions of Americans have migrated to the areas gained in the war, until by the latter part of the twentieth century the state of California (which in 1912 had a population smaller than that of Georgia) had become the most populous state in the Union. If, as the editorialist suggested, this was the United States' "manifest destiny," it was one that Americans themselves took a most active part in achieving.

Chapter 9

The Price for Victory:
The Decision to Use Black Troops

The Problem

Although many leaders in both the North and South denied it at the time, the institution of slavery unquestionably played a major role in bringing on the American Civil War. As slavery intruded into the important issues and events of the day (such as westward expansion, the Mexican War, the admission of new states to the Union, the course charted for the proposed transcontinental railroad, and the right of citizens to petition Congress) as well as into all of the major institutions (churches and schools, for example), an increasing number of northerners and southerners came to feel that the question of slavery must be settled, and settled on the battlefield. Therefore, when news arrived of the firing on Fort Sumter, many greeted the announcement with relief. Lincoln's call for 75,000 volunteers was answered with an enormous response. In Charleston a day of celebration was followed by a night of parades and fireworks.

Yet, for a number of reasons, most northern and southern leaders carefully avoided the slavery issue even after war had begun. To Abraham Lincoln, the debate over the abolition of slavery threatened to divert northerners from what he considered to be the war's central aim, that of preserving the Union and denying the South's right to secede. In addition, Lincoln realized that a great number of northern whites, including himself, did not view blacks as equals and might well oppose a war designed to liberate slaves from bondage. Finally, in large parts of Virginia, North Carolina, Kentucky, and Tennessee and in other pockets in the South, Union sentiment was strong, largely because of the antiplanter bias in these states. But anti-Negro sentiment was also strong in these same areas. With the border states so crucial to the Union both politically and militarily (as points of invasion into the South), it is not surprising that Lincoln purposely discouraged any notion that the war was for the purpose of emancipating slaves. Therefore, when influential editor Horace Greeley publicly called on Lincoln in August 1862 to make the Civil War a war for the emancipation of slaves, the president replied that the primary purpose of the war was to preserve the Union. "My paramount object in this struggle," Lincoln wrote, "is *not* either to save or destroy slavery" (italics added).

> If I could save the Union without freeing *any* slave I would do it, and if I could save it by freeing *all* the slaves I would do it; and if I could save it by freeing some and leaving others alone I would also do that. What I do about slavery, . . . I do because I believe it helps to save the Union; and what I forbear, I forbear because I do *not* believe it would help to save the Union[1] (italics added).

Hence President Lincoln, in spite of his "*personal* wish that all men every where could be free" (italics added), strongly resisted all efforts to turn the Civil War into a moral crusade to eradicate slavery.

1. Lincoln to Greeley, August 22, 1862, in Roy P. Basler, ed., *The Collected Works of Abraham Lincoln*, Vol. V (New Brunswick, N.J.: Rutgers University Press, 1953), pp. 388–389.

On the Confederate side, President Jefferson Davis also had reasons to avoid making slavery (in this case its preservation) a primary war aim. Davis feared, correctly, that foreign governments would be unwilling to recognize or aid the Confederacy if the preservation of slavery was the most important southern reason for fighting. Too, the majority of white southerners did not own slaves, often disliked people who did, and, Davis feared, might not fight if the principal war aim was to defend the "peculiar institution." Therefore, while Lincoln was explaining to northerners that the war was being fought to preserve the Union, Davis was trying to convince southerners that the struggle was for independence and for the defense of constitutional rights.

Yet as it became increasingly clear that the Civil War was going to be a long and costly conflict, issues concerning slavery and the use of blacks in the war effort continually came to the surface. In the North, reports of battle casualties in 1862 caused widespread shock and outrage, and some feared that the United States would be exhausted before the Confederacy was finally subdued — if it was to be subdued at all.[2] Also, many northerners came to feel that emancipation could

2. The following is an estimation of Union casualties (the sum of those killed, wounded, and missing) for the principal engagements of 1862: Shiloh (April, 13,000 casualties), Seven Pines (May, 6,000), Seven Days (June, 16,000), Antietam (September, 12,400), Fredericksburg (December, 12,000).

be used as both a political and diplomatic weapon. Those European nations (especially England, which had ended slavery throughout its own empire in 1833) that had been technically neutral but were leaning toward the Confederacy might, northerners reasoned, be afraid to oppose a government committed to such a worthy cause as emancipation. Too, some northerners hoped that a proclamation of emancipation would incite widespread slave rebellions in the South that would cripple the Confederacy. Not to be overlooked, however, are those northerners (a minority, to be sure) who sincerely viewed slavery as a stain on American society whose eradication was a moral imperative.

Gradually President Lincoln came to favor the emancipation of slaves, although never to the extent that the abolitionists wanted. In early 1862 the president proposed the gradual emancipation of slaves by the states, with compensation for the slave owners and colonization of the former slaves outside the boundaries of the United States. When Congress mandated that Lincoln go farther than that, by passing the Confiscation Act of 1862, which explicitly called for the permanent emancipation of all slaves in the Confederacy, the president simply ignored the law, choosing not to enforce it.[3] But political and diplomatic considerations prompted Lin-

coln to alter his course and support the issuing of the Emancipation Proclamation. So that his action would not be interpreted as one of desperation, the president waited until after the Union "victory" at the Battle of Antietam. While the proclamation actually freed slaves only in areas still under Confederate control (hence immediately freeing no one), the act was a significant one in terms of a shift in war aims.

The second important issue that Lincoln and other northern leaders had to face was whether or not to arm blacks and make them regular soldiers in the Union army. Blacks had seen limited service in the American Revolution and the War of 1812, prompting black abolitionist Frederick Douglass to criticize the United States' initial policy of excluding blacks from the army of the Civil War, saying in February 1862,

Colored men were good enough to fight under Washington. They are not good enough to fight under McClellan. They were good enough to fight under Andrew Jackson. They are not good enough to fight under Gen. Halleck. They were good enough to help win American Independence, but they are not good enough to help preserve that independence against treason and rebellion.

Emancipation of slaves in the South was one thing, but making blacks United States soldiers was another.

3. It was this action of Lincoln that prompted the exchange between Greeley and the president in August 1862.

Such a decision would imply that white northerners recognized blacks as equals. Although most abolitionists preached the dual message of emancipation and racial equality, the vast majority of northern whites did not look upon blacks as equals, a belief that they shared with their president. Would whites fight alongside blacks, even in racially separated units? Were blacks, many northern whites asked, courageous enough to stand and hold their positions under fire? What would blacks want as a price for their aid? Throughout 1862 northern leaders carried on an almost continual debate over whether to accept blacks into the Union army, an issue that had a number of social, ideological, and moral implications.

In the Confederacy the issue of arming blacks for the southern war effort was also a lively one. The northern superiority in population supplemented by continued immigration from Europe put the South at a terrific numerical disadvantage, a disadvantage that could be lessened by the enlistment of at least a portion of the approximately four million slaves. Southern battle casualties also had been fearfully high, in some battles higher than those of the Union.[4] How

long could the Confederacy hold out as its numbers continually eroded? If the main goal of the war was southern independence, shouldn't Confederate leaders use all available means to secure that objective? It was known that some northern whites, shocked by Union casualty figures, were calling on Lincoln to let the South go in peace. If the Confederacy could hold out, many southerners hoped, northern peace sentiments might grow enough to force the Union to give up. If slaves could help in that effort, some reasoned, why not arm them? Yet, as in the North, the question of whether or not to arm blacks had significance far beyond military considerations. Except for the promise of freedom, what would motivate the slaves to fight for their masters? If freedom was to be offered, then what, many surely would argue, was the war being fought over in the first place? Would southern whites fight with blacks? Would some blacks, once armed, then turn against their masters? And finally, if southern whites were correct in their insistence that blacks were essentially docile, child-like creatures, then what conceivable support could they give to the war effort? Interestingly, there were some remarkable similarities in the points debated by the northern and southern policymakers.

In this chapter, your task is to answer five separate but related sets of questions:

4. The following are estimates of Confederate casualties for the principal engagements of 1862–1863: Seven Days (June 1862, 20,000), Antietam (September 1862, 13,700), Fredericksburg (December 1862, 5,000), Gettysburg (July 1863, 28,000).

1. What were the arguments in the North both in favor of and against arming blacks and employing them as regular soldiers? In the South?

2. What were the similarities between the debate in the North and that in the South? What were the differences?

3. What do the similarities and differences tell us about racial opinions in the North and South?

4. What were some of the factors causing the Union to change its policy on arming blacks? The Confederacy?

5. What were the military, social, and ideological implications of the decisions that were finally reached?

The Method

In this chapter you are confronted with two series of speeches, private and official correspondence, reports, newspaper articles and editorials, and laws and proclamations. One series concerns the argument in the North over whether to arm blacks, and the other series deals with the same question in the South. Read and analyze each series separately. Question 1 requires you to list the principal arguments for the North and the South. Questions 2, 3, and 4 require you to compare one set of arguments with

the other. Take notes as you go along, always being careful not to lose track of your central objectives.

By now you should be able with some ease to identify and list the major points, pro and con, in a debate. Jotting down notes as you read the evidence will be extremely helpful. Be careful, for some reports, articles, and letters contain more than one argument.

Several earlier chapters have required that you read between the lines, that is, identify things that are felt or implied although never directly stated. What emotional factors can you identify on both sides of the question? How important would you say these factors were in the final decision? For example, you will see from the evidence that at no time in the debate being carried on in the North are battle casualties mentioned. Were casualties therefore of no importance in the debate? How would you go about answering this question?

In some cases the identity of the author of a particular piece (if known) can give you several clues as to that person's emotions, fears, anxieties, and needs. In other cases, where the identity of the author is not known, you may have to exercise a little historical imagination. What might this person really mean when he or she says (or fails to say) something? Can you infer from the context of the argument any emotions that are not explicitly stated?

The Evidence

NORTH

From James M. McPherson, The Negro's Civil War: How American Negroes Felt and Acted During the War for the Union *(New York: Vintage Books, 1967), p. 33.*

Petition of Some Northern Blacks to President Lincoln, October 1861

We, the undersigned, respectfully represent to Your Excellency that we are native citizens of the United States, and that, notwithstanding much injustice and oppression which our race have suffered, we cherish a strong attachment for the land of our birth and for our Republican Government. We are filled with alarm at the formidable conspiracy for its overthrow, and lament the vast expense of blood and treasure which the present war involves. . . . We are anxious to use our power to give peace to our country and permanence to our Government.

We are strong in numbers, in courage, and in patriotism, and in behalf of our fellow countrymen of the colored race, we offer to you and to the nation a power and a will sufficient to conquer rebellion, and establish peace on a permanent basis. We pledge ourselves, upon receiving the sanction of Your Excellency, that we will immediately proceed to raise an efficient number of regiments, and so fast as arms and equipments shall be furnished, we will bring them into the field in good discipline, and ready for action.

From McPherson, The Negro's Civil War, *p. 162.*

Newspaper Editorial by Frederick Douglass, *Douglass' Monthly,* September 1861

Our Presidents, Governors, Generals and Secretaries are calling, with almost frantic vehemence, for men. — "Men! men! send us men!" they scream, or the cause of the Union is gone; . . . and yet these very officers, representing the people and Government, steadily and persistently refuse to receive the very class of men which have a deeper interest in the defeat and humiliation of the rebels, than all others. . . . What a spectacle of blind, unreasoning prejudice and pusillanimity is this! The national edifice is on fire. Every man who can carry a bucket of water, or remove a brick, is wanted; but those who have the care of the building, having a profound respect for the feeling of the national burglars who set the building on fire, are determined that the flames shall only be extinguished by Indo-Caucasian hands, and to have the building burnt rather than save it by means of any other. Such is the pride, the stupid prejudice and folly that rules the hour.

Why does the Government reject the negro? Is he not a man? Can he not wield a sword, fire a gun, march and countermarch, and obey orders like any other? . . . If persons so humble as we can be allowed to speak to the President of the United States, we should ask him if this dark and terrible hour of the nation's extremity is a time for consulting a mere vulgar and unnatural prejudice? . . . We would tell him that this is no time to fight with one hand, when both are needed; that this is no time to fight only with your white hand, and allow your black hand to remain tied. . . . While the Government continues to refuse the aid of colored men, thus alienating them from the national cause, and giving the rebels the advantage of them, it will not deserve better fortunes than it has thus far experienced. — Men in earnest don't fight with one hand, when they might fight with two, and a man drowning would not refuse to be saved even by a colored hand.

From Roy P. Basler, ed., The Collected Works of Abraham Lincoln, *Vol. V (New Brunswick, N.J.: Rutgers University Press, 1953), pp. 356–357.*

President Lincoln, "Remarks to Deputation of Western Gentlemen," August 4, 1862

A deputation of Western gentlemen waited upon the President this morning to offer two colored regiments from the State of Indiana. Two members of Congress were of the party. The President received them courteously, but stated to them that he was not prepared to go the length of enlisting negroes as soldiers. He would employ all colored men offered as laborers, but would not promise to make soldiers of them.

The deputation came away satisfied that it is the determination of the Government not to arm negroes unless some new and more pressing emergency arises. The President argued that the nation could not afford to lose Kentucky at this crisis, and gave it as his opinion that to arm the negroes would turn 50,000 bayonets from the loyal Border States against us that were for us.

From McPherson, The Negro's Civil War, *pp. 163–164.*

New York Tribune,
August 16, 1862[5]

I am quite sure there is not one man in ten but would feel himself degraded as a volunteer if negro equality is to be the order in the field of battle. . . . I take the liberty of warning the abettors of fraternizing with the blacks, that one negro regiment, in the present temper of things, put on equality with those who have the past year fought and suffered, will withdraw an amount of life and energy in our army equal to disbanding ten of the best regiments we can now raise.

From Basler, ed., The Collected Works of Abraham Lincoln, *Vol. V, pp. 419–425, 436–437, 444, 509–511, and Vol. VI, pp. 149–150, respectively.*

President Lincoln, "Reply to
Emancipation Memorial
Presented by Chicago Christians
of All Denominations,"
September 13, 1862

I admit that slavery is the root of the rebellion, or at least its *sine qua non*. The ambition of politicians may have instigated them to act, but they would have been impotent without slavery as their instrument. I will also concede that emancipation would help us in Europe, and convince them that we are incited by something more than ambition. I grant further that it would help *somewhat* at the North, though not so much, I fear, as you and those you represent imag-

---

5. This was a letter to the editor and did not reflect the opinion of Horace Greeley, editor of the *Tribune* and supporter of racial equality for blacks.

ine. Still, some additional strength would be added in that way to the war. And then unquestionably it would weaken the rebels by drawing off their laborers, which is of great importance. But I am not so sure we could do much with the blacks. If we were to arm them, I fear that in a few weeks the arms would be in the hands of the rebels; and indeed thus far we have not had arms enough to equip our white troops. I will mention another thing, though it meet only your scorn and contempt: There are fifty thousand bayonets in the Union armies from the Border Slave States. It would be a serious matter if, in consequence of a proclamation such as you desire, they should go over to the rebels. I do not think they all would — not so many indeed as a year ago, or as six months ago — not so many to-day as yesterday. Every day increases their Union feeling. They are also getting their pride enlisted, and want to beat the rebels.

Proclamation Suspending the Writ of Habeas Corpus

September 24, 1862

By the President of the United States of America:

A Proclamation.

Whereas, it has become necessary to call into service not only volunteers but also portions of the militia of the States by draft in order to suppress the insurrection existing in the United States, and disloyal persons are not adequately restrained by the ordinary processes of law from hindering this measure and from giving aid and comfort in various ways to the insurrection. . . .

Now, therefore, be it ordered, first, that during the existing insurrection and as a necessary measure for suppressing the same, all Rebels and Insurgents, their aiders and abettors within the United States, and all persons discouraging volunteer enlistments, resisting militia drafts, or guilty of any disloyal practice, affording aid and comfort to Rebels against the authority of the United States, shall be subject to martial law and liable to trial and punishment by Court Martial or Military Commission:

Second. That the Writ of Habeas Corpus is suspended in respect to all persons arrested, or who are now, or hereafter during the rebellion shall be, imprisoned in any fort, camp, arsenal, military prison, or other place of confinement by any military authority or by the sentence of any Court Martial or Military Commission.

To Hannibal Hamlin

(Strictly private.)   Executive Mansion,
                                    Washington, September 28, 1862.

My Dear Sir:

Your kind letter of the 25th is just received. It is known to some that while I hope something from the proclamation, my expectations are not as sanguine as are those of some friends. The time for its effect southward has not come; but northward the effect should be instantaneous.

It is six days old, and while commendation in newspapers and by distinguished individuals is all that a vain man could wish, the stocks have declined, and troops come forward more slowly than ever. This, looked soberly in the face, is not very satisfactory. We have fewer troops in the field at the end of six days than we had at the beginning — the attrition among the old outnumbering the addition of the new. The North responds to the proclamation sufficiently in breath; but breath alone kills no rebels.

I wish I could write more cheerfully; nor do I thank you the less for the kindness of your letter. Yours very truly,

                                    A. LINCOLN

To Carl Schurz

Gen. Carl Schurz   Executive Mansion,
                                    Washington, Nov. 24, 1862.

My dear Sir

I have just received, and read, your letter of the 20th. The purport of it is that we lost the late elections,[6] and the administration is failing, because the war is unsuccessful; and that I must not flatter myself that I am not justly to blame for it. I certainly know that if the war fails, the administration fails, and that I *will* be blamed for it, whether I deserve it or not. And I ought to be blamed, if I could do better. You think I could do better; therefore you blame me already. I think I could not do better; therefore I blame you for blaming me. . . .

6. In the congressional elections of 1862 the Republicans lost three seats in the House of Representatives, although they were still the majority party. Senators were not elected by the people until the Seventeenth Amendment to the Constitution was ratified in 1913.

President Lincoln to Andrew Johnson, March 26, 1863

My dear Sir:

I am told you have at least *thought* of raising a negro military force. In my opinion the country now needs no specific thing so much as some man of your ability, and position, to go to this work. When I speak of your position, I mean that of an eminent citizen of a slave-state, and himself a slave-holder. The colored population is the great *available* and yet *unavailed* of, force for restoring the Union. The bare sight of fifty thousand armed, and drilled black soldiers on the banks of the Mississippi, would end the rebellion at once. And who doubts that we can present that sight, if we but take hold in earnest? If you *have* been thinking of it please do not dismiss the thought. Yours truly

A. LINCOLN

From Dudley Cornish, The Sable Arm: Negro Troops in the Union Army, 1861–1865 *(New York: W. W. Norton, 1966).*

New York Times, March 7, 1864. Editorial.

There has been no more striking manifestation of the marvelous times that are upon us than the scene in our streets at the departure of the first of our colored regiments. Had any man predicted it last year he would have been thought a fool, even by the wisest and most discerning. History abounds with strange contrasts. It always has been an ever-shifting melo-drama. But never, in this land at least, has it presented a transition so extreme and yet so speedy as what our eyes have just beheld.

Eight months ago the African race in this City were literally hunted down like wild beasts.[7] They fled for their lives. When caught, they were shot down in cold blood, or stoned to death, or hung to the trees or the lamp-posts. Their homes were pillaged; the asylum which Christian charity had provided for their

---

7. In mid-1863 demonstrations against conscription in New York City turned into an ugly mob action against blacks, partly because of the blacks' connection, through the Emancipation Proclamation of January 1, 1863, to the war, but also because of economic competition with the poorer whites who comprised most of the rioters.

orphaned children was burned; and there was no limit to the persecution but in the physical impossibility of finding further material on which the mob could wreak its ruthless hate. Nor was it solely the raging horde in the streets that visited upon the black man the nefarious wrong. Thousands and tens of thousands of men of higher social grade, of better education, cherished precisely the same spirit. It found expression in contumelious speech rather than in the violent act, but it was persecution none the less for that. In fact the mob would never have entered upon that career of outrage but for the fact that it was fired and maddened by the prejudice which had been generated by the ruling influences, civil and social, here in New York, till it had enveloped the City like some infernal atmosphere. The physical outrages which were inflicted on the black race in those terrible days were but the outburst of malignant agencies which had been transfusing the whole community from top to bottom year after year.

How astonishingly has all this been changed. The same men who could not have shown themselves in the most obscure street in the City without peril of instant death, even though in the most suppliant attitude, now march in solid platoons, with shouldered muskets, slung knapsacks, and buckled cartridge boxes down through our gayest avenues and our busiest thoroughfares to the pealing strains of martial music and are everywhere saluted with waving handkerchiefs, with descending flowers, and with the acclamations and plaudits of countless beholders. They are halted at our most beautiful square, and amid an admiring crowd, in the presence of many of our most prominent citizens, are addressed in an eloquent and most complimentary speech by the President of our chief literary institution, and are presented with a gorgeous stand of colors in the names of a large number of the first ladies of the City, who attest on parchment, signed by their own fair hands, that they "will anxiously watch your career, glorying in your heroism, ministering to you when wounded and ill, and honoring your martyrdom with benedictions and with tears."

It is only by such occasions that we can at all realize the prodigious revolution which the public mind everywhere is experiencing. Such developments are infallible tokens of a new epoch.

SOUTH

All South evidence except Judah Benjamin piece from Robert F. Durden, The Gray and the Black: The Confederate Debate on Emancipation *(Baton Rouge: Louisiana State University Press, 1972).*

[172]

Montgomery (Ala.)
Weekly Mail,
"Employment of Negroes in
the Army," September 9, 1863

. . . We must either employ the negroes ourselves, or the enemy will employ them against us. While the enemy retains so much of our territory, they are, in their present avocation and status, a dangerous element, a source of weakness. They are no longer negative characters, but subjects of volition as other people. They must be taught to know that this is peculiarly the country of the black man — that in no other is the climate and soil so well adapted to his nature and capacity. He must further be taught that it is his duty, as well as the white man's, to defend his home with arms, if need be.

We are aware that there are persons who shudder at the idea of placing arms in the hands of negroes, and who are not willing to trust them under any circumstances. The negro, however, is proverbial for his faithfulness under kind treatment. He is an affectionate, grateful being, and we are persuaded that the fears of such persons are groundless.

There are in the slaveholding States four millions of negroes, and out of this number at least six hundred thousand able-bodied men capable of bearing arms can be found. Lincoln proposes to free and arm them against us. There are already fifty thousand of them in the Federal ranks. Lincoln's scheme has worked well so far, and if no[t] checkmated, will most assuredly be carried out. The Confederate Government must adopt a counter policy. It must thwart the enemy in this gigantic scheme, at all hazards, and if nothing else will do it — if the negroes cannot be made effective and trustworthy to the Southern cause in no other way, we solemnly believe it is the duty of this Government to forestall Lincoln and proceed at once to take steps for the emancipation or liberation of the negroes itself. Let them be declared free, placed in the ranks, and told to fight for their homes and country. . . .

Such action on the part of our Government would place our people in a purer and better light before the world. It would disabuse the European mind of a grave error in regard to the cause of our separation. It would prove to them that there were higher and holier motives which actuated our people than the mere love of property. It would show that, although slavery is one of the principles that we started to fight for, yet it falls far short of being the chief one; that, for the sake of our liberty, we are capable of any personal sacrifice; that we regard the emancipation of slaves, and the consequent loss of property as an evil infinitely less than the subjugation and enslavement of ourselves; that it is not a war exclusively for the privilege of holding negroes in bondage. It would prove to our soldiers, three-fourths of whom never owned a negro, that it is not "the rich man's war and the poor man's fight," but a war for the most sacred of all principles, for the dearest of all rights — the right to govern ourselves. It would show them that the rich man who owned slaves was not willing to jeopardize the precious liberty of the country by his eagerness to hold on to his slaves, but that he was ready to give them up and sacrifice his interest in them whenever the cause demanded it. It would lend a new impetus, a new enthusiasm, a new and powerful strength to the cause, and place our success beyond a peradventure. It would at once remove all the odium which attached to us on account of slavery, and bring us speedy recognition, and, if necessary, intervention.

General Patrick Cleburne to General Joseph Johnston, January 2, 1864

We have now been fighting for nearly three years, have spilled much of our best blood, and lost, consumed, or thrown to the flames an amount of property equal in value to the specie currency of the world. . . . Our soldiers can see no end to this state of affairs except in our own exhaustion; hence, instead of rising to the occasion, they are sinking into a fatal apathy, growing weary of hardships and slaughters which promise no results. In this state of things it is easy to understand why there is a growing belief that some black catastrophe is not far ahead of us, and that unless some extraordinary change is soon made in our condition we must overtake it. . . .

In view of the state of affairs what does our country propose to do? In the words of President Davis "no effort must be spared to add largely to our effective force as promptly as possible. The sources of supply are to be found in restoring to the army all who are improperly absent, putting an end to substitution, modifying the exemption law, restricting details, and placing in the ranks such of the able-bodied men now employed as wagoners, nurses, cooks, and other employes, as are doing service for which the negroes may be found competent." . . . [W]e propose, in addition to a modification of the President's plans, that we retain in service for the war all troops now in service, and that we immediately commence training a large reserve of the most courageous of our slaves, and further that we guarantee freedom within a reasonable time to every slave in the South who shall remain true to the Confederacy in this war. As between the loss of independence and the loss of slavery, we assume that every patriot will freely give up the latter — give up the negro slave rather than be a slave himself. If we are correct in this assumption it only remains to show how this great national sacrifice is, in all human probabilities, to change the current of success and sweep the invader from our country.

Our country has already some friends in England and France, and there are strong motives to induce these nations to recognize and assist us, but they cannot assist us without helping slavery, and to do this would be in conflict with their policy for the last quarter of a century. . . . But this barrier once removed, the sympathy and the interests of these and other nations will accord with their own, and we may expect from them both moral support and material aid. . . .

Will the slaves fight? . . . The negro slaves of Saint Domingo, fighting for freedom, defeated their white masters and the French troops sent against them. The negro slaves of Jamaica revolted, and under the name of Maroons held the mountains against their masters for 150 years; and the experience of this war has been so far that half-trained negroes have fought as bravely as many other half-trained Yankees. If, contrary to the training of a lifetime, they can be made to face and fight bravely against their former masters, how much more probable is it that with the allurement of a higher reward, and led by those masters, they would submit to discipline and face dangers.

President Jefferson Davis to General Walker, January 13, 1864. Reaction to Cleburne's Proposal.

I have received your letter, with its inclosure, informing me of the propositions [Cleburne's proposal] submitted to a meeting of the general officers on the 2d instant, and thank you for the information. Deeming it to be injurious to the public service that such a subject should be mooted, or even known to be entertained by persons possessed of the confidence and respect of the people, I have concluded that the best policy under the circumstances will be to avoid all publicity, and the Secretary of War has therefore written to General Johnston requesting him to convey to those concerned my desire that it should be kept private. If it be kept out of the public journals its ill effect will be much lessened.

General Joseph Johnston to
General Hardee et al.,
January 31, 1864. Reaction to
Cleburne's Proposal.

Lieutenant-General Hardee, Major-Generals Cheatham, Hindman, Cleburne, Stewart, Walker, Brigadier-Generals Bate and P. Anderson:

GENERAL:

I have just received a letter from the Secretary of War in reference to Major-General Cleburne's memoir read in my quarters about the 2d instant. In this letter the honorable Secretary expresses the earnest conviction of the President "that the dissemination or even promulgation of such opinions under the present circumstances of the Confederacy, whether in the Army or among the people, can be productive only of discouragement, distraction, and dissension." The agitation and controversy which must spring from the presentation of such views by officers high in the public confidence are to be deeply deprecated, and while no doubt or mistrust is for a moment entertained of the patriotic intents of the gallant author of the memorial, and such of his brother officers as may have favored his opinions, it is requested that you communicate to them, as well as all others present on the occasion, the opinions, as herein expressed, of the President, and urge on them the suppression, not only of the memorial itself, but likewise of all discussion and controversy respecting or growing out of it. . . .

Richmond Enquirer,
October 6, 1864

We should be glad to see the Confederate Congress provide for the purchase of two hundred and fifty thousand negroes, present them with their freedom and the privilege of remaining in the States, and arm, equip, drill and fight them. We believe that the negroes, identified with us by interest, and fighting for their freedom here, would be faithful and reliable soldiers, and under officers who would drill them, could be depended on for much of the hardest fighting. . . . Other States may decide for themselves, but Virginia, after exhausting her whites, will fight her blacks through to the last man. She will be free at all costs.

Mobile Register,
November 1864

If the Yankee Government comes at us again with huge armies in the spring, it will become necessary to tap a yet untouched spring of muscle and bone. The question of the use of our slaves as soldiers is one of simple expediency and necessity. If justification were needed, which it is not, the Yankees have offered it in seizing and arming the servants of the South against their masters. If our slaves are to take part in this unhappy conflict, certainly we have a choice as to the side they shall take. The independence of these States and the freedom of the master race is what we are fighting for. If we lose that in the contest, we lose our slaves as a matter of course. If we can save the first at the expense of the last, the result is so much clear gain.

From McPherson, The Negro's Civil War, *pp. 243–244.*

Judah P. Benjamin (Secretary of War, Confederacy) to Fred A. Porcher (an Old Friend and Former Classmate), December 21, 1864

For a year past I have seen that the period was fast approaching when we should be compelled to use every resource at our command for the defense of our liberties. . . . The negroes will certainly be made to fight against us if not armed for our defense. The drain of that source of our strength is steadily fatal, and irreversible by any other expedient than that of arming the slaves as an auxiliary force.

I further agree with you that if they are to fight for our freedom they are entitled to their own. Public opinion is fast ripening on the subject, and ere the close of the winter the conviction on this point will become so widespread that the Government will have no difficulty in inaugurating the policy [of recruiting Negro soldiers].

. . . It is well known that General Lee, who commands so largely the confidence of the people, is strongly in favor of our using the negroes for defense, and emancipating them, if necessary, for that purpose. Can you not yourself write a series of articles in your papers, always urging this point as the true issue, viz, is it better for the negro to fight for us or against us?

Richmond Enquirer, November 4, 1864. Letter to the Editor in Reply to the Editorial of October 6, 1864.

Can it be possible that you are serious and earnest in proposing such a step to be taken by our Government? Or were you merely discussing the matter as a something which might be done? An element of power which might be used — meaning thereby to intimidate or threaten our enemy with it as a weapon of offence which they may drive us to use? Can it be possible that a Southern man — editor of a Southern journal — recognizing the right of property in slaves, admitting their inferiority in the scale of being and also their social inferiority, would recommend the passage of a law which at one blow levels all distinctions, deprives the master of a right to his property, and elevates the negro to an equality with the white man? — for, disguise it as you may, those who fight together in a common cause, and by success win the *same* freedom, enjoy equal rights and equal position, and in this case, are distinguished only by color. Are we prepared for this? Is it for this we are contending? Is it for this we would seek the aid of our slaves? . . . When President Davis said: "We are not fighting for slavery, but independence," he meant that the question and subject of slavery was a matter settled amongst ourselves and one that admitted of no dispute — that he intended to be independent of all foreign influences on this as well as on other matters — free to own slaves if he pleased — free to lay our own taxes — free to govern ourselves. He never intended to ignore the question of slavery or to do aught else but express the determination to be *independent* in this as well as in all other matters. What has embittered the feelings of the two sections of the old Union? What has gradually driven them to the final separation? What is it that has made two nationalities of them, if it is not slavery?

The Yankee *steals* my slave, and makes a soldier and freeman of him to *destroy* me. You *take* my slave, and make a soldier and freeman of him to *defend* me. The difference in your intention is very great; but is not the practice of both equally pernicious to the slave and destruction to the country? And at the expiration of ten years after peace what would be the relative difference between my negro *stolen* and freed by the Yankee and my negro taken and freed by you? Would they not be equally worthless and vicious? How would you distinguish between them? How prevent the return of him whose hand is red with his master's blood, and his enjoyment of those privileges which you so lavishly bestow upon the faithful freedman?

Have you thought of the influence to be exerted by these half or quarter million of free negroes in the midst of slaves as you propose to leave them at the end of the war; these men constitute the bone and sinew of our slaves, the able-bodied between 18 and 45. They will be men who know the value and power of combination; they will be well disciplined, trained to the use of arms, with the power and ability of command; at the same time they will be grossly and miserably ignorant, without any fixed principle of life or the ability of acquiring one. . . .

Howell Cobb, Speech in the Confederate Senate, 1864

. . . if slaves will make good soldiers our whole theory of slavery is wrong. . . . The day you make soldiers of them is the beginning of the end of the revolution.

Robert Toombs, Speech in the Confederate Senate, 1864

. . . the worst calamity that could befall us would be to gain our independence by the valor of our slaves. . . . The day that the army of Virginia allows a negro regiment to enter their lines as soldiers they will be degraded, ruined, and disgraced.

Lynchburg (Va.) *Republican,* November 2, 1864

The proposition is so strange — so unconstitutional — so directly in conflict with all of our former practices and teachings — so entirely subversive of our social and political institutions — and so completely destructive of our liberties, that we stand completely appalled [and] dumfounded at its promulgation.

They propose that Congress shall conscribe two hundred and fifty thousand slaves, arm, equip and fight them in the field. As an inducement of them to be faithful, it is proposed that, at the end of the war, they shall have their freedom and live amongst us. "The conscription of negroes," says the *Enquirer,* "should be accompanied with freedom and the privilege of remaining in the States." This is the monstrous proposition. The South went to war to defeat the designs of the abolitionists, and behold! in the midst of the war, we turn abolitionists ourselves! We went to war because the Federal Congress kept eternally meddling with our domestic institutions, with which we contended they had nothing to do, and now we propose to end the war by asking the Confederate Congress to do precisely what Lincoln proposes to do — free our negroes and make them the equals of the white man! We have always been taught to believe that slaves are property, and under the *exclusive control of the States and the courts. This new doctrine teaches us that Congress has a right to free our negroes and make* them the equals of their masters. . . .

Richmond Examiner, November 8, 1864. Letter to the Editor.

Our enemy has raised its negro army, not as a military, but a political measure — to have the cant of the world on its side — to procure the full and consistent support of the Abolitionist party. With his views and purposes, the creation of the negro soldier is consistent and natural.

But the existence of a negro soldier is totally inconsistent with our political aim and with our social as well as political system. We surrender our position whenever we introduce the negro to arms. If a negro is fit to be a soldier he is not fit to be a slave, and if any large portion of the race is fit for free labour — fit to live and to be useful under the competitive system of labour — then the whole race is fit for it. The employment of negroes as soldiers in our armies, either with or without prospective emancipation, would be the first step, but a step which would involve all the rest, to universal abolition.

Macon (Ga.) Telegraph and Confederate, January 11, 1865

Mr. Editor:

A lady's opinion may not be worth much in such an hour as this, but I cannot resist the temptation of expressing my approbation of "The crisis — the Remedy," copied from the Mobile Register. Would to God our Government would act upon its suggestions at once. The women of the South are not so in love with their negro property, as to wish to see husbands, fathers, sons, brothers, slain to protect it; nor would they submit to Yankee rule, could it secure to them a thousand waiting maids, whence now they possess one. We cannot believe that a loss of one fifth of the negro men would seriously damage our prospects for provisions. For four years, one fifth or more of the negro women on plantations, have been engaged in making clothes. Will not the ladies and misses of our land undertake a part of this necessary labor, and send the negro women to the field, to take the places of the negro men who go to the army. Yes, let every lady and little girl in our land, go to spinning and weaving with all their might; and let the little boys cultivate the gardens. If the city ladies do not wish to spin, or weave, let them send their surplus house servants to the country, to assist in raising provisions, (hire them out if they own no farm) and do more of their house work themselves — better this, than serving a Yankee woman. Some thoughtless women may laugh at this suggestion. I pray God they may never repent not having aided in this struggle for their independence. . . . Listen no longer to the croakings of the skulkers at home, who in the absence of the brave have, alas, done too much towards cooling the patriotism of our noble women.

All legislative and military authority has failed and will doubtless continue to fail in bringing out the "home guards" to their duty. There seems to be but one remedy — the negro — and if our brave and good soldiers are willing to call him to their aid, why not let it be done before it is too late.

Richmond Whig,
February 28, 1865

Mobile, Feb. 14. — One of the largest meetings ever assembled in Mobile was held at the Theatre last night, which was presided over by Hon. Judge Forsyth.

Resolutions were unanimously adopted declaring our unalterable purpose to sustain the civil and military authorities to achieve independence — that our battle-cry henceforth should be — "Victory or Death" — that there is now no middle-ground between treachery and patriotism — that we still have an abiding confidence in our ability to achieve our independence — that the Government should immediately place one hundred thousand negroes in the field — that reconstruction is no longer an open question.

**Confederate Congress, "An Act
to Increase the Military Force
of the Confederate States,"
March 13, 1865**

The Congress of the Confederate States of America do enact, That in order to provide additional forces to repel invasion, maintain the rightful possession of the Confederate States, secure their independence, and preserve their institutions, the President be, and he is hereby, authorized to ask for and accept from the owners of slaves, the services of such number of able-bodied negro men as he may deem expedient, for and during the war, to perform military service in whatever capacity he may direct.

Sec. 2. That the General-in-Chief be authorized to organize the said slaves into companies, battalions, regiments and brigades, under such rules and regulations as the Secretary of War may prescribe, and to be commanded by such officers as the President may appoint.

Sec. 3. That while employed in the service the said troops shall receive the same rations, clothing and compensation as are allowed to other troops in the same branch of the service.

Sec. 4. That if, under the previous sections of this act, the President shall not be able to raise a sufficient number of troops to prosecute the war successfully and maintain the sovereignty of the States and the independence of the Confederate States, then he is hereby authorized to call on each State, whenever he thinks it expedient, for her quota of 300,000 troops, in addition to those subject to military service under existing laws, or so many thereof as the President may deem necessary to be raised from such classes of the population, irrespective of color, in each State, as the proper authorities thereof may determine: *Provided,* that not more than twenty-five per cent of the male slaves between the ages of eighteen and forty-five, in any State, shall be called for under the provisions of this act.

Sec. 5. That nothing in this act shall be construed to authorize a change in the relation which the said slaves shall bear toward their owners, except by consent of the owners and of the States in which they may reside, and in pursuance of the laws thereof.

Approved, March 13, 1865.

General Robert E. Lee to Ethelbert Barksdale (Confederate Congressman from Mississippi Who Favored Arming Slaves), February 18, 1865

I should therefore prefer to rely upon our white population to preserve the ratio between our forces and those of the enemy, which experience has shown to be safe. But in view of the preparations of our enemies, it is our duty to provide for continued war and not for a battle or a campaign, and I fear that we cannot accomplish this without overtaxing the capacity of our white population. . . . I think, therefore, we must decide whether slavery shall be extinguished by our enemies and the slaves be used against us, or use them ourselves at the risk of the effects which may be produced upon our social institutions. My own opinion is that we should employ them without delay. I believe that with proper regulations they can be made efficient soldiers. They possess the physical qualifications in an eminent degree. Long habits of obedience and subordination, coupled with the moral influence which in our country the white man possesses over the black, furnish an excellent foundation for that discipline which is the best guaranty of military efficiency. Our chief aim should be to secure their fidelity.

There have been formidable armies composed of men having no interest in the cause for which they fought beyond their pay or the hope of plunder. But it is certain that the surest foundation upon which the fidelity of an army can rest, especially in a service which imposes peculiar hardships and privations, is the personal interest of the soldier in the issue of the contest. Such an interest we can give our negroes by giving immediate freedom to all who enlist, and freedom at the end of the war to the families of those who discharge their duties faithfully (whether they survive or not), together with the privilege of residing at the South. To this might be added a bounty for faithful service.

We should not expect slaves to fight for prospective freedom when they can secure it at once by going to the enemy, in whose service they will incur no greater risk than in ours. The reasons that induce me to recommend the employment of negro troops at all render the effect of the measures I have suggested upon slavery immaterial, and in my opinion the best means of securing the efficiency and fidelity of this auxiliary force would be to accompany the measure with a well-digested plan of gradual and general emancipation. As that will be the result of the continuance of the war, and will certainly occur if the enemy succeed, it seems to be most advisable to adopt it at once, and thereby obtain all the benefits that will accrue to our cause.

Presidential Order,
"General Orders, No. 14,"
March 23, 1865

[*Sections I–III dealt with the setting up of a machinery for recruiting slaves.*]

IV. The enlistment of colored persons under this act will be made upon printed forms. . . . No slave will be accepted as a recruit unless with his own consent and with the approbation of his master by a written instrument conferring, as far as he may, the rights of a freedman, and which will be filed with the superintendent. The enlistments will be made for the war, and the effect of the enlistment will be to place the slave in the military service conformably to this act. The recruits will be organized at the camps in squads and companies, and will be subject to the orders of the General-in-Chief under the second section of this act.

[*Sections V–VIII dealt with reporting recruitment progress, appointment of officers, and mustering of volunteers.*]

IX. All officers who may be employed in the recruiting service, under the provisions of this act, or who may be appointed to the command of troops raised under it, or who may hold any staff appointment in connection with them, are enjoined to a provident, considerate, and humane attention to whatever concerns the health, comfort, instruction, and discipline of those troops, and to the uniform observance of kindness, forbearance, and indulgence in their treatment of them, and especially that they will protect them from injustice and oppression.

Questions to Consider

At this point, it is helpful to review the questions asked in the Method section of this chapter. Questions 1 and 2 are straightforward, the first asking for a list of pro and con arguments on each side, and the second for a comparison of the arguments of the North and South to discover similarities and differences.

Questions 3, 4, and 5, however, require some historical imagination and a considerably broader look at the evidence. For Question 3, you must determine how whites in the North and the South felt about blacks and racial equality. In order to do this, you will have to look behind the evidence for underlying or unstated opinions. For example, on the surface President Lincoln's remarks on September 13, 1862, give no hint of any racial feelings. A closer examination, however, reveals Lincoln's attitudes about blacks and their ability to fight. By employing such care with each piece of evidence, you will gradually form a composite picture of racial opinions in the North and the South.

Question 4 requires you to use the evidence in another, distinctly different, way. As you will see, the evidence will tell you different things depending on the question that you ask. Here you are instructed to identify and analyze some of the factors influencing the shifts of policy in the North and in

the South regarding the use of blacks as soldiers. It will not be possible for you to determine with certainty which argument was the most important, largely because we do not have any evidence to suggest why Lincoln and Davis changed their positions. You will, however, be able to identify some of the important factors.

As an example of how asking different questions can elicit different responses from the evidence, look again at Lincoln's remarks of September 13, 1862. Earlier you were asked to use this piece of evidence to try to detect any racial opinions the president possessed. Now look again at the same remarks, asking why Lincoln refused in 1862 to approve the use of black soldiers. With this question in mind, examine each piece of evidence again.

Finally look at Question 5. In many ways this is the most difficult question, for its ask you to assess the implications of the decisions. The military implications are not hard to discover (see the Epilogue for help). But the social and ideological implications are considerably more difficult to measure. To begin with, go back to Questions 1 and 4. What do the answers to these questions have to say about social and ideological implications? For example, did whites accept the idea that enlisting blacks as soldiers would make them equal? Did the North and South differ in this regard? What does this tell you? How can the evidence

[185]

written by blacks (the northern blacks' petition and Frederick Douglass' editorial) help you here? In other words, except for the military situation, was it likely that the arming of blacks would lead to a change in their social ranks or in whites' perceptions of blacks? Why or why not? Supplementary reading may be extremely helpful here, especially in providing background on the status of blacks and on white racial opinions *after* the Civil War.

Epilogue

Even after northern leaders adopted the policy that blacks would be recruited as soldiers in the Union army, many white northerners still doubted whether blacks would volunteer and, if they did, whether they would fight. Yet the evidence overwhelmingly demonstrates that blacks rushed to the colors and were an effective part of the Union war effort. By the end of the Civil War, approximately 190,000 black men had served in the United States Army and Navy, a figure that represents roughly 10 percent of all the North's fighting men throughout the entire war. The blacks participated in approximately four hundred engagements, including thirty-nine major battles. Black casualties were high: over one-third of the black soldiers were killed or

wounded, although the majority of deaths, as with white soldiers, came from disease rather than from battle wounds. The percentage of desertions among blacks was lower than for the army as a whole. Moreover, twenty-one black soldiers and sailors were awarded congressional medals of honor, the nation's most distinguished award to military personnel.

Yet there is another side to the story of black service in the Union army and navy. Black volunteers were rigidly segregated, serving in all-black regiments, usually under white officers. At first black troops received less pay than their white counterparts. However, after many petitions and protests by black soldiers, Congress at last established the principle of equal pay for black soldiers in June 1864. Unfortunately racial incidents within the Union army and navy were not uncommon.

Within the Confederacy, the adoption of the policy to recruit black soldiers came too late, the last gasp of a dying nation that had debated too long between principle and survival. In the month between the approval of the policy and the end of the war at Appomattox Court House, some black companies were organized, but there is no record that they ever saw action. For a conflict that had raged for four agonizingly long years, the end came relatively quickly.

The debate over the use of black troops points out what many abolitionists had maintained for years: while slavery was a moral concern that consumed all who touched it, the institution of slavery was but part of the problem facing black — and white — Americans. More insidious and less easily eradicated was racism, a set of assumptions, feelings, and emotions that survived long after slavery had been destroyed. The debate in both the North and the South over the use of black troops clearly demonstrates that the true problem confronting many people of the Civil War era was their own feelings, anxieties, and fears.

Chapter 10

Reconstructing Reconstruction: The Political Cartoonist and the National Mood

The Problem

By early 1865 it was evident to most northerners and southerners that the Civil War was nearly over. While Grant was hammering at Lee's depleted forces in Virginia, Union general William Tecumseh Sherman broke the back of the Confederacy with his devastating march through Georgia and then northward into the Carolinas. Atlanta fell to Sherman's troops in September 1864, Savannah in December, and Charleston and Columbia, South Carolina, in February 1865. Two-thirds of Columbia lay in ashes. Meanwhile General Philip Sheridan had driven the Confederates out of the Shenandoah Valley of Virginia, thus blocking any escape attempts by Lee and further cutting southern supply routes. The Union naval blockade of the South was taking its fearful toll, as parts of the dying Confederacy were facing real privation. Hence, although northern armies had suffered terrible losses, by 1865 they stood poised on the brink of victory.

In the South all but the extreme die-hards recognized that defeat was inevitable. The Confederacy was suffering in more ways than militarily. The Confederate economy had almost completely collapsed and Confederate paper money was nearly worthless. Slaves were abandoning their masters and mistresses in record numbers, running away to Union armies or roaming through the South in search of better opportunities. In many areas civilian morale had almost totally deteriorated, and one Georgian wrote, "The people are soul-sick and heartily tired of the hateful, hopeless strife. . . . We have had enough of want and woe, of cruelty and carnage, enough of cripples and corpses."[1] As the Confederate government made secret plans to evacuate Richmond, most southerners knew that the end was very near.

Yet, even with victory almost in hand, many northerners had given little thought to what should happen after the war was over. Would southerners accept the life-style changes that defeat would almost inevitably force on them (most especially the end of slavery)? What demands should the victors make upon the vanquished? Should the North assist the South in rebuilding after the devastation of war? If so, should the North dictate how that rebuilding, or reconstruction, should take place? What efforts should the North make to insure that the former slaves were receiving the rights of free men and women? During the war few northerners had seriously considered these questions. Now that victory was within their grasp, they could not avoid them.

One person who had been wrestling with these questions was Abraham Lincoln. In December 1863 the president announced his own plan for reconstructing the South, a plan in keeping with his later hope, as expressed in his second inaugural address, for "malice toward none; with charity for all; . . . Let us . . . bind up the nation's wounds."[2] In Lincoln's plan a southern state could resume its normal activities in the Union as soon as 10 percent of the voters of 1860 had taken an oath of loyalty to the United States. High-ranking Confederate leaders would be excluded, and some blacks might gain the right to vote. No mention was made of protecting the civil rights of former slaves, and it was presumed that this would be left to their former masters and mistresses.

To many northerners, later known as Radical Republicans, Lincoln's plan was much too lenient. In the opinion of these people, a number of whom had been abolitionists, the South, when conquered, should not be allowed to return to its former ways and life-style. Not only should slavery be eradicated, they claimed, but freed blacks should be assisted in their efforts to attain economic, social, and political equity. Most of the Radical Republicans favored education for blacks, and some advocated carving

---

1. The letter probably was written by Georgian Herschel V. Walker. See Allan Nevins, *The Organized War to Victory, 1864–1865*, Vol. IV of *The War for the Union* (New York: Charles Scribner's Sons, 1971), p. 221.

2. The full text of Lincoln's second inaugural address, delivered on March 4, 1865, can be found in Roy P. Basler, ed., *The Collected Works of Abraham Lincoln*, Vol. VIII (New Brunswick, N.J.: Rutgers University Press, 1953), pp. 332–333.

Chapter 10
Reconstructing
Reconstruction:
The Political
Cartoonist and the
National Mood

the South's plantations into small parcels to be given to the freedmen. To implement these reforms, Radical Republicans wanted detachments of the United States Army to remain in the South and favored the appointment of provisional governors to oversee the transitional governments in the southern states. Lincoln approved plans for the Army to stay and supported the idea of provisional governors. But he opposed the more far-reaching reform notions of the Radical Republicans, and as president was able to block them.

In addition to having diametrically opposed views of Reconstruction, Lincoln and the Radical Republicans differed over the constitutional question of which branch of the federal government would be responsible for the reconstruction of the South. The Constitution made no mention of secession, reunion, or reconstruction. But Radical Republicans, citing passages in the Constitution giving Congress the power to guarantee each state a republican government, insisted that the reconstruction of the South should be carried out by Congress.[3] For his part, however, Lincoln maintained that, as chief enforcer of the law and as commander in chief, the president was the appropriate person to be in charge of Reconstruction. Clearly a stalemate was in the making, with Radical Republicans calling for a more reform-minded Reconstruction policy and Lincoln continuing to block them.

President Lincoln's death on April 15, 1865 (one week after Lee's surrender at Appomattox Court House),[4] brought Vice-President Andrew Johnson to the nation's highest office. At first, Radical Republicans had reason to hope that the new president would follow policies more to their liking. A Tennessean, Johnson had risen to political prominence from humble circumstances, had become a spokesperson for the common white men and women of the South, and had opposed the planter aristocracy. Upon becoming president, he excluded from amnesty all former Confederate political and military leaders as well as all southerners who owned taxable property worth more than $20,000 (an obvious slap at his old planter-aristocrat foes). Moreover, Johnson issued a proclamation setting up provisional military governments in the conquered South and told his cabinet he favored black suffrage, although as a states' rightist, he insisted that states adopt the measure voluntarily. At the outset, then, Johnson, appeared to be all the Radical Republicans had hoped

3. See Article IV, Section 4, of the Constitution. Later Radical Republicans also justified their position using the Thirteenth Amendment, adopted in 1865, which gave Congress the power to enforce the amendment ending slavery in the South.

4. The last Confederate army to give up, commanded by General Joseph Johnston, surrendered to Sherman at Durham Station, North Carolina, on April 18, 1865.

for, far preferable to the more moderate Lincoln.

Yet it did not take Radical Republicans long to realize that President Johnson was not one of them. Although he spoke harshly, he pardoned hundreds of former Confederates who quickly captured control of southern state governments and congressional delegations. Many northerners were shocked to see former Confederate generals, officials, and even former Confederate vice-president Alexander Stephens returned to Washington. The new southern state legislatures passed a series of laws, known collectively as black codes, that so severely restricted the rights of former slaves that they were all but slaves again. Moreover, Johnson privately told southerners that he opposed the Fourteenth Amendment to the Constitution, which was intended to confer full civil rights on the newly freed slaves. He also used his veto power to block Radical Republican Reconstruction measures in Congress and seemed to do little to combat the general defiance of the former Confederacy (exhibited in many forms, including insults thrown at Union occupation soldiers, the desecration of the United States flag, and the formation of organized resistance groups such as the Ku Klux Klan).

To an increasing number of northerners, the unrepentant spirit of the South and Johnson's acquiescence to it were nothing short of appalling. Had the Civil War been fought for nothing? Had over 364,000 federal soldiers died in vain? White southerners were openly defiant, blacks were being subjugated by white southerners and virtually ignored by President Johnson, and former Confederates were returning to positions of power and prominence. Radical Republicans had sufficient power in Congress to pass harsher measures, but Johnson kept vetoing them and the Radicals lacked the votes to override his vetoes. Indeed, the impasse that had existed before Lincoln's death continued.

In such an atmosphere the congressional elections of 1866 were bitterly fought campaigns, especially in the northern states. President Johnson traveled throughout the North, defending his moderate plan of Reconstruction and viciously attacking his political enemies. However, the Radical Republicans were even more effective. Stirring up the hostilities of wartime, they "waved the bloody shirt" and excited northern voters by charging that the South had never accepted its defeat and that the 364,000 Union dead and 275,000 wounded would be for nothing if the South was permitted to continue its arrogant and stubborn behavior. Increasingly, Johnson was greeted by hostile audiences as the North underwent a major shift in public opinion.

The Radical Republicans won a stunning victory in the congressional election and thus broke the stalemate between Congress and the president.

Chapter 10
Reconstructing
Reconstruction:
The Political
Cartoonist and the
National Mood

Armed with enough votes to override Johnson's vetoes, the new Congress proceeded rapidly to implement the Radical Republican vision of Reconstruction. The South was divided into five military districts to be ruled by martial law. Southern states had to ratify the Fourteenth Amendment and institute black suffrage before being allowed to take their formal places in the Union. The Freedmen's Bureau, founded earlier, was given additional federal support to set up schools for blacks, negotiate labor contracts, and, with the military, help monitor elections. Only the proposal to give land to blacks was not adopted, being seen as too extreme by even some Radical Republicans. Congressional Reconstruction had begun.

President Johnson, however, had not been left completely powerless. Determined to undercut the Radical Republicans' Reconstruction policies, he issued orders increasing the powers of civil governments in the South and removed military officers who were enforcing Congress's will, replacing them with commanders less determined to protect black voting rights and more willing to turn the other way when disqualified white southerners voted. Opposed most vigorously by his own secretary of war, Edwin Stanton, Johnson tried to discharge Stanton. To an increasing number of Radicals, the president would have to be removed from office.

In 1868 the House of Representatives voted to impeach Andrew John-son. The president was tried in the Senate, where two-thirds of the senators would have to vote against Johnson for him to be removed.[5] The vast majority of senators disagreed with the president's Reconstruction policies. Yet they feared that impeachment had become a political tool that, if successful, threatened to destroy the balance of power between the branches of the federal government. The vote on removal fell one short of the necessary two-thirds, and Johnson was spared the indignity of removal. Nevertheless, the Republican nomination of General Ulysses Grant and his subsequent landslide victory (running as a military hero, Grant carried twenty-six out of thirty-four states) gave Radical Republicans a malleable president, one who, although not a Radical himself, could assure the continuation of their vision of Reconstruction.

By 1872 a renewed Democratic party believed it had a chance to oust Grant and the Republicans. For one thing, the Grant administration had been rocked by a series of scandals, some of them involving men quite close to the president. Although honest himself, Grant lost a good deal of popularity by defending the culprits and naively aiding in a cover-up of the corruption. These actions, along with some of his other policies, triggered a revolt within the Republican party, in

5. See Article I, Sections 2 and 3, of the Constitution.

which a group calling themselves Liberal Republicans bolted the party ranks and nominated well-known editor and reformer Horace Greeley to oppose Grant for the presidency. Hoping for a coalition to defeat Grant, the Democrats also nominated the controversial Greeley.

Greeley's platform was designed to attract as many disparate groups of voters as possible to the Liberal Republican–Democratic political fold. Greeley favored civil service reform, the return to a "hard money" fiscal policy, and the reservation of western lands for settlers rather than for large land companies. He vowed an end to corruption in government. But the most dramatic part of Greeley's message was his call for an end to the bitterness of the Civil War, a thinly veiled promise to bring an end to Radical Reconstruction in the South. For their part, Radical Republicans attacked Greeley as the tool of die-hard southerners and labeled him as the candidate of white southern bigots and northern urban Irish immigrants manipulated by political machines. They took one of Greeley's phrases, "Let us shake hands over the bloody chasm" (a phrase with which Greeley intended to state his hope for an end to sectional hostilities), and warped that utterance almost beyond recognition. By contrast, Grant was labeled as a great war hero and a friend of blacks and whites alike. The incumbent Grant won easily, capturing 55 percent of the popular vote and 286 electoral votes. Greeley died soon after the exhausting campaign.

Gradually, however, the zeal of Radical Republicanism began to fade. An increasing number of northerners grew tired of the issue. With their commitment to full civil rights for blacks never strong, they had voted into office Radical Republicans more out of anger at southern intransigence than out of any lofty notions of black equality. Hence northerners said little when, one by one, southern Democrats returned to power in the states of the former Confederacy.[6] As a mark of how little their own attitudes had changed in the years since the Civil War, white southerners labeled these native Democrats "Redeemers." Yet, as long as southern Democrats made no overt moves to subvert the rights of blacks, most northerners were willing to put the whole agony of Reconstruction behind them. Hence, while much that was fruitful and beneficial was accomplished in the South during the Reconstruction period (most notably black suffrage and public education), some of this was to be temporary, and many opportunities for progress were lost. By the presidential election of 1876, both candi-

6. Southerners regained control of the state governments in Tennessee and Virginia in 1869, North Carolina in 1870, Georgia in 1871, Arkansas and Alabama in 1874, and Mississippi in early 1876. By the presidential election of 1876, only South Carolina, Louisiana, and Florida were still controlled by Reconstruction governments.

Chapter 10
Reconstructing
Reconstruction:
The Political
Cartoonist and the
National Mood

dates (Rutherford B. Hayes and Samuel Tilden) promised an end to Reconstruction, and the Radical Republican experiment to all intents and purposes was over.

Many Americans formed their opinions about the events surrounding Reconstruction from newspapers. Especially influential were editorial cartoons, which captured the issues visually, often simplifying them so that virtually everyone could understand them. Perhaps the master of this style was Thomas Nast, a political cartoonist whose career, principally with *Harper's Weekly,* spanned the tumultuous years of the Civil War and Reconstruction. Congratulating themselves for having hired Nast, the editors of *Harper's Weekly* once exclaimed that each of Nast's drawings was at once "a poem and a speech."

Apparently Thomas Nast developed his talents early in life. Born in the German Palatinate (one of the German states) in 1840, Nast was the son of a musician in the Ninth Regiment Bavarian Band. The family moved to New York City in 1846, at which time young Thomas was enrolled in school. It seems that art was his only interest — one teacher admonished him, "Go finish your picture. You will never learn to read or figure." After unsuccessfully trying to interest their son in music, his parents eventually encouraged the development of his artistic talent. By the age of fifteen, Thomas Nast was drawing illustrations for *Frank Leslie's Illustrated Newspaper.* He joined *Harper's Weekly* in 1862 (at the age of twenty-two), where he developed the cartoon style that was to win him a national reputation, as well as enemies. One of Nast's favorite targets, political boss William Marcy Tweed of New York's Tammany Hall, once shouted, "Let's stop these damn pictures. I don't care so much what the papers say about me — my constituents can't read; but damn it, they can see pictures!"

It is obvious from his work that Thomas Nast was a man of strong feelings and emotions. In his eyes, those people whom he admired possessed no flaws. Conversely, those whom he opposed were, to him, capable of every conceivable villainy. As a result his characterizations were often terribly unfair, gross distortions of reality, and more than occasionally slanderous. In his view, however, his central purpose was not to entertain but to move his audiences, to make them scream out in outrage or anger, to prod them to action.

Your task in this chapter is twofold:

1. By examining selected political cartoons of Thomas Nast dealing with Reconstruction, determine how Nast attempted to influence public opinion on Reconstruction's major issues.

2. By contrasting each cartoon with the treatment of Reconstruction in the introduction to this chapter and in supplementary readings, determine the extent to which Nast's illustrations

did or did not reflect northern public opinion at different times on the issues of Reconstruction.

Note carefully that the task is a dual one. All political cartoonists attempt to influence public opinion. Sometimes they are successful, sometimes not. To complete both parts of the assignment, you will have to do the following:

1. Read the introduction to this chapter and supplementary texts carefully to identify the principal issues of Reconstruction. You will want to make a list of those issues.

2. Examine closely the cartoons presented to determine where Nast stood on those issues.

3. Return to your readings to determine how the general public responded to those issues *at different times* during the Reconstruction period.

4. Finally, assess the extent to which Nast's illustrations did or did not reflect northern public opinion at different times on the issues of Reconstruction. Remember that public opinion shifts and changes. The public's stand on an issue at one point in time may not be its position at another point in time.

Public opinion is not always easy to measure. But we do have certain clues. Election results, for example, are a good gauge of public opinion. So are audience responses to speakers

(recall the audiences that President Johnson faced in 1866). As you read, looking for public opinion, be sensitive to these clues.

The Method

Although Thomas Nast developed the political cartoon into a true art form, cartoons and caricatures had a long tradition both in Europe and America before Nast. English artists helped to bring forth the cartoon style that eventually made *Punch* (founded in 1841) one of the liveliest-illustrated periodicals on both sides of the Atlantic. In America, Benjamin Franklin is traditionally credited with publishing the first newspaper cartoon in 1754, the multidivided snake (each part of the snake representing one colony) with the ominous warning "Join or Die." By the time Andrew Jackson sought the presidency, the political cartoon had become a regular and popular feature of American political life. Crude by modern standards, these cartoons influenced some people far more than did the printed word.

As noted above, the political cartoon, like the newspaper editorial, is intended to do more than objectively report events. It is meant to express an opinion, a point of view. Cartoons often praise or ridicule. Those who create them want to move people, anger them, make them laugh, or spur

Chapter 10
Reconstructing
Reconstruction:
The Political
Cartoonist and the
National Mood

them to action. In short, political cartoons are poor devices for learning what was happening, but they are excellent devices for portraying popular reaction to what was happening.

How, then, can we analyze political cartoons? To begin with, cartoons almost always portray events. As you examine the cartoons in this chapter, try to determine what event is being portrayed. Often a cartoon's caption, dialogue, or other clues will help you to discover the event in question. By careful scrutiny, can you discern what the cartoonist's opinion of the event is? Is he or she approving or disapproving? How did you reach that conclusion?

Examine the people in each cartoon. Is the cartoonist aiming for a true likeness? Is he or she portraying the people sympathetically or unsympathetically? Nast often placed his characters out of their historical context (in Roman circuses, for example). Why did he do this? What did he intend to show? Sometimes cartoonists accentuate their subjects' physical features. Why do they do this?

After you examine a cartoon in detail, try to determine the message the cartoonist is trying to convey. What reactions does he or she hope those who see the cartoon will have? What do you think people's reactions might have been at the time the cartoon was published?

Before you begin the exercises in this chapter, it might be well to familiarize yourself both with the method discussed above and with Nast by making a "trial run" on one of Nast's cartoons on another subject, that of public subsidy of private schools.

In 1868 the New York state legislature ruled that public funds could be made available to private schools. Most of the schools that benefited from this law were parochial schools of the Roman Catholic Church. Shortly thereafter, Roman Catholics complained about the compulsory use of the King James Version of the Bible in public schools.

The cartoon shown in Figure 1 appeared in *Harper's Weekly* on September 30, 1871. It graphically shows Nast's opinion on the issue. Examine the cartoon carefully. How are Roman Catholic clergymen portrayed? In the upper right, who is the woman being led to the gallows, and who is leading her? To the left of that, who are the adults at the top of the cliff and what are they doing? In what condition are the public schools? What is Tammany Hall (upper left), and what is the building intended to look like? In the foreground, what is stuck in the largest child's coat? What are the reactions of the children? Finally, what was Thomas Nast's opinion of Tammany Hall? The Irish Americans? The New York state legislature? The Roman Catholic Church? What feelings was Nast trying to elicit from those who saw this cartoon?

As you can see, a political cartoon must be analyzed to the most minute detail in order to get the full meaning

FIGURE 1 *(From Morton Keller, The Art and Politics of Thomas Nast (New York: Oxford University Press, © 1968), Plate 108. Courtesy of the publisher.)*

THE AMERICAN RIVER GANGES.

The Priests and the Children.

September 30, 1871.

[197]

Chapter 10
Reconstructing
Reconstruction:
The Political
Cartoonist and the
National Mood

the cartoonist is trying to convey. From that analysis, one can discover the creator's full meaning or message and can imagine the emotions the cartoon was likely to evoke.

Now you are ready to begin your analysis of the Reconstruction period through the cartoons of Thomas Nast. As you analyze each cartoon, be aware of the collective message of *all* of the cartoons. Most subscribers to *Harper's Weekly* saw all of the cartoons. What was their general reaction likely to be?

The Evidence

Figures 2 through 9 from Morton Keller, The Art and Politics of Thomas Nast *(New York: Oxford University Press, © 1968), Plates 14 (Figure 2), 55 and 56 (Figure 3), 22 (Figure 4), 27 (Figure 5), 32 (Figure 6), 47 (Figure 7), 48 (Figure 8), and 50 (Figure 9). Courtesy of the publisher. Figure 10 from J. Chal Vinson,* Thomas Nast, Political Cartoonist *(Athens: University of Georgia Press, © 1967), Plate 103. Courtesy of the publisher.*

FIGURE 2

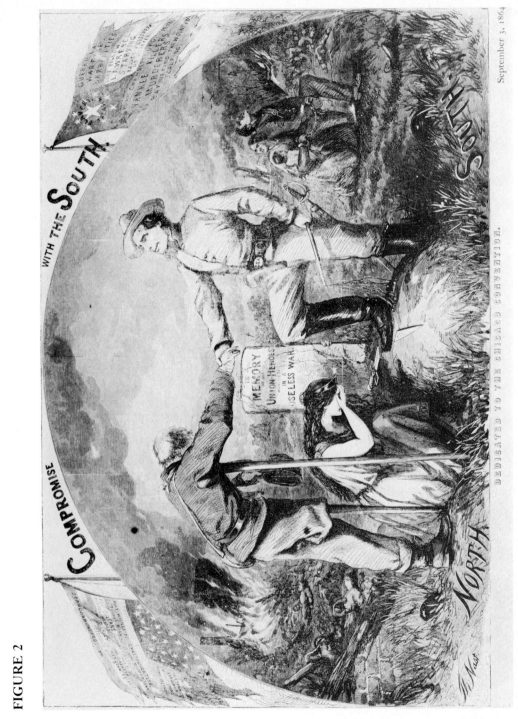

Chapter 10
Reconstructing
Reconstruction:
The Political
Cartoonist and the
National Mood

FIGURE 3

PARDON.

Columbia.—"Shall I Trust These Men,

FRANCHISE.   August 5, 1865

And Not This Man?''

Chapter 10
Reconstructing
Reconstruction:
The Political
Cartoonist and the
National Mood

FIGURE 4

THE CONTRAST OF SUFFERING ANDERSONVILLE & FORTRESS MONROE.

TREASON MUST BE MADE ODIOUS.

June 30, 1866

FIGURE 5 *The Evidence*

September 5, 1868

"This Is a White Man's Government."

"We regard the Reconstruction Acts (so called) of Congress as usurpations, and unconstitutional, revolutionary, and void."—*Democratic Platform.*

FIGURE 6

The Modern Samson.

FIGURE 7 *The Evidence*

Baltimore 1861–1872.

"Let Us Clasp Hands over the Bloody Chasm."

August 3, 1872

FIGURE 8

"Let Us Clasp Hands over the Bloody Chasm."—Horace Greeley.

FIGURE 9   *The Evidence*

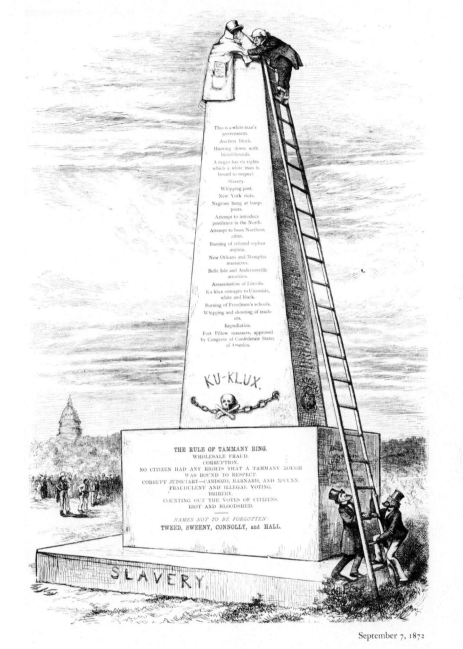

This is a white man's
government.
Auction block.
Hunting down with
blood-hounds.
A negro has no rights
which a white man is
bound to respect.
Slavery.
Whipping-post.
New York riots.
Negroes hung at lamp-
posts.
Attempt to introduce
pestilence in the North.
Attempt to burn Northern
cities.
Burning of colored orphan
asylum.
New Orleans and Memphis
massacres.
Belle Isle and Andersonville
atrocities.
Assassination of Lincoln.
Ku-klux outrages to Unionists,
white and black.
Burning of Freedmen's schools.
Whipping and shooting of teach-
ers.
Repudiation.
Fort Pillow massacre, approved
by Congress of Confederate States
of America.

KU-KLUX.

THE RULE OF TAMMANY RING.
WHOLESALE FRAUD.
CORRUPTION.
NO CITIZEN HAD ANY RIGHTS THAT A TAMMANY ROUGH
WAS BOUND TO RESPECT.
CORRUPT JUDICIARY—CARDOZO, BARNARD, AND M'CUNN.
FRAUDULENT AND ILLEGAL VOTING.
BRIBERY.
COUNTING OUT THE VOTES OF CITIZENS.
RIOT AND BLOODSHED.

NAMES NOT TO BE FORGOTTEN:
TWEED, SWEENY, CONNOLLY, and HALL.

SLAVERY

September 7, 1872

The Whited Sepulchre.

Covering the monument of infamy with his white hat and coat.

[207]

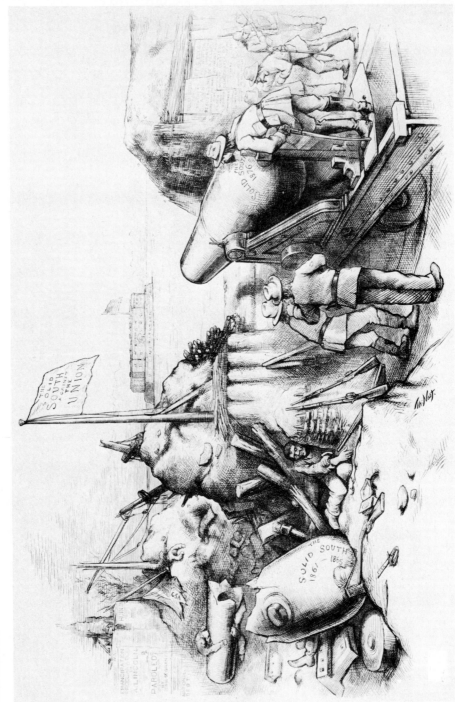

FIGURE 10

Questions to Consider

A review of the process you must use to complete this exercise should prove helpful. First, you are to identify the principal issues of the Reconstruction period. Second, determine where Nast stood on each of those issues. Third, describe how the general northern public stood on these issues at different times during the period (using clues such as election results). And, fourth, determine the extent to which Nast's illustrations did or did not reflect northern public opinion at different times on each of these issues. The process readily lends itself to a chart:

Issues:

Nast's Position:

Public Opinion:

Did Nast Reflect?

A close reading of the introduction to this chapter and supplementary texts will provide the data for the first and third rows, and an examination of Nast's cartoons will help you fill in the second row. Then, by comparing the second and third rows, you should be able to answer the question, "Did Nast reflect?"

Figures 2 to 6 represent Thomas Nast's view of the immediate aftermath of the Civil War and the early years of Reconstruction. The next three figures (7, 8, and 9) focus on the presidential election of 1872, and the last cartoon (Figure 10) evaluates the South of the late 1870s, at the end of Reconstruction. You will be looking at these cartoons first individually and then in relation to one another.

Look at the title and date of the cartoon in Figure 2. To what event was Nast referring? Who are the two men shaking hands? How do you explain the contrast in their appearances? Who is the woman by the grave, and why is she crying? What is being shown in both the right and the left background? What do the two flags symbolize? When the cartoon is taken as a whole, what emotions was Nast trying to arouse in his readers?

Figure 3 must first be examined for its symbolism. Who is Columbia? What emotions do her two different poses suggest? Who are the people asking for pardon in the first frame? Now look carefully at the black man in the second frame — who does he represent? Can you formulate one sentence that summarizes the message of both parts of Figure 3?

Chapter 10
Reconstructing
Reconstruction:
The Political
Cartoonist and the
National Mood

Figure 4 is more complex: two drawings within two other drawings. If you do not already know, consult a text on this time period, an encyclopedia, or a good Civil War history book to discover what purpose Andersonville and Fortress Monroe served. Then look at the upper left and right outside drawings. Contrast the appearance of the man entering with the man leaving. Now examine the lower left and right outside drawings the same way. What was Nast trying to tell you? The explanation of the contrast is found in the larger inside drawings. What were the conditions like at Andersonville? At Fortress Monroe? What did the cartoonist think were the physical and psychological results?

Each of the three people standing in Figure 5 represents part of the Democratic Party coalition, and each has something to contribute to the party. Can you identify the groups that are being represented by the man on the right and the man in the center? What do they offer the party? Notice the facial features of the man on the left as well as his dress, particularly the hatband from Five Points (a notorious slum section of New York City). Who is this man supposed to represent, and what does he give the party? Notice what the black man lying on the ground has dropped. Who does he represent? What is he reaching for? What is happening in the background of the cartoon?

Figure 6 also explores the question

of rights for freed blacks, this time within the setting of the well-known story of Samson and Delilah. Who is Nast's Delilah, and what has she done? Who are her supporters at the left? What other things do they advocate? Now look carefully at the figure in the upper right-hand corner. Who is he? What has he promised blacks? What has he done?

Figures 7, 8, and 9 were all published just before the election of 1872. Who is the plump little man with the white beard and glasses who appears in all three cartoons? What part of this character's campaign did Nast find especially objectionable? Why? What is wrong with what the character is trying to do? (Since these cartoons show many reasons for Nast's disgust, you might find it helpful to keep a list as you study each separately.)

The last cartoon (Figure 10) shows Nast's opinion of the South in 1876, near the end of Reconstruction. What scene was Nast re-creating? Of what significance is this? How is the black man depicted? What was Nast trying to show?

You should now return to the questions asked in the Problem section of this chapter (and perhaps to supplementary readings). What were the major issues and events of the Reconstruction period? Who were the principal personalities? Think about all of Nast's cartoons collectively. In what ways did Nast try to influence public opinion about these events, issues, and people? How did he want his readers to feel about them? In Nast's view, what were the worst failures of Reconstruction? Historians have sometimes characterized this era's Republican politics as "waving the bloody shirt." Can you explain why?

Epilogue

Undoubtedly Nast's work had an important impact on northern opinion of Reconstruction, the Democratic Party, Horace Greeley, the Irish Americans, and other issues as well. Yet gradually northern ardor began to decline as other issues and concerns eased Reconstruction out of the limelight and as it appeared that the crusade to reconstruct the South would be an endless one. Radical Republicans, who insisted on equality for the freed slaves, received less and less attention, and southern Democrats, who regained control of southern state governments, were essentially allowed a free hand as long as they didn't obviously violate the Constitution and federal law. By 1877 the South was once again in the hands of white Democrats.

Yet as long as blacks did not insist on their rights, white southern leaders allowed them to retain, in principle, all that the Civil War and Reconstruction had won. In other words, as long as black voters didn't challenge the Redeemers, they were allowed to retain their political rights. Economically, many blacks gradually slipped into the status of tenant farmer, sharecropper, or even peon. The political structure, local courts, and law-enforcement agencies tended to support this arrangement. For his part, black leader Booker T. Washington was praised by white southerners for urging that blacks seek education and economic opportunities but not "rock the boat" politically in the white-controlled South.

In the 1890s the farmers' revolts that swept through the South and Midwest threatened southern white Democratic control, for the revolts threatened to unite white and black farmers in a political coalition that could drive the Redeemers from power. In response, southern white Democrats moved to restrict formally the rights of blacks, taking away the right to vote as well as racially segregating educational facilities, public transportation, parks, restaurants and theaters, elevators and drinking fountains. Not until the 1950s did these chains begin to be broken.

As the reform spirit waned in the latter years of Reconstruction, Nast's popularity suffered. The public appeared to tire of his anger, his self-righteousness, his relentless crusades. The new publisher of *Harper's Weekly* sought to make the magazine less political, and in that atmosphere there was no place for Nast. He resigned in 1886.

Chapter 10
Reconstructing
Reconstruction:
The Political
Cartoonist and the
National Mood

Nast continued to do freelance work for a number of magazines and tried unsuccessfully to start his own periodical, *Nast's Weekly*. Financially struggling, he appealed to friends who influenced President Theodore Roosevelt to appoint Nast to a minor consular post in Ecuador. He died there of yellow fever in 1902.

Yet Thomas Nast was a pioneer of a tradition and of a political art form.

His successors, people such as Herbert Block (Herblock), Bill Mauldin, Oliphant, and even Garry Trudeau ("Doonesbury"), have continued to prick the American conscience, fret and irritate newspaper readers, and assert through their art the proposition that no evildoer can escape the scrutiny and ultimate justice of the popular will. Sometimes they are effective, sometimes not.

Acknowledgments continued from page iv.

Pages 38–46: Extract from *The Legal Papers of John Adams*, Vol. 2, by H. B. Zobel, ed., reprinted by permission of the Belknap Press of Harvard University Press, Cambridge, MA. Copyright © by The President and Fellows of Harvard College.

Pages 120–126: From B. A. Botkin, *Lay My Burden Down*. Used by permission of The University of Chicago Press. Copyright 1945 by The University of Chicago. All rights reserved. Published in 1945.

Page 127: Songs IV and V from S. Stuckey, "Through the Prism of Folklore," *Massachusetts Review*, 1968, reprinted by permission of the Editors of *Massachusetts Review*.

Pages 141–142, 144–146: Extracts from Glenn W. Price, *Origins of the War with Mexico*, reprinted by permission of the University of Texas Press.

Pages 166–167, 168, 177–178: Excerpts from pages 33, 162, 243–244 from James McPherson, *The Negro's Civil War*, reprinted by courtesy of Pantheon Books, a Division of Random House, Inc.

Pages 167–171: All letters by Lincoln from *The Collected Works of Abraham Lincoln* edited by Roy P. Basler. Copyright 1953, by the Abraham Lincoln Association. Permission courtesy of Rutgers University Press.

Pages 171–172: Selections are reprinted from THE SABLE ARM, Negro Troops in the Union Army, 1861–1865, by Dudley Taylor Cornish, by permission of W. W. Norton & Company, Inc. Copyright © 1966 by W. W. Norton & Company, Inc. Copyright © 1956 by Dudley Taylor Cornish.

Pages 173–177, 178–184: From Robert F. Durden, *The Gray and the Black*. Reprinted by permission of the publisher, Louisiana State University Press.